Contents

Foreword to this Edition — xi

Eco-Twisters are Everywhere — 1

Chapter 1 — 7

When the left hand does not know what the right hand is doing

> Living at other people's expense
> *Where the cream is creamed off*
>
> The Men of Gotham at work
> *Monk seals without a future*
>
> Here's dust in your eye
> *Woodland clearances on afforestation funds*
>
> Money down the drain
> *Another dream island bites the dust*
>
> The destructive power of stupidity
> *How wrong investments destroy nature*

Chapter 2 — 34

Head in the sand

> My home is my castle
> *Marble for the affluent citizen*
>
> Accelerating into Chaos
> *The cult of mobility*
>
> Spellbound into the abyss
> *Death freighters on the high seas*

Just like the ostrich
You can't see an ozone hole

Chapter 3 53
Money rules, O.K.?

Put money in thy purse
The scam of the nature reserves

The privatised environment
Destroying the rivers – not only the Amazon

Many trees do not make a forest
Dual standards in environmental conservation

Chapter 4 69
The lust for adventure

I want my fun
No hope for the Elbe beaver

The lust for killing
Making a killing at the sales

Chapter 5 78
The illusion of the possible

Rules where there is nothing to regulate
The Eurocracy's mania for standardisation

Aid which does not help
Why the woods are burning in Southern Europe

For they know not what they do
Nestos – damned from Here to Eternity

Going for uniformity
All is not nature that is green

Sweeping your own doorstep
Europe also violates its rivers

Chapter 6 102
Looking after Number One

> Exporting your mistakes
> *From exploitation to sell-off*
>
> Don't get it right, don't stop the wrong
> *Regarding the logic of no aid for Eastern Europe*
>
> You have to have something in the bank, Frank
> *The wood in the gas chamber*

Chapter 7 122
Everyone longs for The Land of Cockayne

> Don't look beyond your own plate
> *Asparagus – from wherever*
>
> Never mind what I said yesterday
> *The suffering of the marine giants*
>
> The instant feast
> *Yes, we have no bananas*
>
> Better look this gift horse in the mouth
> *Death freight equals humanitarian aid –*
> *Pesticides for Albania*
>
> I could eat you up
> *From smallholding to the agrarian factory*
>
> More, more, more – means less
> *Agricultural policy which is no policy*

Chapter 8 156
Driving out the Devil with Beelzebub

> Planning with blinkers on
> *Why Attica is so bare*
>
> Refusing to learn from one's mistakes
> *Super-Power in the Rhodope Mountains*

> Big, cheap and cheerful
> *Peasant farmers on the Danger List*

Chapter 9 — 172
The battle against one's own inertia

> The beam in one's own eye
> *Can Brussels create an environmental State?*
>
> None so blind . . .
> *Data graveyards save no forests*
>
> The art of waiting
> *The silent death of the frogs*

Chapter 10 — 184
Even what the eye does see, the heart doesn't grieve about

> Two minds in one body
> *The question of birdcatching*
>
> Sweeping it under the carpet
> *The North Sea – a patient with no future?*
>
> Animals as merchandise
> *Europe's way with living creatures*
>
> Out of sight, out of mind
> *The garbage avalanche goes rolling on*

Chapter 11 — 207
The spirit is willing, but the flesh is weak

> The unbearable heaviness of becoming
> *Pacta sunt servanda – agreements must be kept*
>
> The spirits I called up
> *Theory and practice in Eurocracy*
>
> But you can't see the ones in the dark
> *The sharp (blunt) sword of the Union*

Twenty years – and little (none?) the wiser
EU – the end or the turning point?

What the individual can do	235
Addresses	238
Bibliography	243
Index	249
List of authors	251
Acknowledgements	253

Foreword to this Edition

'Eco-Twisters are everywhere' is the heading of the introductory chapter of this book. A book that puts a finger on the ecological failures of the European Union: a Union which claims to be evolving from an economic into an environmental Union; which declares that, following on the main task of the '80s, the creation of the European Common Market, it must be the crucial task of the '90s to solve the ecological problem.

However, the signals we receive from Brussels meanwhile have no connection with consistent environmental protection, or with the ideas and concepts agreed at the 1992 Conference for the Environment and Sustained Development in Rio.

As before, 85% of the 68 billion ECU of the European Commission's budget continues to flow into the guaranteed fund for agriculture and into the structural fund. Agricultural reform has not managed so far to implement actual ecological reforms in agriculture. Merely the grossest excesses of spraying and fertilising may have been slightly curbed, but the structural changes in agriculture will go forward quite consciously and deliberately. The laying off of farmworkers and fields is praised as 'reform'. At the same time mass livestock farming assumes ever more grotesque dimensions, and genetic engineering invades agriculture . . . 200 million ECU for the promotion of environmentally sound methods of production, e.g. encouraging environmentally sustainable farming, as against 37 billion ECU for continuing up the wrong path. It is not the environmentally-friendly smallholding products which are encouraged, but the agri-business farming. And the billions of structural funds are spent on furthering regional developments which, subscribing to the concept that all growth is good, which destroys the environment, human beings and quality of life in equal measure.

Money is the crux. No better way to assess the relative value given environmental protection than by examining the bare budget figures. The environment item in the EU budget for 1993 (Budget item B 4–3) was exactly the same amount as the Budget item 'Reimbursement [i.e. export subsidies] for grain exported in the form of designated alcoholic beverages'; it came to a bare 100 million ECU, ca. 0.16% of the total EU budget. The European Environment Financing instrument, the LIFE-Programme named by the Australians as their chief reason for voting to join the Union – because one really wanted to participate in that – is financially endowed to the same extent as the 'subsidy for the use of olive oil in vegetable – and fish – preserves'. Fully 60 million ECU were provided for this in 1994. 35% of this sum went to nature protection, i.e. 20 million. Among 12 member states! Since 1985 the EU has funded just 11 nature conservation projects. The number of environmentally destructive initiatives across the whole of Europe is inconceivable.

The tomato-processing industry collects a mere £0.45 billion from the Brussels coffers – every year, that is. So that it will utilise European sugar as raw material instead of buying on the world market the chemical industry receives four times as much as is available for nature protection.

All this is the reality of Brussels. There is talk of the environment, but action is against the environment. Resources flow from the new Cohesion Fund and are labelled environmental investments, meaning such projects as dams and water diversion projects. The list could be extended indefinitely; this book *Eco-Twisters* can only describe some of the almost unimaginable misdeeds.

But let us be fair: Brussels is not a self-contained political enclave. Policy development in Brussels is not detached from or out of the control of the member states. On the contrary, ultimate responsibility for the decisions which inflict such manifold damage on our natural heritage and the environment rests with the Council of Ministers, which consists of the respective departmental ministers of member states. So there is no decision from Brussels which does not have the blessing of the member states. We must stress that EU policy cannot be more ecological than the policies of member states.

There have even been some environmentally useful measures developed in the offices of the Commission, but they have met with fierce resistance, or else indifference, from member countries. The CO_2- and energy-tax, which has made no progress in years, is one example. The Bird Protection Directive is another. No other directive has been so trampled on by individual member countries, no other EU legislation has been so frequently contravened, as this European nature protection measure. The very recent Flora-Fauna-Habitat Directive, too, is already in trouble.

So kindly note, dear readers, that the Eco-Twisters are not all sitting in Brussels: it is not 'Europe' itself which is environment-hostile. It is the policies which damage nature and the environment. But policy is decided by the member states and therefore, indirectly, by all of us.

Nevertheless we consider it vital – even in the face of all the propaganda on the subject of Europe – to write this book, to inform you about the shortcomings of European policy. For there has to be a decisive change. It is not necessary to invest 400 billion ECU in new traffic and energy structures to initiate a fatal economic growth. 'Sustainable development', environmentally-friendly long-term development, has been declared, and the politicians make much play with this.

In line with what member countries are doing, or failing to do, with regard to environment policy, Brussels will also decide.

Thus Eco-Twisters are indeed everywhere: in Brussels, in the member states, in local communities. And perhaps even in our own houses? It does not have to be like that for ever, and that is why *Eco-Twisters* is a rallying call for change. A change, not back into the past, but forward into a future with a better quality of environment and life.

Eco-Twisters are Everywhere

The book you are holding should not exist. And all the scandals and environmental crimes, stinking to high heaven, which it describes should exist even less. If everything went according to the laws, decrees, directives and other regulations as well as the authoritatively announced political aims of the various local governments, individual countries or, indeed, the European Union we would have a sane and healthy world. That is the conclusion one must reach after listening to the constantly reiterated pronouncements of politicians who try to convince us with a glib flow of words that the ecological framework is in good order, or at least – where damage is admitted – can be brought under control. Again, if our society – from its smallest unit, the family, up to the top decision makers in all the various departments – were to act according to the dictates of common sense, the economic and ecological future of Europeans and the survival of succeeding generations on our Continent would be assured.

Greed, combined with ecological ignorance, misguided faith in progress, the illusion of technical feasibility, and the laziness which prevents a change of direction when things go wrong, ensures that the basis of our lives is being destroyed at a galloping rate, and with it the irreplaceable natural and cultural heritage of Europe. All this is done with our taxes: income which could be used to improve the quality of life and future perspectives on the Continent.

That is why this book, *The Eco-Twisters*, is needed. On our many research trips in the most varied landscapes and regions of Europe, we encountered such numerous and incredible scandals – some blatantly obvious, others sneaky and unrecognised – that one could easily compile a multi-volume encyclopaedia on the sell-out of nature and environment in Europe. So with this book we hope to show by selected and typical examples exactly what goes on in Europe. We want to raise consciousness and create a new awareness before it is too late. The book is directed at all who no longer want to remain passive as our common heritage is squandered. We therefore name not only the deeds but the perpetrators. It is high time that people in all parts of Europe awoke from their lethargy and realised that Europe should be a Europe for its citizens, not just for the bureaucrats.

For this it is essential that we learn once more to read the landscapes, to recognise and understand what actually belongs where, to be alert to changes for the worse. Have you noticed that landscapes in Europe are becoming more and more alike? For instance, one spring there might be brilliant yellow rape growing everywhere. Another year in summer there will be sunflowers in bloom as far as the eye can see. This is no accident, but the result of agricultural policy emanating from Brussels, which has long since forced farmers into a vicious circle of subsidies, guaranteed prices, dependency and intensive cultivation, confining farmworkers to the role of agrarian factory hands. The casualties are not only peasant farming, but landscape diversity, the soil loss and the water table depletion.

Have you ever driven through Spain or Portugal or Calabria? Then you must have noticed the extensive forests. However, many of these are no longer natural indigenous woodlands, but plantations of eucalyptus trees – an alien species – which, through lowering the water table and altering the landscape, are systematically destroying the original environment. But as we grow up and live ever further removed from nature, we have become blind to such changes. A dangerous development, because it gives full encouragement to the Eco-Twisters. Who exactly are the Eco-Twisters?

For a start, they are those individuals and groups who could not care less about the basis of our life and our future and are only concerned with their own advantages. Yet, working on this book, we had to recognise that other elements in our society could also be regarded as Eco-Twisters: all the machinery designed to frustrate and ultimately bring to a halt any efforts at improvement, preventing genuine progress.

Take, for instance, faulty organisation and lack of co-ordination. You doubtless see it in your own family, problems arise because the left hand does not know what the right hand is doing. This can lead to grotesque situations, as no one knows any longer what it is really all about. When it comes to the fundamental basis of life, lack of co-ordination makes for an unprecedented waste of tax monies and an ecological game of chance. Is it not ludicrous when on the one hand money is allocated for afforestation in Spain – which everyone thinks a virtuous measure – while on the other hand these funds, because appropriate mechanisms of control do not exist, or are not invoked, or simply do not function, are used for countryside-destroying clearances?

Another example. You must have met the head-in-the-sand syndrome. The facts are known, environmental data established, all the problems of environment destruction are evident, and yet everyone carries on as if no one knew anything. One might call it the ostrich policy. Although everyone in Europe should long have been aware of the devastating consequences for the environment and the economy that ensue from the exploitation of rivers and brooks. In Spain further dams, water diversions and irrigation systems are planned for an agriculture which already produces surpluses in Europe. All this even though the cost of water is far less in Spain than in, say, Italy, Holland or Germany. The ecological cost – the cost of nature destroyed – does not enter into the calculations. But is there not the danger of repeating the very mistakes whose consequences we are now trying to remedy – at huge expense – in Central Europe?

Add to this the greed for profit, the shameless incentive of never having enough. Nature is regarded as a mere self-service store, and everything possible is grabbed for one's own pocket. Never mind the losses. Nor is that the end of it. All these problems and syndromes are also being transported to other regions of Europe, with all the smug conviction of the successful. Instead of bringing aid we set out to dump the often ecologically disastrous system of the West on the East. What we call aid in the long run often causes damage. The danger is that we are replacing communist exploitation with an ecological market-economy sell-off.

Ultimately the whole world yearns for the Land of Cockayne. That longing for the fairy-tale instant feast is yet another devastating eco-twister. Because we can never gorge ourselves enough and lust for ever more exotic delicacies, creatures have to suffer and die throughout Europe and all over the world. Yet so much could be done to preserve the European natural heritage. There seems to be plenty of money available, but it is wrongly applied.

Billions are poured into schemes which destroy the environment and merely enrich a few speculators in criminal fashion. Checks of any kind are lacking. Tests for environment compatibility are almost never carried out within the European Union, and there are only lax controls, or none at all, on what is actually done with the funds in individual recipient countries. Some development blunders are well known. That is why the Audit Office of the European Union purposefully recommended a better co-ordination of the various measures at a local as well as a national level, and severely criticised the impenetrability surrounding the division of responsibilities among individual member countries. The financial watchdogs of the Community also pointed out the danger that certain projects financed out of EU structural funds ultimately 'react to the detriment of the environment, or at least produce not inconsiderable negative effects'. They said it! But note: although all these developments are known, nothing changes. On the contrary: inertia governs environmental action in Europe – irrespective of whether inside or outside the EU.

Europe likes to pose on the world scene as the ecological moralist of the environment. That has long ceased to be the true picture. Not only in Amazonia or the Far East are rivers violated and forests destroyed, but right here, on our own doorstep. All this has unforseeable consequences for the natural world, above all for the people living in these regions. If the funds assigned to such idiocies as the Acheloos-diversion in Greece were rerouted, both environment and human beings would benefit. The construction of sewage works would be more appropriate than senseless road and dam building projects – or the development of nature-oriented tourism in areas which threaten to go to the dogs because of EU agricultural policy.

Is it not ludicrous that milk from Denmark, Holland or Belgium is carted off to Spain to be made into butter or cheese, while the indigenous peasants – in Cantabria in Northern Spain, for instance – do not know where to turn for their livelihood? Because of the quota systems for milk all over Europe and the consequent collapse of prices they have had to slaughter their landscape-adapted native breeds of cattle. There is something very wrong with present-day Europe.

All the mechanisms described here show that Eco-Twisters essentially arise out of a wrong-headed attitude. Out of selfishness, greed for profit, ignorance, or any other (all too human) motives whatsoever. Many of the scandals described in this book are absolutely legal, financed by taxpayers. What is missing is simply a clear public awareness of these wrongs. It is up to all of us, therefore, to create and strengthen such an awareness in our daily lives that the Eco-Twisters in our own and other minds do not gain the upper hand. For if the Eco-

Twisters were to go further, so much would be lost – cultural and natural diversity, billions of tax monies, and the quality of life for the inhabitants of our Continent. An unscrupulous contempt for life should not be allowed to destroy the basis of our lives or the future of generations to come.

Nevertheless, this is not a book against Europe, but a book in favour of a truly united Europe. The natural world, the landscape, and above all the people of the continent deserve the natural and cultural heritage that has been entrusted once and for all time to our care. Environment conservation is a question of majorities and also of the value we place on ourselves. These examples, many researched over a period of years and often reading like crime thrillers, are meant to disturb and to create watchfulness. The dossier on the European environment should have no further sombre chapters of destruction added to it. That is how we see the suggestions for necessary changes and initiatives, to which every one of us can contribute. Only thus can the mansion of Europe acquire a green garden and rest on ecologically sound foundations.

Chapter 1

When the left hand does not know what the right hand is doing

Carelessness and indifference, lack of concentration and commitment, are the sources of devastating misjudgments. What goes for the individual is also valid for more complex structures and organisations. Through mismanagement and inadequate or missing information, billions in tax income are squandered. To repair the economic or ecological damage thus caused is hardly possible or else costs many times as much as a sensible use of economic and ecological resources would require. Why do we do this to ourselves?

Living at other people's expense
Where the cream is creamed off

He appealed to all of us, 'Marlboro Man', that cowboy on horseback who sought to convince us that there can be no true freedom for man without the consumption of a certain brand of cigarette.

There will be no more photographs of him, he died of cancer.

On his deathbed Marlboro Man campaigned fiercely against smoking, which had made him rich and famous – and mortally ill. Whether in this fight he enjoyed the support of EU Ministers is not known. They certainly warn about the consequences of smoking. Every hoarding advertising tobacco, every tin of tobacco, cigarette packet or cigar box carries a government health warning: 'Tobacco can seriously damage your health.' The dangers to health linked with smoking are known to all. They are constantly brought to everyone's notice. Cigarette packets may even bear the additional message: 'Smoking causes heart diseases.'

So there *is* an EU campaign to point out the harmful consequences of tobacco consumption. In Germany tobacco advertising is banned, in France many bars prohibit smoking. But now wait for the pay-off: what scandalous double standards possess our politicians? The same EU Council of Ministers which at some stage decided – possibly as a result of those endless marathon conferences at which often not only the tempers light up – to attach warnings to all tobacco products for sale, at the same time promotes tobacco cultivation in Europe on an unimaginable scale.

The budget of the European Union provides a full cornucopia for the tobacco industry. Chapter B1–17 is devoted to tobacco. 1.131 billion ECU (ca. £0.9 billion) is the grant assigned for the cultivation of tobacco in Europe. But that is not all. 68 million ECU (ca. £55 million) are provided for subsidising tobacco export, because our own smokers are not too keen on the taste of European tobacco. So it has to be exported. However, as even with a £0.9 billion subsidy it is still too expensive for non-European markets. The export itself has to receive an additional subsidy.

Of course one must not imagine that the tobacco is processed and used, or exported, immediately after harvesting. Publicly sponsored intermediate storage facilities have to be procured, because the free market cannot afford them. The poor tobacco industry presents itself as in need of a public handout. The European Community is ready and generous with its aid. To the tune of 9 million ECU – £7.3 million – for the technical expenses of public storage, and 2 million ECU – £1.6 million – for the financial cost, the EU – i.e. we the taxpayers – willingly share the burden.

Altogether the EU package for tobacco in the year 1993 amounted to 1274 m ECU, rather more than in 1992, less than in 1991. A budget item made up of our taxes, including those of non-smokers, to maintain the European tobacco industry. A good thing, too. What else would the Health Ministries issue warnings against?

In the face of this schizophrenia one cannot but ask whether the Eurocracy's left hand has any idea at all what the right hand is up to. Of course it does know but the head is not able to put an end to the mischief. Or simply not willing, because the lobby of those who profit from this lunacy is huge. Questions of environment, nature conservation or health are immaterial. Money rules the world, and policy.

The case of tobacco is but one instance of many such subsidies to be found in the EU economy in general and in the agrarian economy in particular.

Did you know that Germany exports rice? Of course it is not grown locally. But the export of rice grown in Southern Europe is an important trade item. The EU agricultural budget for 1993 provided 88 million ECU as reimbursement for the export of rice. As with tobacco rice grown in Europe is more expensive than rice on the world market. It is more costly even with public subsidies for production: not for every kind of rice, but for *Indica* rice there is 15 million ECU (roughly £12.2 million). So, of course new planting will be of rice eligible for subsidy. The EU agricultural budget, through its promotion programme, determines what is or is not planted in our countrysides.

In order that our fellow European citizens in the French Overseas Department of La Réunion neither totally reject home-grown European rice, nor have to dig too deep into their pockets to buy it, EU taxpayers, represented by the EU bureaucracy, are fleeced once again. They provide 4 million ECU in rice aid for the European exclave.

Even that is not enough of a rice subsidy. Rice, as we know, grows in water, and water is in very short supply in Southern Europe. But that is no problem for the EU. Structural funds can deal with these 'disadvantages', the natural deficiencies of each region are overcome by technology, the countryside is geared to the production. Whether it is the dams and water projects planned on the Nestos or Acheloos in Greece – on which there will be more in this book – or the extensive plans for dam-systems in Spain – everywhere the EU is prepared to 'help' with structural funds or perhaps the new 'cohesion funds'. With billions pumped into large-scale projects, landscapes are devastated in order to build a system of agriculture which is hostile to environment and communities, and often totally unsuited to the region. The delusion is no accident, but quite deliberate. There is an enormous amount of money behind it. Let us stay with rice for the moment, and with other subsidised products. For the sake of completeness we should not omit the cost of storage, necessary for rice as for tobacco (see above), for grain (ca. 800 million ECU), for sugar (ca. 500 m ECU), for olive oil (ca. 30 m ECU), as for beef (ca. 500 m ECU), and other agricultural products. Money which gives nothing to the environment or the farmers except the vexations of the struggle to produce from the land.

The smallest part of the agricultural budget goes where it is most needed: to the peasant farmers, who, despite rising public expenditure on agriculture, have ever-diminishing incomes. Why is this? Very simple: most of the funds are creamed off by exporters, distributors and industrialists. Only about a third of the annual ca. £32 billion expenditure on agriculture goes to farms, not fairly distributed either. 20% of the farmers collect 80% of the residual funds which filter down to the actual farms. The main profit is made by the 6% of grain growers who own half of all the grain-growing area and on it produce 60% of the total income; by the 15% of the dairy farmers who produce 50% of the milk (in bulk); or the 10% of fatstock farmers who produce 50% of all the meat. So the ones who chiefly profit are those agrarian industrialists who most pollute our environment, whose intensive production is responsible for many environmental scandals and the suffering of animals.

It is thus not surprising that agricultural subsidies gravitate to those countries where the most intensive and environment-hostile methods prevail, in which factory farming has wrested all power from peasant farmers. An example is Holland, where the Dutch tomato is possibly the world's most tasteless vegetable. Mocking spirits have called it the fourth state of density of water. In the Netherlands there are still 280,000 workers on the land. Adding up all the subsidies which accrue from the agricultural resources to Holland (including export, storage, etc.), this makes over 13,000 ECU per worker. In Portugal, which still has a smallholding, labour-intensive and environmentally-friendly agriculture, each of the 940,000 farmworkers receives only the equivalent of 370 ECU, i.e. a mere 2.8% of what goes to Holland.

Thus it is not the farmers who skim the cream from the EU agricultural subsidies. The profiteers are sitting comfortably ensconced in industry and trade. Can you imagine what benefit actual workers on the land can get from a budget item of 10 m ECU 'Grant for pineapple preserves'? Or from 'Grants for processed strawberries' (1 m ECU), or from the 'Reconstruction of the sardine processing industry' (Budget item B 2–232).

There are three ways to make quick money – clean up (you might say in a dirty way): drugs, arms, and food. But in the latter case the option is only open to those who know how to turn the EU regulations to their own advantage, legally or illegally. EU rules are made for the processing industry, for the exporters, distributors and marketeers, but not for the farmers. These days money may be made out of agriculture, but not by it.

Those who export surplus produce from Europe can make money, and plenty of it. Our surpluses are caused, inter alia, by over-intensive cultivation. But surpluses can also be caused by trade agreements. In the budget of the EU one reads: 'In accordance with the sugar report of the AKP-EWG agreement and the separate agreement with India the Community imports roughly 1.3 million tonnes of sugar per year: as it has surpluses of its own, it must export a corresponding amount; the cost of export reimbursements (Par. B1–110) for the year 1993 was assessed at 618 million ECU.' Set out fully in words: Six hundred and eighteen million ECU – five hundred and four million pounds sterling – agricultural expenditure, none of which goes to farmworkers.

Clearly such programmes, and such sums, will attract villains as a dungheap attracts flies. One exporter of butter overreached in this game. He had applied for export reimbursement for delivery of EU butter to the Vatican. The Vatican is not a member of EU, and therefore anyone who exports a subsidised product like butter to it can get reimbursed for export expenses to the full amount. But in this scam the amount exported was hugely exaggerated, the documents were forged. Every inhabitant of the Vatican would have had to eat 375 grams ($^3/_4$ lb.) of butter every day for a year to accommodate the stated quantity . . .

It is rare for the authorities to uncover such illegal manipulations. They do spend millions to fight fraud – rightly, we think – but the wilderness of regulations is so tangled and the controls so lax that the door is wide open to scams.

A quick stop should be put to the legal scandals which not only represent wasted taxes but cause environmental problems. The money could be used more efficiently than for a wrongheaded, environmentally and socially harmful industrial agriculture.

We cannot change until we reach the point where the EU economy has a majority of politicians who actually consider it monstrous to warn against smoking and at the same time subsidise tobacco cultivation. They cannot talk of 'peasant farming' and mean 'agrarian industry'. Here is a tip for those who would like to climb on the lucrative EU-subsidy bandwagon: If you don't have sufficient land to profit from the

687 million ECU which the EU lays out for cotton production, why not breed silkworms and their eggs? Reluctant officials may be referred to Regulation (EEC) 827/68 which created a Common Market organisation for silkworms and silkworm eggs. If you can get Regulation (EEC) No. 845/72 of the Committee of 24.4.72 dealing with special measures to encourage silkworm rearing (OJ No. L 100 of 27.4.72, P 1), recently amended by Regulation (EEC) No. 2059/92 (OJ No. L 215 of 30.6.92), and study these, you will soon be an expert on the subject. A silk tie of your own production – supported by funds from budget item B1–142 'Silkworms' to the tune of 1 million ECU (in 1991 there was only a third as much available) – would certainly be worth having. And environmental pollution from cultivation is guaranteed minimal – it would not make you an Eco-Twister.

The Men of Gotham at Work
Monk seals without a Future

The marble shines bright in the glaring sun of the Aegean. Nearby the deep blue sea froths against the shore of the Greek island of Alonnisos, one of the Northern Sporades and among the most beautiful places to be found in Hellas. A spacious mansion which bears the title of Biological Institute has a sombre background that led to its foundation and is inextricably linked with the island. For this building was intended for the protection and study of one of the rarest animal species in Europe, indeed, in the world – the monk seal, that legendary creature which, in the guise of 'the Sirens', supposedly enchanted the lost heroes of the Odyssey. Almost as hard to understand are the circumstances surrounding the creation of this alleged refuge and research centre for the monk seal on the Sporadic island of Alonnisos.

In 1987–8 construction of the Institute began on this island in the Marine National Park of the Northern Sporades, partly financed by the European Union, without whose aid the Greek Ministry of the Environment could not have started such a project. Appropriately the Centre was also sponsored by the MEDSPA programme of the EU, which aims to support worthy pilot projects for nature and environmental conservation in the Mediterranean region. The project then duly evolved from pilot project to pilot ruin, an instructive example of how not to do it.

Anyone wanting to visit the ghost Institute on Alonnisos will have difficulty finding someone to take him. The drive from the island's main village of Patitiri leads over many kilometres of rough track to the other end of the island, and many a driver fears, not without cause, that his vehicle could sustain damage. When after a real boneshaker of a journey, one finally reaches the Bay of Gerakas, one immediately sees the Institute, radiant in the bright Aegean light and giving an impression of having dropped from the sky.

Looking more closely at the building, the first thing that strikes one is the fine marble-clad terraces. Strolling along these terraces was meant to bring inspiration to the scientists working here, and it would also be a great place for cocktail parties – thus malicious commentators sneer at the terrace landscape.

The merciless critics of the Centre go on to complain that the laboratory looks more like the washroom of a youth hostel and the lecture theatre is absolutely minute in comparison with the oversized 'party room'. Who can wonder that the architects are offended by what they regard as 'unjustified criticism'.

But it is beyond a joke, for ultimately the Institute is a travesty of what it was meant to be – a contribution to the protection of nature. Even the choice of site shows no regard for the environment and the local inhabitants. Rather it humoured the fanciful whim of scientists who dreamed up a project for breeding monk seals in the Bay of Gerakas. In fact these were local suggestions to build the Centre nearer to existing settlements on the island, where an adequate infrastructure was already in place. Now the Centre, though in practice unused, necessarily produces the appurtenances of an infrastructure and thus becomes a 'pole of development' in the hitherto untouched North of the island. Recently electrification reached the Institute, and soon a proper road will be constructed to it. Apart from the spur to development given by the Institute, it has also made a more direct contribution to the disfigurement of nature. The lumps of rock excavated while digging the hole for the foundations were simply dumped into the Bay of Gerakas. The huge sums invested in the useless building could have funded far more sensible measures for the preservation of the endangered monk seal.

Nevertheless, some will say it's not all that bad. The Institute has been built, and there must be some use for it. So now a Greek environmental organisation tries to arrange several seminars a year there. Unfortunately the Biological Institute is not a unique example of the EU's structural promotions policy, which indirectly poses a big threat to the Mediterranean monk seal, as such programmes enable the destruction of nature on a grand scale even in poor countries like Greece.

Of course there are some positive initiatives of EU structural policy, like the environment programmes MEDSPA and ENVIREG, but what is the value of these if – like the Biological Institute – they degenerate into promotions for the regional construction industry and fail to meet long-term environmental goals. Thus it is common enough in Mediterranean countries for sewage works to be built with EU aid, but then to lack funds for running them. Moreover, in countries like Greece the authorities and ministries are often short of qualified experts, and officials are either hopelessly out of their depth with the programmes or exploit them to satisfy their political contracts. Overextended, too, are most of the EU officials of the Environment Management Board in Brussels, whose departments are understaffed and unable to monitor individual projects adequately.

But nobody draws the logical conclusions, and so the

'messing about' goes merrily on, and it is no surprise that with such Kafkaesque set-ups, despite good intentions, often produce nothing.

However, to return to the monk seal, one of the world's most endangered species, whose total population is now estimated at barely 500. Half these animals live in the Western Atlantic around Madeira and off the Western Sahara, the other half mainly in Greek territorial waters. One of the most important populations, roughly 40 individuals, is found in the Northern Sporades Marine National Park on the Island of Alonnisos where the Biological Institute was built. But also monk seals may be found anywhere in the Aegean or Ionian Seas, and the population in the Northern Sporades has a chance of survival only if the entire Greek stock can be protected.

The Marine National Park of the Northern Sporades consists of a group of deserted islands; Alonnisos is the only inhabited one. The National Park is due to the initiative of a German biologist who developed the idea together with the local fishermen of Alonnisos. Of course one must realise that the fishermen themselves still constitute the biggest threat to monk seals in Greece. The traditional coastal fishermen are still killing monk seals because the latter eat fish out of their nets, often causing considerable damage. As the Mediterranean has been hopelessly overfished, the competition between the few remaining monk seals and the many inshore fishermen (around 20,000 in Greece) grows more ruthless every day. Yet the real enemies of the fishermen are not the monk seals but the trawlers and the so-called *Gri-Gri* boats, who fish at night with headlights and circular drag nets and empty large areas of fish at the same time destroying the small fry. Then there are dynamite fishers and tourists fishing illegally with harpoons, causing devastation in the deep sea world. As the coastal fishermen have no defence against their real enemies, the monk seal is made the scapegoat, and it pays with its life.

But things are different in the National Park of the Northern Sporades, where, thanks to the persuasive work of conservationists, fishermen are no longer killing monk seals. For the enemies of traditional fishermen, the *Gri-Gri* boats, are now banned from fishing in the National Park. This indirectly compensates the coastal fishermen for any loss caused by the monk seals, whom they are now actively protecting. After lengthy teething troubles, surveillance of the Park works well, not least because international and local conservationist organisations like the *Stiftung Europäisches Naturerbe* (European Natural Heritage Fund) and the Ecological and Cultural Movement of Alonnisos by intensive lobbying over the years exerted pressure on the Greek authorities and on the EU. It has been a thankless and expensive task, receiving no financial support from either the European Union or the National Government. The foundations are accused of just making difficulties and hampering the 'work' of the administration. Indirectly there is also the intermittent threat that the foundation cannot expect grants if it goes on behaving so awkwardly.

But ultimately the crisis of traditional inshore fishing around Greece exposes the whole disaster area of EU structural policy for the fishing industry in general, which is largely responsible for present day problems. At the beginning of the '80s the European Union gave financial support to an expansion of fishing fleets throughout the EU. Note that it was not the traditional coastal fishermen but the big trawlers and the *Gri-Gri* boats which received support; and now in the '90s it suddenly appears that maybe such policy was exceedingly shortsighted and has led to a dangerous overfishing of the Mediterranean. So now one has to pay subsidies for reducing the previously built up excess capacity. Again there is little to spare for the more environmentally-friendly inshore fishermen. In Brussels the current idea is to reduce excess capacity by subsidising the big boats to do their fishing in the Atlantic off the West Coast of Africa. One cannot reproach the hard-working officials with lack of imagination in proposing such a self-parodying 'solution' to serious problems.

Not only the EU aid policy for fishing but many EU programmes in general harm the monk seal indirectly, for instance, Brussels funding for regional development or forestry. With EU money roads are built to remote coasts where formerly the timid monk seals could survive relatively undisturbed, at least by tourists fishing illegally or by the native population. It is positively wrongheaded to build forest roads, ostensibly to combat forest fires, on inaccessible shores. Essentially these roads are built only because EU funds are available and therefore have to be spent. Often the motto of the local developers is no longer 'What is needed?' but 'For what can we get money from the EU?' Obviously this will lead to misguided initiatives, and it is made worse by mingling EU funds with 'national' ones, so that the EU no longer accepts responsibility for the way the money is spent. Nevertheless, all this would not be possible without the EU, and so the European Union is and should be held ultimately responsible. Yet it totally rejects such responsibility, arguing that the member state, not the EU, is responsible for correct use of the funds. Inevitably this leads to a system of 'organised irresponsibility'. It is almost like giving a drug addict opium and then arguing it is his responsibility whether he takes it or not. However, no one in the EU seems aware of this, or those responsible simply will not admit it, otherwise the Biological Institute on Alonnisos would never have been built.

Compared with the money the EU spends on encouraging commercial development, what the conservationists get for protecting the monk seals is 'peanuts'.

Conservationist organisations are hopelessly under-powered when trying to defend the species against the apparatus of 'organised irresponsibility'. Sometimes they even become part of that apparatus: thus the Greek section of a famous international conservation organisation which runs a monk seal project supported by the EU looked on in silence when one fisherman shot a monk seal, although the incident was observed by witnesses and reported to the local harbour police.

The action violated and disregarded the Berne Convention for the Protection of Endangered Species in the most blatant fashion.

Owing to a perjury the prosecution of the fisherman collapsed, and the environmental foundation, although in full possession of the facts, made no move against the perjurer. The local management of the Monk Seal Campaign, who demanded a public stand from the conservation organisation against the perjurer, was simply not employed again. The fact is that no one wants problems with the monk seal. Problems are swept under the carpet. The main thing is that the monk seal as a subject is duly 'dealt with', meaning 'studied'. The European Union mostly finances scientific programmes about the monk seal in Greece, programmes which hurt nobody but do little to preserve the animal (studied by Aristotle, too, in his day). Agreed, it is better than doing absolutely nothing, but it will not be enough. What is really needed is to orientate both fishing and regional development in areas where monk seals depend on their protection. The demand may sound excessive, conservationists run mad, but in the end it is the only way to stop the overfishing of that sea and lay the foundations for a truly 'sustainable development': for no other species epitomises the well-being or sickness of the Mediterranean better than the monk seal.

What is needed is a network of functioning nature reserves along the lines of the Northern Sporades Marine National Park (hopefully without Biological Institute), but also of the exemplary monk seal reserve on the Desertas near Madeira. In its Habitat Directive the EU has now forged an instrument for attaining this goal. If this Directive is really carried out and not, as so often, merely a paper tiger, the monk seal could be saved in Greece. If the Directive is not carried out, the EU will certainly blame the Greek government once again – and admittedly the latter is far from a star pupil as regards nature and environmental protection. The EU, which shows such creativity in furthering the aims of industry, must develop ways and means of implementing the Directive for the good of our common European natural heritage. Anyhow, conservationist organisations will give the EU and the regional governments no peace until this ambitious aim has been achieved, and Europe's rarest mammal once more has a chance of survival – and with it the whole marine world of the Mediterranean.

Here's dust in your eye
Woodland clearances on afforestation funds

Deeply disturbed, we see on Television and in magazines pictures of the destroyed rain forest. Cut down, burnt, bulldozed. Every year all over the world 170,000 square kilometres of primeval forest are destroyed – in Brazil alone a round 34,000 square kilometres. We know the danger of destroying the great oxygen producers of Plant Earth. We know about the loss of priceless gene reservoirs – animal and plant species eradicated before they have even been discovered.

The fight against rain forest destruction in South America, Asia and Africa has long ceased to be an insider topic of environment activists. Indeed, awareness of the rain forest has reached peak status. The rain forest – and of course that is a good thing – has become a presentable preoccupation. These days schoolchildren can tell you which indigenous groups are endangered, and glossy magazines report on the threat to jaguar, sloth, and brilliantly colourful vegetation. All this is vital if things are ever to change and the abuses made to stop.

However, a similar commitment is as cruelly necessary for the preservation of many woodland regions in Europe. For here, on our own doorstep, woods are being destroyed piecemeal, with monstrous speed and brutality: with them we lose oxygen producers, habitats, climate regulators and water stores. Acid rain and forest sickness?

No, that punishment for decades of ecological folly by our industrial societies is not the only cause. In quite a different way and almost unnoticed forests are being destroyed in Europe. A scandal in itself. But an even bigger scandal is the fact that the taxpayers of the European Union are expected to finance this. The essential scandal is the barely credible situation that public money intended for afforestation is used in Spain, for example, to systematically clear intact natural forest and then replant with landscape-alien monocultures. It is worth pursuing the course of events in detail. The folly that is enacted here could scarcely be thought up by the most inventive satirist. Let us consider the case of Spain.

For the 'development of less advantaged regions', as the budget item for Spain puts it, in the years 1989–93 a round billion Pesetas were provided (1 million Pesetas roughly equivalent to £5676). One of the regions receiving such support (essentially from EU funds) is the Extremadura in South-West Spain. There is a 'programme for environment protection and conservation of natural resources in the Extremadura'. That sounds good. But looked at more closely, it conceals an environmental destruction of gigantic proportions. 900 million Pesetas, probably also largely from EU funds, are earmarked for reafforestation. Anyone acquainted with conditions in Southern Europe and its lack of wooded areas will immediately feel that afforestation is a good thing. Unfortunately in this instance the reverse is true.

According to the government plan projects for reafforestation in Maquis regions are intended to 'improve' the low economic value of the (natural) woodland. But the Maquis – ecologists are agreed on this – is a valuable habitat. It harbours lynx, imperial eagles and black vultures. The vegetation protects the fragile soil and provides resources for the local population – such as grazing areas, honey and firewood. What is termed reafforestation in reality means the complete clearance of the slopes by heavy machinery. This is to make room for monocultures, where trees – often species alien to this area, such as pines – are planted at regular intervals. Most of these saplings die soon after planting. The valuable but vulnerable soil is then exposed completely unprotected to wind and rain. Fatal erosion is the consequence, and as much as 20 tonnes of soil are lost per hectare. Brooks and rivers in the mountains of the Extremadura get muddied and blocked, and the ecosystems of the waters are in the long run destroyed, like the original woodland.

But it is not only in the Maquis areas that the woods of the Extremadura are dying, silently and thus unnoticed. Hardly a tourist penetrates to the mountain regions where he could see the heavy bulldozers executing their fell work in the forests. Large parts of the region have already been 'cleared' in this criminal manner for pseudo-reafforestation schemes, according to Isabell Bermejo, one of the most respected conservationists in Spain. But definite cause for complaint to the EU is only provided where such activities are started in a protected habitat. Many habitats of great value are not protected because the regional government of the Extremadura is not interested. And why are the local President of the Council, Juan Carlos Rodriquez Ibarra, and his minions not interested in creating protected reserves? The answer is obvious when one knows that these are the same people to help push ahead and cover up the wrongheaded development projects. Thus one of the most ecologically valuable regions of Europe is threatened with destruction.

The autonomous region of Extremadura (comparable with a German Land) covers an area of roughly 4 million hectares and is very sparsely populated by about 1 million people. Due to its borderland position and a shortage of raw materials it is among the 'less advantaged' regions – at least, according to standard classification. This takes account solely of the income per head of population and the regional productivity, but not of other factors such as quality of life and environment. And both of these the Extremadura has (still, just) in plenty.

There in the South-West of Spain a unique bioreserve has maintained itself. Lynxes and wolves still inhabit inaccessible mountain regions. But it is not only the wooded mountains that are ecologically important; on the plains of the extensive, richly structured countryside millions of migrant birds from Central, Western and Northern Europe spend the winter. (Ring doves from Central Europe winter here, as do the black redstart and many of our familiar species.) The Extremadura woods are particularly worth protecting for that reason alone. But above all, in mountain areas and on steep slopes, which are very prone to erosion, a dense Mediterranean forest with luxuriant undergrowth has survived. This woodland protects the soil, stores ground water, and at the same time regulates the climate.

Since the Bronze Age a savannah-like landscape has evolved on the plains: a quasi-combination of Central European orchard-meadow, English park landscape and African savannah. These light-dappled woods of cork- and sessile oak, which the Spaniards call 'dehesa', at present still cover many square kilometres of the Extremadura. They form both a natural and a cultural heritage which over the centuries has been extensively used by the inhabitants for grazing land and for grain cultivation. The oak trees were regularly coppiced for charcoal burning, and the acorns used for pig fodder. These parts of the Extremadura also have international importance. Roughly 50,000 cranes from Germany, West Poland and Scandinavia spend the winter here, as do hundreds of thousands of lapwings, numerous red and black golden plovers, and a number of other migrant species.

The traditional form of land use through adaptation to environmental conditions has produced a particular diversity of landscape with a great wealth of flora and fauna. Besides the birds of passage the Extremadura shelters the world's largest stock of endangered species, such as black vultures, imperial eagles and great bustards. Despite the inestimable ecological importance of this South-west Spanish region both the extensive oakwoods and the primeval mountain woodlands are being destroyed. Many Dehesa-areas have been cleared to make room for large-scale irrigation projects promoted by the government. Often many centuries-old trees were uprooted, and within a few days and weeks bare mass-production fields took over, such as we know from other parts of Europe. On these areas monotonous expanses of maize, asparagus and other intensive crops were planted. High grade agricultural products of the Dehesas have in many cases lost their markets to the cheaper products of this industrial farming.

We must learn once more to understand landscapes in their original form. Only then can we comprehend the lunacies that take place in such regions. There is not much time. Development proceeds very fast and soon further areas could be cleared. In future people could drive through this country – perhaps on the way to a holiday in Portugal – and no longer see that there was anything wrong. They will have gotten used to the bleak landscapes of intensive monocultures, as we have become used to them in so many other parts of Europe. And people will forget, as we have all forgotten, that a portion of our natural heritage has been lost purely and simply through political folly and business deals.

Indeed, the Dehesa-woods of the Extremadura die in silence and virtually unobserved. And already the next dam has been erected as a water reservoir to irrigate an area of 5,000 hectares. To this end a small river, the Ambroz, has been dammed. There is still some resistance from an alliance of conservationists and smallholders. For the latter the destruction of the woods and the intensification of agricultural land use brings no good. They lose their present countryside-adapted jobs, they are degraded into unskilled labour, forced to emigrate to the cities – in every way they lose their cultural, regional identity.

The scant soil, unsuited to intensive cultivation, deteriorates very quickly. The investment in irrigation projects, for which the Dehesa woods had to make way, is already proving uneconomic, as well as an ecological catastrophe for the locality. Gains from such projects are for the few, who of course are totally blameless and point to the high cost of planning and construction. So they do all right in any case, no matter whether the projects are worthwhile. And the taxpayers of the

EU are asked to bear the cost.

Work on the Amroz has been halted by the EU, following representations by groups of environmentalists and farmers. But the responsible officials in the Regional Government of Extremadura – above all the Regional Minister President Ibarra – continue to put the brake on ecological action while coming down with the heavy foot of private interest on the destructive accelerator pedal of – magic word – *progress*.

Under cover of 'ecological development' even worse horrors occur. And where the criteria for complaints to the EU are fulfilled, most of the time these get bogged down in the numerous nooks and crannies of the impenetrable and inflated EU bureaucracy. The officials of the Brussels General Committee XI which deals with environment protection point proudly to huge box files of documents which, owing to constant office moves, have not been unpacked for three years. In this way a complaint by Spanish conservationists – pointing out the senseless clearances of protected stretches of Maquis immediately below or very close to the nests of imperial eagles – sank without trace in the shifting sands of Brussels bureaucracy. What is the use of putting a protection order on rare animal species of Europe if their habitats are then systematically and almost legally destroyed with the bureaucratic blessing – and the funds – of the European Union?

Poor old Europe! We look at South America and lament the loss of the rain forests, and then we allow our own natural woodlands to be destroyed with our own money. Where are the Commissions which ought to be looking into such lunacy on the spot? What is the use of the German Chancellor uttering fine words at the UNO Global Environment Conference and causing funds to be released for the rain forest if nobody takes any notice of the silent death of our European woods?

Worse is to come. A further investment of 910 million Pesetas in the Extremadura woodlands is to encourage forestry in areas where the climate is unfavourable. Nature is to be helped, so the argument goes. Yet if the woods of the region require support, i.e. measures for improvement, as Isabell Bermejo points out it is not on account of an unfavourable climate, but to compensate for the consequences of mistaken investment and inadequate forestry practices.

One absurdity is the granting of funds for cleansing and tidying up woods in the cause of preventing and fighting fires. The result is to 'clean up' the woods; all the undergrowth is cleared away by heavy machinery. Once again the soil is helplessly exposed to erosion. With the methods of traditional management such 'cleansing' in eco-Stalinist style had not been necessary. The people of the Extremadura exploited the mountain woodlands, but with consideration for nature. Firewood was continually gathered, the woods were carefully grazed and controlled by individual tree felling. That is woodland management such as one can ideally visualise for the South American rain forests and their aboriginal inhabitants.

It once worked well enough in Europe. While the changes in the South American rain forest are now well known, very few are aware of the events in South Western Europe. Unfortunately these few have not the power to change matters. Conservation is a question of majorities. And most people are just not concerned about the devastation of the woods on their own doorstep. How would they know about these crimes against nature and the Eco-Twisters responsible?

Today the population is cut off from sustainable utilisation of the woods. Machinery and soil destruction and senseless investment of tax monies are given preference. As in the example of the Dehesas, only a few benefit. They are paid for senseless plans developed in offices many miles removed from the actual landscape. They profit from the employment of machinery. The losers are the people of the Extremadura, the countryside itself, and all of us who are ultimately dependent on intact ecosystems in all parts of the Continent.

Erosion is not the only consequence of this insensate development: there is also an increase in forest fires. Afforestation is usually done with foreign trees unsuited to the existing ecosystems. Pines simply do not have protective features against fires like the thick bark of the cork oak, the leathery leaves of holm oak or sessile oak, or the regenerative powers of other species. As a result forest fires have markedly increased. True, they are sometimes started deliberately by the population to regain the grazing areas. As part of the deal expensive helicopters and other mechanical aids are supplied for fire fighting, instead of attacking the causes.

Conservation experts in the Extremadura point out that all this would be quite superfluous if the woodlands were once again turned over to traditional use by the local inhabitants. Also, there is the building of firebreaks – 10–15 metre wide strips cleared of trees and shrubs which have been slashed through the woods as a protection against conflagrations. Investment in these help only the entrepreneurs and owners of machines who carry out the work. The joke is that, thanks to the firebreaks and forest roads intended as such, arsonists as well as poachers can penetrate into areas which natural conditions had previously rendered inaccessible to them.

For unnecessary forest roads alone 144 million Pesetas have been provided in the plan for the region. And that is only the published programme. Most investments of this kind are not announced in advance, but negotiated behind closed doors. So it is almost accidental when conservationists, for all their vigilance, actually discover some concrete figures. One instance is the nonsensical river channelling taking place in the Extremadura under the guise of fighting erosion. But that is another story from the new seemingly endless file of Crimes against the European Environment.

Money down the drain
Another dream island bites the dust

Shrouds of mist hang over steeply rising mountains, the deep clefts of valleys, the whole strange, exotic landscape mosaic.

Here in the highlands of the Canary Island La Gomera, in the midst of the National Park Garajonay, the world still seems in good shape.

Beardlike drifts of lichen drip from the misty, outlandish laurel trees. Down in the barrancos, those typical deep canyons making for the sea, time seems to have stood still. The steep slopes are terraced with painstakingly assembled natural stones, and the gigantic boulders of the Cyclops walls give rise to the wildest flights of speculation. Was it really human beings of our own planet who achieved this incredible interlacing of nature and human skill? Scenic perfection is achieved where dozens, indeed hundreds, of Canary date palms give a final touch of exotic magic to the landscape.

Driving through the at times very wild, ravined interior of the island we pass only a few sleepy settlements. La Gomera, this advance guard of Africa yet part of Spain, seems a little fragment of long-lost paradise in our hectic present. No wonder that some time around the late '70s the island was discovered as a precious secret by European individualists and dropouts. But shock, horror! Unfortunately the idyll is deceptive, here as so often. And once again it is the structural funds of the European Union which by their misguided 'Development Support' threaten to destroy nature and culture alike.

The island – where Colombus is said to have stopped to take water on board before the decisive stage of his voyage on to the South America he did not expect – could soon be doomed to fall victim to mistaken development policy and irresponsible speculation. Everywhere one can see the blue tin signs with the white or yellow stars symbolising the European Union's money which in the long run, unhappily, brings only misery. Such signs are always put up where a development policy is being carried out which the self-styled proponents of progressive ideas (a.k.a. ambitious officials) have thought up in the interests of short-term boom and quick profits.

But enough of gush and lamentation. This is serious. So

serious that, to understand the whole enormity fully, we must look closely at the developments up to now. It all started with the entry of Spain into the European Union in 1986 – which opened the opportunity for the country to share in the EU development funds. The Canary Islands were classed as 'underdeveloped' in the European sense, where Eurocrats think in terms of making everything the same. To this end, without the necessary co-ordination, all kinds of measures are put forward.

Far-sighted people began setting up an ECOPLAN for La Gomera, which does indeed lack infrastructure. This plan visualised an ecologically oriented preservation of resources supported by UNESCO as part of the Man-and-Biosphere programme. However, the plan could not overcome the political obstacles and eventually foundered. What transpired instead of that far-sighted plan has been terrible for the island. Since 1989 a programme has been running, backed with EU funds, called 'Operativo Integrado' (POI/Operational Action Programme), which is seen as part of the European structures development policy.

The island of La Gomera is almost circular, with a diameter of 22–25 kilometres, easy to survey. With a population of barely 16,000 it should have been possible to preserve the unique structure of the island as an ecological as well as economic basis for an assured future. But once again the opposite has happened. So far – and this has been proved by a special study – the EU initiative has produced only ecological irreparable damage. Roads have been built in districts which had no need of them, and from Calera to Vueltas, at the lower end of the scenically, culturally and ecologically magnificent Valle Gran Rey, pathways of composition-stonepaving and marble slabs make a broad promenade down to the beach, where – like a string of beads – new hotels and holiday home estates are continually springing up. Even the market square of the small, sleepy main town of San Sebastian has been remodelled. The old square had to give way to the same boring paved paths and look-alike monotony. Nothing was improved thereby. Rather the small settlements were robbed of part of their identity to be made into the tedious developments we know all too well from certain coastal areas of France and Spain.

That is called progress. Progress paid for with the individuality of this long-remote island, with a piece of unique natural and cultural heritage. But far more ominous than the monotonous paving slabs along the new wannabe promenades are the equally EU-subsidised roads ruthlessly cut into the slopes. Sites of irreplaceable indigenous plant species, found only on this island and on these sites, were destroyed in the process without a second thought. Studies for environmental compatibility simply did not take place – although the EU has laid down regulations regarding this. Mountains were dynamited, valleys filled in, and all kinds of other follies committed.

Take only the single example of the airfield. Though La Gomera can be reached from Tenerife in half an hour by ferry, an airport is built at a cost of £25 million, half the cost paid by the EU and half by the Canaries' Regional Government. Although the Government under Felipe Gonzalez had rejected the building of an airport as late as 1985 – now a runway of 1800 metres was constructed – which would do for a jumbo jet. And that for an island 22–25 km. across! Anyone who has ever visited La Gomera can imagine what that means for the island. The *Frankfurter Allgemeine Zeitung* has accurately detailed what will happen. In future those wishing to reach La Gomera by air will be subjected to the following experiences: They will land on the Airport (Reina Sofia) for Tenerife South. By taxi or bus they will be driven for two hours beyond the island capital of Santa Cruz to the far North Airport of Los Rodeos. There they will have a further wait, another check-in (at least 1 hour), and then the flight to Gomera (45 minutes). There you have to change to a taxi or bus again and suffer another one and a half hours' drive to the tourist centre of Valle Gran Rey. And to get to the scenically attractive regions around Hermigua or Agoulo in the North will take correspondingly longer.

The industrial management consultant Professor Frederico

Aguilera Klink of the Institute for Applied Economics of the University of Tenerife finds (the FAZ goes on) that the airport can only pay for itself if the planned two flights per day are fully booked for 30 seats per plane every day of the year and every visitor to Gomera then spends roughly £110 per day on the island – although the airport was supposedly built for the population. Anyone who has visited La Gomera knows that won't work. Insiders maintain that commonsense played no part in these plans. On the contrary: Not a single member of the island's population (which suffers badly from unemployment – 25% in 1992) found work at the biggest building site on the island. The reason is the population's lack of adequate qualifications from a Central European point of view. Work for which the Gomeros are qualified, such as a landscape-suited vegetable cultivation, was not being promoted. A true vicious circle of economic underdevelopment, illiteracy, unemployment and dependency on foreign aid. Nor is there better hope for the future. The reformed structures policy of the European Union promises no new solutions. Even the Finance Minister of the Canaries Government announced in an open letter to the local Press that he warned the Island Administration and the building contractors of the island against misusing the support funds from European national resources.

Once again nature is sacrificed to greed for profit and the refusal to learn from mistakes made elsewhere. An officially approved petition from the Foundation for European Natural Heritage against the above-mentioned road building elicited the curt reply that the case would be investigated by inquiries to the relevant EU Commission. In the meantime the excavators and the bulldozers go rolling on, and the wheeler-dealers are tirelessly at work. On their way they crush a mature island structure, a unique cultural heritage, and an irreplaceable natural heritage. And nobody stands up to them.

The destructive power of stupidity
How wrong investments destroy nature

A picture-book landscape lies before our eyes. We are standing on high ground overlooking the North Atlantic coast of Spain. Here in Cantabria the warm Gulf Stream makes for a temperate, mild climate, which in turn has produced a landscape of infinite variety. Round about us this October there are juicy green meadows – in this fortunate countryside spring is several months early. Here at Tina Menor there is a particular diversity. Besides the lush meadows there are steep scrub-covered slopes down to the sea. And then there is a wide, idyllic expanse of water: we are at the estuary of the River Nanza. Here the world still seems in good shape. Then our Spanish friend Jesus Garzon alerts us to the fact that the river no longer flows wild into the sea, but has been dammed at the very mouth.

Our curiosity aroused, we start asking questions, and discover that once more the Eco-Twisters have been at work, aided by EU funds. Possibly in this case it was not speculators that were harming nature and landscape, but the sheer stupidity or thoughtlessness of the responsible authorities. Once more a precious part of natural heritage is being lost, even though a cursory look at the view does not show it. So what is happening?

The River Nanza has been dammed in order to turn the resulting lake in to a plaice farm. But the plans of those who put public money into this venture did not work out. As the river now has only an up-river outlet to the sea, the former shallow but many-armed estuary has quickly silted up. Nor was that the only consequence. As the water exchange with the adjacent sea was no longer possible, an ecosystem built up over millennia was destroyed. For plaice farming there is simply not enough sea water in the silted-up area. It soon transpired that the fish breeding project financed with public money could not possibly pay its way. But, as usual, it is not the men responsible who suffer the consequences, but nature. For at the same time the nursery of many sea fish, crabs and other creatures adapted to that environment was lost.

To sum up: Before enterprises are promoted with public money, their environmental compatibility must be tested to the limit. Maybe it would be a good thing to test the intelligence of those who think up and implement such new departures.

Chapter 2

Head in the sand

It is almost unbelievable, but bitter reality: Even when they know about dangers and threats with a devastating effect on body and mind, people tend to close their eyes to disagreeable facts and continue undeterred. That is more than frivolity, it is stupidity. 'It won't affect me,' they think, regarding themselves as exceptional. One only has to look around in Europe: the ostrich attitude knows no limits; after all, it makes life so much more carefree . . .

My home is my castle
Marble for the affluent citizen

Asbestos? No thanks! CFCs? For heaven's sake! Composition panels? No way. We have all become environment-conscious and will be increasingly so. Only natural materials for us.

Here is an example. The hall needs renovating, new flooring is required.

'What might you be wanting?' asks the builders' merchant, whose business is visibly prospering.

I hesitated. In the showroom panels of the finest materials hung on the walls: slate, granite, every kind of marble . . .

'I would take Thasos marble,' said the man. 'You could hardly do better.'

I took it. Thirty square metres. Environment-conscious and guilty at the same time.

'Fire on Thasos.' Who worries about such a minor news item in the face of the huge forest fires reported every year round the Mediterranean, on French, Italian and Greek islands? Natural disasters or arson? The causes of the devastation of Mediterranean woods are many and various.

There have been fires on Thasos, too, many times. Greek friends had alerted us that there was something special about this island off Northern Greece. The marble was to blame for everything, they said, and spoke of a secret war between the 'marble breakers' and the hotel owners on the island. A war without human dead or wounded, but with great damage to the environment. To Thasos, then!

Going from Thessaloniki eastwards to Thracia, if you then choose to go via Drama to the regional capital of Kavalla and thence to Thasos, do not fail to visit the Cave of Maraa – before it is too late. The gigantic cave, still only partly explored, is under European nature protection. Its underground river is mentioned in Classical sources. But it is in acute danger. On the mountain ridge above the cave marble is being quarried: in fact, marble is being blasted out, and the vibrations shake the rocks below. Cracks in the roof of the cave are an unmistakable indication.

It all began 65 million years ago. That, according to the geologists' estimates, is when the high mountain ranges of Central and Southern Europe were formed. The process was accompanied by 'breakthrough of magmatic rock masses and isolated volcanic eruptions'. Everywhere the hot rocks touched and melted the layers of chalk above, precious marble was formed. This Northern Greek marble is among the most valuable and microscopically pure in the world. Its quarrying became a significant economic factor in this not very affluent part of the world. The white patches on the mountain tops, visible from afar, are therefore not natural phenomena but the opposite. They signal the destruction of the environment – accompanied by the background music of blasting detonations which a visitor travelling through the region has constantly in his ears.

In the evening, sitting in a little fish restaurant in the port of Keramoti we have a heated discussion. Are economics and ecology really irreconcilable? Can one blame the Greeks if to our eyes they have not developed a proper environmental awareness? As long as we are taking marble from North-East Greece, we too are Eco-Twisters. Environmental conservation is for rich countries, my Greek friend maintains. When we protest we are reminded of our own sins, and charged with sitting in a glass house with regard to this discussion.

The next morning we cross to Thasos. This is the finest marble of all, the marble dealer in Germany had said. Part illegally quarried, to be sure, but universally desirable. On the ferry we continue the previous evening's argument. 'You'll see!'

We heard!

In the little seaport of Limenas we climbed the narrow alleys up to the classical amphitheatre, and enjoyed the view over the island, and the silence – an apparent silence, but broken at intervals by detonations as from a distant battlefield. The marble! There was indeed a battle going on with great gains involved. Later on we saw the wounds, as at Maraa the day before bare, white-shining patches on the mountains, among ravaged areas of woodland.

'The European Union has a finger in every pie,' said a friend we visited. 'Most of the machines for quarrying the marble are financed by EU funds.' He pointed to the mountain slope opposite. Black, charred tree stumps made a picture of desolation. The wood is completely destroyed; the fire only stopped when it reached the leafy edge of the wood. That was in 1989, four years after the first disastrous fire on Thasos. 'It was an inferno. One has to accept that it was arson. Nature and environment here are purely objects for speculation.'

Our friend knows what he is talking about. In Brussels, too, they know that marble quarrying on Thasos is illegal by European and Greek law and that there have been no environmental compatibility studies. The Greek politicians' attitude was ambivalent. There were opponents of the savage exploitation, but also some who favoured it. After all, the business was worth millions. Even the Arab countries and Italy, 'that land of marble', bought from the Island what they could get. Tilting against windmills?

Our friend wants to save what was once 'green Thasos'. He has started a 'Citizens' Initiative Thasos'. 'Every block of marble exported is a piece of our Macedonian homeland lost,' is the message he sends out, in several languages. He speaks of 'malignant tumours in our woods,' and of 'a catastrophe for the whole island.' He pleads with ministers and other politicians and rehearses a riot when the marble-entrepreneurs make propaganda for their point of view with a symposium illustrated with classical sculptures. 'A shameless misuse of classical art,' he writes to the authorities in Thessaloniki and Athens. 'The marble quarries drive our visitors away,' is one of his arguments followed by the observation that the Greeks are only slowly learning to resist the despoiling of their countryside.

On Thasos those who are already fighting vehemently are the hoteliers, who are afraid that the tourists will not come back again. Among then is the Mayor of Prinos, Theodoros Hatziandreou. He and his wife have just opened a new hotel, and they support plans to build up a kind of eco-tourism on the island, which remains attractive with its long sandy beaches, its appealing hilly landscape, the ancient olive groves and the deep valleys of broad-leaved woodland.

What is best for Thasos? Tourism, or marble-quarrying? Or can they co-exist? Opinion on the Island is divided on these questions. The hotel owners and conservationists want an unspoilt world – without forest fires, detonations and ugly white bald patches on the mountains. The 'marble-people' put up economic arguments against that: more than 700 jobs in the quarries with high earnings meaning great spending power, a considerable export income for the best marble in Greece, benefits for the whole island through improvements in infrastructure – for example, roadbuilding and modernisation of the ferries – as well as new enterprises like transport firms and repair workshops.

The marble quarriers defend themselves vehemently against the reproach that they are insensitive to nature and ruin the environment. They insist the opposite is the case, and they even claim that the marble quarries are a sight to attract tourists.

That surely is rather far-fetched. The fact is that once the marble has been removed there has been no recultivation to date, and it is also true that beside the legal quarrying there is a high proportion of illegal cutting.

So there is war on the Island of Thasos. But Thasos must not die. Ecology and economics must be brought into accord, the rules for marble quarrying made more effective, the recultivation of quarries made obligatory, and the burnt and mutilated woods reafforested.

This is a meaningful task for the structural funds of the European Union.

Accelerating into chaos

The cult of mobility

'Just in time' or 'just at the turn of the tide'? The question comes up ever more sharply since the 'tin god' not only transports more and more people on ever more unnecessary new roads and the degree of motorisation in Europe is higher than ever before, but also as the craziest marathon feats of transport keep increasing. The whole absurdity of 'borderless' HGV-Europe today is typified by the North German potatoes which – transport being cheaper than labour costs – are driven across the Alps to Italy to be washed before being brought back for sale in North Germany. Or, did you know that, as a study by the *Wuppertal Institute for Climate, Environment and Energy* shows, the components of a tasty strawberry yogurt have travelled a distance of 7,695 km. before they reach the consumer?

Such kilometric achievements, which provoke the periodical *fairkehr* of the Verkehrsclub Deutschland (VDC) to the apt comment 'We are all road hogs' no longer surprise when one remembers that the strawberries have to find their way from distant Poland to Aachen and thence to Stuttgart, the foil for the container comes from France, and the cardboard from the German North Sea coast. This works out at a proud 10 km. HGV-performance for every serving of yogurt ... But the yogurt is by no means exceptional if one knows that North Sea shrimps are driven to Poland to be peeled, then driven back to Germany to land on the counters of gourmet shops. The bill is made out on a purely financial basis, reckoning without the 'host' – nature – and thus without human cost. Is this folly, this traffic chaos, a mere fad of the '80s and '90s? No, the system is self-perpetuating. And the name of this murderous system is Business as usual, time is money, don't interfere with transport. This (mainly) EU development could have us all out of breath. It is the scandal of making your deal and devil take the hindmost. Ecology does not appear on the balance-sheets of the Eco-Twisters, otherwise they would look very different.

When the EC in summer 1992 argued the necessity for 12,000 km. of new motorway for infrastructurally underdeveloped regions (as they put it in statements from official Europe), inter alia Greece, Spain, Portugal and Ireland, even the last sceptic must have realised where the train – or rather, the motorcade – of European transport policy was heading.

So the Prague Transport Conference, which pleaded for a change of direction in favour of railways, was not really worth the price of tickets for the journey. That demand for the concreting over of valuable landscapes, not hitherto cut by too many roads or asphalted, and often of outstanding importance for ecology and culture, reveals the official transport-policy ideology of the EU Commission, and the Council of Ministers which influences it, like an ominous fixed star in the sky above the Common Market and the European economy. So far there is no hint of a change in transport policy in favour of the environment and observance of the EU's own conservation legislation which would apply to many of the endangered countrysides, e.g. the Bird Protection Directive and the Flora-Fauna-Habitat Directive; the socially desirable encouragement of railways and the vital reduction of motor traffic are nowhere in sight. On the contrary, the expected transfer of responsibility for transport policy to the EU must be regarded with some dread. There is a striking resemblance in certain pronouncements (the demand for further motorways in the allegedly 'underdeveloped' EU countries) to what was raised ten years ago by industrial groups like the 'Round Table of Industry' with their Missing Links and Scan Links proposals. And these same lobbyists now scent a lead-impregnated dawn, in which they will find willing advocates of a car-oriented policy like the first United Germany Minister of Transport, Krause, once dubbed a 'motorway Stalinist' by the watchful VCD traffic activists, and fortunately soon replaced.

Already there is a call for a whole network of new motorways in the direction of Eastern Europe; even lunatic projects presumed defunct, like the extremely nature-destructive North German coastal Autobahn heading for Poland, have been resurrected. For the sake of completeness one should mention that this policy of road-building after German unification is not due solely to the German Motorways Minister. It would not be possible if there were more resistance from the Federal German regions, often governed by politicians who call themselves 'ecologists'.

Again, consider the acquiescence of Rhineland-Palatinate in the traffic communications facilitation law – another region ruled by local politicians who apparently support the 'ecological reconstruction of industrial society' – all political correctness. The same goes for Lower Saxony, which presents itself as being exceptionally environment-conscious. The Lower Saxons actually undertook the task of facilitating the 'great' coastal motorway to the East, even though they keep denying it. Yet no less than the Minister for Economic Affairs (and Transport) of that North German Federal Region came out in favour of the so-called Weser Tunnel north of Bremen, to such good effect that the Tunnel was promptly made an 'urgent need' priority of the Federal Communications Plan. Politics in some Federal lands appear to proceed according to the principles of Mr Facing-Both-Ways. It is especially revealing where a regional government in opposition to the Federal government advocates 'complete ecological reform' even for transport policy. Germany as the outrider of a United Autoland?

The first All-German Federal Communications Plan points clearly to the future course of European transport policy: roads, roads, roads, plus many dishonest statements about transport policy reversal. Since 1989 there has been a vast change in the chief lines of communication in Europe. After the disappearance of the Iron Curtain there began tentative turning away from the North-South-Axis to an East-West alignment which reinforced the existing streams of traffic.

Since 1989 the lorry-borne goods traffic has proliferated in East-West transit through Germany. According to the calculations of the Federal Ministry of Transport transport of goods alone, East to West and vice versa, in the year 2010 will have reached more than four times the figure for 1988, while North-South traffic will have increased 2.7 times. A drastic increase in general goods traffic is clearly the writing on the wall for the European Economic area. Clearly prognoses of a 100% increase in lorry traffic by the year 2010 are by no means in the realm of fantasy, but simply show exactly what is heading towards people and their environment – overrunning, flattening them . . .

One prominent victim of the transfer of goods transport to the roads will be the railways. Their transport tariffs will stand no chance in competition with road transport once all restrictions of customs, licence and concessions duties have been lifted. Wholly in accordance with the EU's maxim of 'free passage of goods' all haulage contractors of all member states will be at liberty to send their goods from any point to any other within the European Union.

Moreover, the EU Commission is playing an ever more dubious role in the matter of climate conservation, so closely bound up with transport policy. This was shown just before the Rio Earth Summit. The widely acclaimed tax on climate killing CO_2, which would at last have laid a financial burden on motor transport, was postponed, because for the EU to go it alone might not have been opportune, a fact which throws some doubt on the environmental credibility of the EU Commission.

And again world policy is turning somersaults. That long-standing environment policy twister and largest energy user in the world, the United States, announced the introduction of an energy tax which would put a 5% purchase tax on every barrel of oil. The question as to whether this would be enough to noticeably reduce mineral oil consumption does not present itself: the announcement was never translated into fact. Research in the mid '80s for the German Federal Republic showed that even a considerable rise in the price of petrol to 3 or even 4 DM per litre would have no decisive effect on driving habits.

But to return to the railways. What at first looked hopeful – the chance to get better control of regional interests and requirements – has now at EU level developed into what amounts to preparations for abandoning trains. The EU Commission wanted to initiate 'a new order of market conditions' for rail policy by means of a liberalising directive. That noble principle must, however, be viewed with great scepticism as regards its realization in individual European countries. For the Transport Ministers of European countries such as Germany and UK have long set dangerous tracks for the future of their national railways. While the privatisation of British Rail has already begun, in Germany only the first tracks have been laid for branching off into three joint-stock companies. The greatest imposition is the delegating of responsibility for regional and local domestic services to the Lands and the local communities. All this is with a positively minimal financial provision of an estimated six or seven billion DM from the

Federal budget – while up to 2005 the Federal Transport Minister's budget for road building alone should amount to 200 billion DM. Money is invested against the railways, further weighting the alleged open competition to their disadvantage. It is all too plain what is in store for local rail passenger services: an unprecedented orgy of line closures which will shrink the rail network (already halved in West Germany since 1945) in dramatic fashion.

What else does the rail- and communications policy of the EU Commission propose? In the main there are the so-called Trans-European networks, motorways, high-speed trains, conventional railways, inland waterways, sea- and airports, as well as combined services. In the case of high-speed trains it is vital to demand that these services undergo tests for social and environmental compatibility. Is it acceptable to work on 300 km/hr. stretches involving huge financial outlay (spacious underpass tunnels, devouring of landscapes, vast use of energy for the motive power, highly intensive in Germany at exceptional speeds, so that any advantage against motor traffic is largely sacrificed), while in East Germany rail passenger local services are collapsing with not even the most essential line repairs carried out?

Apart from the time element – it would take decades to build up such a network – once again only the symptom would be treated. Official EU Europe clearly does not want railways for Europe as the real necessities – First Aid to deal with transport- and environmental collapse – fall victim to Brussels' catastrophic environmental policy.

Spellbound into the abyss
Death freighters on the high seas

Police reports show it all the time. Evidently nothing is more fun than to see the aftermath of an accident, in which – of course – one is not personally involved. The statistics mention increasing numbers of onlookers and growing difficulties with rescue work. To be on the spot when catastrophes happen, or to watch them live on television, means a lot to many people.

An example of disaster-tourism is the Shetland Isles to the North of Scotland, where on 5 January 1993 – one month after the shipping disaster outside the Spanish port La Coruna – the oil tanker *Braer*, sailing under the Liberian flag with a cargo of 84,000 tonnes, ran on to rocks in a storm and broke up. The tanker became unmanoeuvrable when at windforce ten sea water got into the fuel tanks and put the engines out of action.

Strange as it sounds the immediately threatened major environmental catastrophe in this important bird sanctuary actually was averted due to the cause of the accident. Storms and high waves quickly dispersed the oil leak and largely kept it away from the coast. Nevertheless thousands of birds died, and there would have been more if animal conservationists had not saved many of the endangered creatures with a 1600 km. air-lift.

The first photos taken after the storm showed the broken parts of the tanker rearing picturesquely out of the sea close to the shore. Months later only the bow of the 241-metre-long ship was visible. Target for numerous tourists who, judging by the sudden increase in bookings, came to the Shetlands solely for this; the macabre consequence of an increasing trend to voyeurism. For the inhabitants of the Islands this meant good coming of evil, for money was certainly needed to rehabilitate the polluted beaches and detoxify the grasslands for sheep.

One continues to wonder how such things can happen? There are frequent tanker disasters on the same pattern as the *Braer*. The Shetlands may have just escaped the worst, but that cannot be said of most tanker accidents.

These disasters seem to obey some series law, caused by a diabolical mixture of carelessness, human error and technical deficiencies. The log of tanker shipping is a pure catalogue of disasters. More than 200 large tankers have come to grief in the last 25 years on the high seas. They were rammed, drifted on to rocks with their steering gone, broke up in storms, and leaked their cargo of oil into the sea.

The cost to the environment in most cases is devastating. Beaches polluted for years, the death of many thousands of seabirds, fish, whales, seaturtles, otters and seals, and health problems for the coastal inhabitants.

A few names from the horror serial of tanker disasters still send a shiver down the spine, even today:

Torrey Canyon: In March 1967 there occurred the greatest oil pestilence up to that time in the history of world shipping, when the 120,000-ton Liberian tanker broke up off the coast of Cornwall, contaminating large areas of coast in England, France and Holland.

Amoco Cadiz: In March 1978 the Liberian giant tanker ran aground outside the French port of Brest. Its 230,000 tonnes of oil contaminated 200 km. of beaches in Brittany. 15,000 seabirds died.

Exxon Valdez: In March 1989 outside the harbour of Valdez in Alaska the American supertanker struck a reef. 42,000 tonnes of oil poured out and caused the USA's greatest environmental catastrophe in Alaska's richest fishing grounds. The death toll was around 580,000 seabirds and 5,500 otters, seals, whales and sealions. The aftereffects of this oil pestilence are felt to this day. A recent study showed considerable long-time damage to flora and fauna.

Haven: In April 1991 the Cypriot oil tanker exploded off the coast of Genoa. 50,000 tonnes of oil poured out, causing heavy damage.

Havoc caused by storm and weather is in a way explicable. But there can be no understanding the disaster that occurred two weeks after the *Braer* in the Straits of Malacca, the busiest sea passage between Europe and the Far East, traversed daily by about 400 big ships and 1500 local craft and ferries. In January 1993 on a calm sea and with clear visibility the 322-metre-long Danish supertanker *Maersk Navigator* with a load of 225,000 tonnes of oil was rammed amidships by the empty Japanese tanker *Sanka Honour*. The *Maersk Navigator* burned for five days before the fire could be extinguished. Massive quantities of oil poured into the sea off the coast of Sumatra.

For a long time tanker accidents were classed as 'natural disasters'. One accepted them, with regret and sympathy for the region affected, but, as it were, resigned to fate. With growing environmental awareness and ever more massive presence of conservationists there has meanwhile been a real change of attitude; the limits of pain and tolerance have been reached. Suddenly there is a world-wide demand for action, even governments and politicians have been frightened, not least in Europe. The 'floating timebombs' on the seas must be tackled; there was a hectic search for the causes and initiators of catastrophes – and facts soon emerged. In 90% of all marine disasters the 'human factor' is the basic cause. But add to that the superannuated ships and inadequate technical and security resources.

In plain language: On the oceans of the world there are constantly around 4,000 tankers travelling with an annual load of 1.4 billion tonnes of crude oil. Many of the ships are totally superannuated, often having seen more than 25 years' service. Most of the over 700 giant tankers were commissioned and built 20 years ago, after the *Yom Kippur* War in the Middle East, when the Suez Canal was closed and, taking the route around South Africa, only huge capacities made the transport of oil profitable. Many of these ships have been poorly serviced and maintained, and are manned by crews coming from all over the world who have no common language and are marked by sharp social divisions. The officers are often insufficiently trained and at odds with modern technology. Then along comes a great storm, engine trouble, or some other crisis. The *Braer* which ran aground off the Shetlands was 18 years old, the critical age for a tanker.

The Americans have already drawn their conclusions from the *Exxon Valdez* disaster and now allow only double-hulled tankers into their territorial waters. Accidents can result in unlimited sums in damages. That has had some effect.

The Europeans are now following suit. In the port of Rotterdam a marine Technical Supervision Authority (TöV) has existed for a long time. A most efficient body, equipped with experienced experts and wide powers, it makes sure that the port is not endangered by incoming damaged ships. The controllers are uncompromising. Ships which do not conform to international safety regulations have to be repaired on the spot before they are permitted to leave again. That can cost a fortune, including harbour dues. Rotterdam can afford such measures, for this Dutch port is the most important port of call for imports to Europe from all over the world. The TöV of Rotterdam could be a model for the avoidance of tanker disasters on Europe's doorstep. Such an authority has already been called for by international insurance, led by Europe's largest insurance group, the *Alliance* – shaken as they have been by the most recent chain of disasters.

It really is astonishing: the most terrible things have to happen before bureaucrats and politicians are ready to react. But at least that seems to be happening now. The EU member states have, through the International Maritime Organisation to which 130 members belong, required that newly built tankers have to pass more stringent conditions.

Council of Ministers, EU-Commission and European Parliament are acting in concert. Thus there is to be an obligatory pilot service where shipping routes run close to EU coasts. Further there is consideration of a ban on tankers more than 15 years old in European ports. EU territorial waters will in future be closed to tankers without a double hull. Other requirements: one single language spoken on board, obligatory training of crews in safety procedures, inspection of ships in EU harbours, and sanctions against infringement of EU regulations. It has been long overdue for the European Union, the greatest economic power in the world, to show its teeth and put an end to coffin ships sailing under flags of convenience.

Just like the ostrich
You can't see an ozone hole

Greetings from the suicide society. Because politicians could not agree industry would not yield an inch and really all of us were not keen to recognise the explosive nature of the problem. We stumbled like lemmings, open-eyed, to destruction. Ever more natural disasters, a general deterioration of climate, an increase in skin cancer and cataracts in some parts of the world; these are the writing on the wall for the unbounded recklessness that threatens to make victims of us all. The full extent of the consequences of that recklessness, for people, animals and plants, is still not fully recognised.

We are talking about the so-called ozone hole; nobody knows its actual size, but many fear that it is bigger than so far assumed. We are talking about the continuing disappearance of the triatomic oxygen molecule, ozone, which forms a dense protective layer around the Globe and shields – or should one say, shielded – life on Earth from the destructive effect of 'hard' short-wave ultraviolet rays of the sun. In recent decades this protective layer has become thinner and is still continuing to decrease. This is the result of a complex chemical reaction which we humans started unwittingly at first, but are still carrying on, wantonly and self-destructively, despite all warnings.

This portentous drama takes place at a great height, about ten kilometres above the Earth's surface, and extends into inner space – almost up to 50 km. In this 'belt' there was, until a few decades ago, a more or less stable equilibrium. Oxygen and ozone molecules were split up by the action of the ultraviolet rays and then reconstituted, absorbing part of the dangerous radiation in the process. That, briefly, is the scientific explanation.

That equilibrium has now been seriously disturbed. The elements chlorine and bromine intervene with chemical aggression in the atmospheric events and attack the ozone molecule: killers which destroy the ozone without any harm to themselves. With refined methods of measurement, above all by satellite observation and the findings of the space ferry 'Discovery', the process of erosion in the Earth's atmosphere can be proved and followed very accurately. First traced above the Antarctic, an ozone hole has now also been discovered above the Arctic. The term 'ozone hole' is actually misleading, not meant to be more than a fanciful description of the reality as seen by meteorologists, physicists and chemists. These have diagnosed a steadily progressive thinning of the ozone layer, damage increasing steadily from the Equator to the Poles, where it has assumed alarming proportions. Above Germany at the end of 1992 researchers recorded a frightening 'loss' of almost 40%.

Those responsible – the Eco-Twisters among them – are situated several kilometres below in Spaceship Earth and behave like someone who has taken the roof off his house and is surprised to find the rain coming in. Ignorant or careless, they produce or use aerosol sprays, refrigerators and air conditioning plants which all have one thing in common: they work on chlorofluorohydrocarbons, those valuable but fiendish propellant gases which under the abbreviation CFCs are now known to virtually every child and have for some years been banned by the international community. However, with only partial success.

Already in 1978 the USA banned the use of CFCs in sprays; Sweden, Norway and Canada quickly followed suit. In the German Federal Republic, thanks to pressure from industry, at first voluntary restrictions were tried – understandably with hardly noticeable effects. In 1990 a law was passed to abandon the use of CFCs by 1995, but this date was soon put forward to the end of 1993.

Belatedly, but at last sensibly, the initially reluctant German Chemical Industry changed its negative attitude, and now also sees speedier relinquishing as unavoidable, in the face of increasing public pressure and the hardening realisation of the catastrophic consequences of ozone destruction. Car manufacturers, the building industry and the electrical industry are now pulling in the same direction and have given up using CFCs. The Federal Republic can pat itself on the back: after long hesitation, it has embraced the concept of dropping substances that harm the ozone layer.

It was of course clear from the start that the whole problem could only be solved satisfactorily by international cooperation. That was a good opportunity for politicians and governments everywhere to opt for protecting the Earth's atmosphere and the environment at spectacular international conferences all over the Globe with more or less concrete demands. There was at first general agreement to ban the 'dangerous propellants' only from the year 2000.

But then the alarming reports from the 'ozone front' led to a concerted and drastic reaction. 81 countries resolved in 1992 at the Fourth Ozone Conference of UNO in Copenhagen to advance the date of the ban on the ozone killers to the 1 January 1996. Halons, such as were used in fire extinguishers, have not been in use since 1994. Thus the deadlines agreed in Montreal in 1987 and in London in 1990 were significantly amended. In Canada the signatory states, including the EU, had committed themselves in what was known as the Montreal Protocol to cut the production of certain important CFC gases by degrees to half by 1999. However, a supplementary agreement negotiated in London mandates a total ban by the year 2000.

The search for substitutes and the switch to less aggressive variants of the CFCs was no simple matter. They are known as part-halogenated hydrocarbons (HCFCs), these neat little half-strength killers, which following on the Copenhagen agreement are to be reduced by one third by 2004 and totally banned by the year 2030. There was no choice. Probably it cannot be done more quickly. An industrial society must abide by its own laws, even where it faces its own destruction.

A special interest at these international conventions is represented by the Third World. Special rules have been and must be made in dealing with it. And here comes the 'cloven hoof'. The Third World countries have been hit hardest financially by the change to less dangerous substitute materials. Therefore in London all the 87 signatory states of the 'Montreal Ozone Protocol' agreed to set up a permanent aid fund to make it easier for developing countries to give up ozone-damaging materials. It will be financed, however reluctantly, by the rich industrial countries who were the main causers of the ozone crisis. These funds were secured only until 1993.

In Copenhagen the financial requirement for saving the ozone layer globally was given as 2 to 7 billion dollars, a pretty vague assessment. Of this at least 2 billion dollars should, according to the UNO Environment Organisation, go as minimum contribution to the Third World. On this question a battle of basic principle flared between the delegations from North and South. It concerned the continued financing and administering of the fund which ran out in 1993. In London an equitably composed committee of industrial and developing countries was proposed for distributing the aid money. Against this in Copenhagen there was a small but influential block led by the EU countries UK, France, Italy and Holland. They want the 'Ozone Fund' incorporated in the Global Environment Fund under the aegis of the World Bank, where they have a stronger say than do the representatives of the Third World. The latter promptly spoke of a 'breach of trust'. Others were even blunter: they called it an elegant breakdown of the Conference.

At the moment, beside many serious efforts, we are also experiencing a whole series of sham fights and shadow-boxing in the matter, so vital for all of us, of 'Saving the Ozone Layer'. But one thing has become clear to all those involved or affected – and that means everyone on earth: the self-healing power of nature – which includes the atmosphere – can only take effect when the ruthless exploitation is curbed, or, better still, stopped altogether. Scientists have as good evidence that the atmosphere is capable of regeneration as for the causes of its destruction.

It would be most desirable if we could say one day with a great sigh of relief: Well, we've escaped that one.

Chapter 3

Money rules, O.K.?

Money makes the world go round. With sufficient banknotes the world evidently can be turned in any direction. We all know business is business. Who pays, consumes, and we comfort ourselves that money always comes up smelling of roses. Is it really worthwhile to do anything and everything for money?

Put money in thy purse
The scam of the nature reserves

Often it is simple ignorance, inadequate controls or lack of sensitivity to ecological matters that cause our environment to be endangered and nature destroyed. Unfortunately often it is also greed for profit, coupled with unbelievably brazen lies to the public.

Take the question of the nature reserves. Again and again, amid great fanfares and after much pressure from conservationists, nature reserves are designated, only to be wrested from nature again later, basically as cheap building sites. The many encroachments on the new national parks, nature parks, wildlife reserves and sites of special scenic beauty in the new Federal region are a sad example of this. Let us take a further instance which shows that all is not, and should not be, gold that glitters. As you read these lines, perhaps you should ask yourself whether you really want to spend your next holiday on one of the Balearic Islands. For it if were up to leading politicians like the Governor President of the Balearics, Canellas, and some of his party comrades, soon the last remaining attractive and unspoilt areas of Majorca, Minorca and Ibiza could be sacrificed to commercial greed. But now for the incredible scandal which shows once again that through such irresponsible greed and slick manipulations the cause of landscape preservation and ecology is merely used as a shuttlecock for financial and power-political interests – just as it happens to suit these people's plans.

In 1989 Spanish and international conservationists thought they had scored a notable success. The Regional Government of the Balearics, after much urging by the conservationists and the association of the hoteliers, issued a truly exemplary law for the designation of protected areas. By this law about a third of the islands' total area was placed under protection. The initiative was greeted with acclaim from all sides, and even received the World Aware Award – a prize for sensitive treatment of nature and culture – from the British tour operators Thomson. Even the politicians tirelessly lobbied for their new law under the slogan 'an exemplary conjunction of nature and tourism'. Busily the new line was marketed in advertising brochures. And – says Marion Cavanna of ECOTRANS in Spain – they would have had a perfect right to do so, had not the Conservative Party of the Balearics succeeded by a tiny majority in remodelling the law in 1992. What had happened?

The answer is very simple. The powerful families of the President of the Balearics and the EU Commissioner Abel Matutes are planning to build tourist developments in bays which, under the law, are actually in protected areas. So as nature conservation – though they themselves had proclaimed it in the past – has got in the way of the noble gentlemen and their family clans, they want to remould the basic tenets and slaughter the districts which should be protected on the sacrificial slab of commercial greed and speculative enterprise.

In contrast to its politicians, the population of the Balearics has however realised that on the Islands the limits of the tourist trade have been reached, nay, exceeded. In November 1992 the biggest ever demonstration in the history of the Balearics took place. Over 26,000 people gathered to protest against the modification of the law and demanded protection for the last remaining nature reserves. They had recognised that the natural life and landscape of the Balearic Islands represented important ecological capital for their own economic future. Of the areas designated as nature reserves in 1989, three on Majorca, one large area on Minorca and three on Ibiza would be wholly or largely taken out of protection. That is not the last of it. To crown it all, on Ibiza as well as Formentera the building regulations and limitations of development were so vaguely and flexibly framed that in unprotected areas there could be no less than seven times as much building as was allowed for in 1989.

So when advertising brochures and travel guides tell you that a holiday resort has conservation areas, wildlife reserves or national parks, look closely, dear readers, if you care about those landscapes. Often protected areas only last as long as it suits the speculators – or as long as we all stand together to defend them.

The privatised environment

Destroying the rivers – not only the Amazon

The Amazon, lying far away from the Old World, has caught the European imagination. We visualise giant trees hung with lianas leaning over the shallow flowing water – a multifaceted paradise, threatened with death by chainsaws. As a synonym for the threat to nature, to the rivers of Paradise, one feels this is the river that must be preserved. Above all the thought is intolerable that the river is being sacrificed to private interests. Yet there is no need to go as far as South America to find circumstances where a river seems in danger of becoming a private possession. Similar things on a smaller scale are happening on our very doorstep, in EU-Europe, in Germany, in a cultural enclave which prides itself on having the fiercest environment regulations in the world, and the most enlightened politicians. Moreover, within the jurisdiction of EU legislation. Such events mark the political and social anomalies to which structurally weak regions are particularly exposed.

This excursion into harsh reality could actually begin like a fairy tale, a fairy tale relating how an ingenious gentleman succeeded, even in the hardest of times, in looking after all the people who sat in his boat. And this same gentleman, one of the most respected dignitaries of the whole region, could negotiate the trickiest rocks that beset the economic straits of his country. But that would present just one side of the action, or rather, just one of the protagonists. The other protagonist, equally involved, has not yet been mentioned: a river. This river is not one of the most imposing in Germany, let alone Europe, but neither is it a mere rivulet – it is the River Ems.

Situated in the Ems region at Papenburg, in one of the structurally weakest parts of Germany with above average unemployment figures, the Meyer-Werft (Shipyard) survives as the last of what were almost two dozen large shipyards in the region. And, wholly counter to the current trend of great shipyards' mortality, Meyer-Werft and its eponymous owner have so far managed to present full order books and an expanding site. More than 1800 workers find employment here, and many ancillary suppliers also draw their income from Meyer's. In a way the whole area around the little town of Papenburg is therefore dependent on this shipyard. So it is not surprising that politicians of all parties, up to the highest ranks, come to pay their respects to the shipyard, for its enterprising owner has always known how to maintain useful connections with friends in high places.

But that is only one side. The other side is that matter of regarding nature as private property. While most shipyard locations experienced stagnation or even decline, the Meyer-Werft could hitherto pride itself and amaze the public at large with the splendid orders that kept coming in. Large passenger ships are built in the town on the Ems, and to the astonishment of the whole industry there are always more follow-up orders. This must be largely due to the dauntless spirit of the shipyard, especially in coping with an obstacle which for years has resembled the many headed Hydra: the Ems itself. For the navigable depth of the river has consistently hampered new construction, being insufficient for the proverbial 'hand's breadth of water under the keel' needed to take the ships the mere 70 km. to the mouth of the Ems at the Dollart. So with beautiful regularity the call was heard for a deepening of the Ems – at the taxpayers' expense. In the past its depth at Papenburg was a bare 3 metres; now it is a proud 6.30 metres, and is to be made deeper still. If the shipyard has its way, not only to the 6.80 metres applied for, but to 7.30 metres – for the ships commissioned from Meyer-Werft are getting steadily bigger. Technology is not being adapted to nature, nature has to adapt to technology. The chain of deepening operations – all, mark you, carried out with public money, including the necessary maintenance dredging – seems to be endless, the conservation societies complain. The development of ship size for domestic navigation, from small craft such as the 1000-tonner to the European ship of 1350 tons had already necessitated a steady deepening and widening of the Ems. The focus now is on the lower Ems. The Meyer Shipyard, with the argument 'River extension or loss of worksite' as its bargaining counter, always gets a hearing from the politicians. At least to date . . .

Very much to the dismay of the conservationists, Meyer's calculation seems to be working so far. It is obvious that no politician can come out against the apparently vital deepening of the Ems without having the whole region against him. The Regional Government based in Oldenburg soon saw what that meant. They were considering the demand for deepening the river to 6.80 metres – with even greater 'dredging tolerance', i.e. expected deviations, as the conservation societies warn – when in summer 1992 they suddenly found themselves besieged by 1800 shipyard workers, who had come to the regional capital to press their demand for further works on the Ems. Such a demonstration had never been seen before. Accordingly the authorities made heavy weather of the ecological classification of the application. So far, it was repeatedly stressed, there had been no adequate ecological report on the river works. The conservationists impute 'premature obedience' to the regional authority and to the land of Lower Saxony. The latter took on a guarantee of a generous 500 million DM for the new works. It is not hard to visualise that even a depth of 6.80 metres will not be the end of the line. For it is the Region that has to decide, via the local authority, whether deepening is or is not ecologically justifiable. Those concerned for the river ask themselves, 'Can one expect a sufficiently disinterested consideration?'

'It is a monstrous thing,' the conservationists complain, 'and unworthy of a responsible society, for a shipyard to come and call upon the State to promote their purely business interests.' Politicians should no longer act as obliging aides to Meyer-Werft. Rather the River Ems should be 'granted its rights'. For every added construction work so far had added more damage to nature, and fishermen and farmers also complained of losses. The catch of sought-after eels had declined noticeably after the dredging. With catches small at best, this could pose a threat to the survival of the few remaining Ems fishermen, who have always managed to co-exist with 'their' river.

The deepening of the Ems, the conservationists say, has considerably increased the speed of flow, with the result that more pieces of the banks were broken away and riparian erosion grew worse. Also certain protected reed beds, which cannot survive in a strong current, are especially endangered. The deepening of the Ems that was carried out in 1982 already led to sizeable encroachments in the well-known nature reserve of the Tunxdorf Peninsula. Again and again there was flooding of the wetlands, which immediately makes it impossible for endangered grassland birds to breed there. But even more devastation is threatened by further works. One must expect further deepening to lead to diminished water levels in the area of the estuary, so that the tide would come in more strongly, causing considerable variations in the lower course. Conservationists are therefore concerned about the few remaining outer-dyke areas and foresee erosion of the banks. Reed beds cannot maintain themselves here. The sufferers would be bird species (such as bluethroat and marsh harrier) protected under the Bird Protection Directive and German Conservation Law.

The questions are to whom does a river 'belong', and what is the actual use of nature protection laws. An added hazard is the dangerous products of dredging, as already some heavily polluted mud has to be disposed of in the course of the cycle of maintaining the navigation depth. More deepening would again produce gigantic quantities of dredger silt.

For conservationists the route of advance (or should it be the direction of the current) is clear. They demand no further deepening or widening of the river, and they will explore all legal means to stop it. Above all they demand genuine testing for environmental compatibility to meet the criteria of the EU directive. That it is not, all the societies stress, at public expense – at the expense of every one of us – that we should continually give in to the demands of an entrepreneur. The conservationists realise that this will cause discomfort to many an official. To escape from the vicious circle of 'loss of workplace or enlargement of the Ems', they have for years suggested a course that sounds plausible: to resite the shipyard in a place which already has the requisite seagoing depth. This could be done by a partial relocation of the shipyard to nearby Emden, or by moving the whole enterprise, which at present, with its massive engine shed is undoubtedly one of the most impressive edifices on the flat plain where the Ems region meets East Friesland.

It has also been suggested that relocation be to one of the focal points of economic decline in North Germany: to

Wilhelmshafen, which already has the right seagoing depth of navigable water and enormous space which will become available soon when the navy is cut. Rostock, too, is a frequent suggestion for the East German metropolis on the Baltic has a long tradition of shipbuilding, and at present is going through the most desperate crisis since shipbuilding began in the old Hanseatic city.

The Meyer Shipyard itself once thought of moving, but its plans would not have pleased the conservationists. Just after the 'change' in East Germany, when Federal regions had just been set up in the former DDR, the bombshell exploded in 1991: Meyer-Werft wanted to settle in Mukran on the island of Rügen, not far from the Jasmund National Park with its famous forest and its chalk cliffs. An 'island' was to be built out into the sea, with huge dimensions of 300 metres in length and 400 metres in breadth, and this area of nearly 60 hectares would enable hangers to be erected up to a height of 63 metres. They would have towered 40 metres above the nearby cliff! And as the watchful Citizens' Initiative for Rügen, which received the European Environment Prize in 1992, pointed out accusingly, the 'planning' was to proceed at an unprecedented, galloping pace which, the Rügen conservationists feared, would hardly allow for serious spatial dispositions . . .

This aroused all the horror one would imagine, and throughout Germany there was active opposition to the Meyer-Werft proposal. Swiftly signatures were collected – more than 160,000 – and all the conservation societies protested to the Regional Government in Schwerin, and even the EU-Commission was rung up. For nobody could see why the Island of Rügen, whose only asset from the time of Caspar David Friedrich to the present day was its largely unspoilt scenery and consequently whose only chance of development was through soft tourism, should be ruined by such a stampede while in nearby Rostock huge areas of navigable depth for seagoing ships sank into stagnant decline.

The far-sighted attitude of the Rügen population – rejecting the supposed allurements of Meyer-Werft, unmasked for the deadly nightshade it was – has not so far found a parallel in any other part of the countryside in Germany. It is thanks to the obstinate persistence of the people of Rügen and the support of numerous nature lovers all over Europe that this attack on Rügen was fought off. The project 'Meyer-Werft in Mukran' was finally shelved just before Whitsun 1992. The Meyer Shipyard abandoned its building plans, allegedly on account of the EU decision to cut down on shipbuilding capacity. But conservation organisations are sure that the intrinsic value of the landscape around the Ems will one day also find the consideration it deserves. Otherwise the spiral of Ems deepening will experience further turns of the screw – to the detriment of nature, human beings, and the credibility of EU legislation for the environment.

Many trees do not make a forest
Dual standards in environmental conservation

Imagine a virgin forest, many centuries old, is to be cut down to make wood pulp – wood pulp for a declining world market where the prices are dropping right down to the cellar. Oddly enough the same country where the ancient forest is to go has plentiful reserves of commercially managed woodland – with a higher rate of regrowth than a year's felling can deplete. A farce? A satire? No, this is reality – in Europe, in Finland, to be precise.

The Nordic countries like to present themselves to nature lovers and observers as the most ecologically intact, as they are also the richest in woodland, on the Old Continent. Dark fir woods, midsummernights on the tundra, low-growing trees, and elk loping across the road make up the cliché picture, largely thanks to the native tourist industry. In fact Scandinavia really is one of the most densely wooded regions of Europe. Thus Sweden is 60% woodland, and the most north-easterly country on the Arctic Circle region, Finland, 90%. Germany has only 29%.

This apparently positive balance-sheet, however, boils down to a basic value which does not tell you much about ecological diversity. One has to look behind the facade of forestry and above all query the handling of the most valuable woodland in Scandinavia. Of course the wood, apart from its function as a habitat for plants and animals and its role as a guarantor of ground water, also has the important task of acting as a 'climate conditioning chamber'. By means of massive evaporation it moderates temperatures and binds carbon dioxide (CO_2), synthesising it into new plant material. So, with some justice, there is constant clamour for large-scale afforestation, to counteract, at least partially, the greenhouse effect. Notably before the Rio Earth Summit these demands proliferated, and the EU certainly thinks along these lines. Why not plant forests to bind carbon dioxide and at the same time create 'woods for the future' which will also provide recreation for city dwellers? The EU Directive (No. 2080/92) even proposes extra subsidies for afforestation with particularly fast-growing species. That is trying to do what gave Scandinavia its original rich stock of woodland. But afforestation and forests are two different things.

Of course every plant absorbs carbon dioxide, filters dust and harmful substances from the air, and improves the climate. But only site-specific woods offer true living conditions for native wildlife. Exotic, alien trees, not so much planted as 'built' into plantations, can merely supply food and space for breeding and development to a few all-purpose species. Take Europe's woods of the post-war period: dark plantations of Douglas fir cover wide stretches of the Continent, though these trees come from North America and are really a sylvan fake. There is hardly any wildlife in these plantations, and the ground is virtually free from undergrowth and vegetation. Birds have little chance of finding a nesting place. There are no tree hollows or food resources for European fauna. The same goes for other imported tree species.

The Canadian hybrid poplar is an extreme example. This tree was planted in preference to the native black poplar because of its rapid growth, and thereby has brought one of the most colourful native butterflies to the verge of extinction. The Purple Emperor lays its eggs on poplar leaves. The caterpillars emerge straight into their food store, but only where the indigenous poplars are concerned. Canadian hybrid poplars have significantly tougher leaf edges, which the caterpillars cannot masticate. So the caterpillars starve to death on the very leaves.

The woods in Scandinavia do not merely show a parallel development to those in Central Europe, but have taken an even more ecologically disastrous turn. A dreary commercial woodland sets the scene over large tracts of the Nordic countries. These 'commercial asparagus woods' are still being planted wherever possible. Splendidly large yields of wood can be achieved in this way, and one can readily argue that enormous quantities of carbon dioxide are tied up – but that is no use to native animal and plant life.

The picture of Scandinavian woodlands is increasingly determined by industrial forestry. Automatic tree-felling machinery, where the driver can make headway on the darkest night and over trackless ground and 'harvest' trees by floodlight, has become the sorry norm. At lightning speed the same monstrous machinery not only saws off the trees but strips them of twigs and bark and shreds them at any time of day or night. What would have taken half a dozen woodcutters several hours in the past, the machine does in a few minutes. It is acceptable that the self-propelling monsters cost an enormous amount – the quantity of timber garnered soon recovers the investment.

These masses of wood processed into wood pulp for years have swamped the world market. The supply has become so extensive – also through the plundering of tropical rain forests, often by Japanese concerns – that prices for woodpulp have virtually tumbled into the basement. Thus countries like

Sweden and Finland find it increasingly difficult to achieve adequate prices for their wood pulp, what with ever-rising quotas for waste paper recycling in many parts of the Western world (Germany is aiming at roughly 80% recycling from 1 July 1996) – which unfortunately does not tell us much about the utilisation of the waste paper. Conservationists fear that a large part will be burnt, if the market cannot cope with such quantities. The result is that more and more wood, and more and more processed wood pulp, are flung on this overextended world market – with ever less consideration for nature.

In Finland the consequences of the great wood sell-off are especially palpable, in a manner both tragic and dramatic for man and nature. Finland, whose woodlands are in any case more than 95% commercial, has since the beginning of the present decade made moves to sacrifice the last remaining virgin forests, primary forests and hitherto almost untouched, for quick money – or perhaps to gain a few thousand votes in the run-up to the Finnish parliamentary elections. Harald Helander, activist speaker and driving force of the wildlife movement in Finland, must be given the credit for alerting the European public to this threat of denuding Paradise. Helander, a widely travelled engineer, and deeply involved with 'his' woods, after a restless wandering life returned a few years ago to settle down in his Finnish homeland. He built himself a log cabin at the bend of a river in the midst of the forest. But peace and isolation were rudely disturbed, and the great battle of Harald Helander for Kessi and Hammastunturi, the two primeval forests on the Arctic Circle, began. News had got about that the Finnish Government, in the cause of job creation – which would at best mean a few dozen workers – wanted to authorise logging in these centuries-old forests. The reason for this initiative was, of course, purely financial, but it was swiftly claimed that it was also environment-friendly, wholly in accordance with the motto: Woods need managing; and in any case Finland is 'the land of forests'. The most hypocritical reason given, however, was the reference to the Finnish

Common Land Law. Under this an area of 1.5 million hectares of woodland are protected in any case, and only traditional utilisation as by the ethnic minority of Lapps is permitted. All other activities in regions covered by the Common Land Law must fulfill the criteria of environment-friendliness.

In fact, Harald Helander says, reality looks depressingly different. About 88% of the areas protected by the Common Land Law are bare mountainsides or moorland where tree-felling would hardly be worthwhile. The vegetation consists mainly of scrub birches, whose cutting down would not interest any forester. Besides, the Finnish woods today have a rate of regrowth of a good 80 million cubic metres of timber per year, while the necessary felling amounts to only about 50 million, so there is actually an ample surplus of regeneration, which makes tampering with the virgin forest seem totally absurd. And as regards the Lapps, the Government seems to have put one over on the conservationists, palming the ethnic ace like a card-sharper. The Lapps have absolutely no interest in tree felling – their reindeer culture requires no clearances.

Meanwhile the discussion ranges around the forests of Kessi and Hammastunturi, both habitats in which wolverines, buzzards and golden eagles live, and where the sturdy ancient trees have not grown very high on account of the extreme climatic conditions. There is discussion about alleged protection under the Common Land Law, nature-friendly tree felling, and the profitability of intervention. 'One thing has not been considered,' Harald Helander warns, 'which is the displacement southwards of the forest limits. These are unique forests, which once destroyed may never be recreated. The tree line could migrate southwards, and there is no telling what that could mean for climate, ecology and people.'

Nevertheless the Finnish Government, or to be precise the 'Woodland Administration', the top Finnish forestry authority, held fast to its clearance plans for Kessi and Hammastunturi. Desperately the activists of the Wildlife Movement tried to stop the deforestation. They could testify that the Common Land

Law is no protection for nature, but a way to make quick money. For barely 60,000 hectares, just half a percent of the total woodland area of the Lappland region of Finland, were marked out for invasion – valuable areas like Kessi and Hammastunturi. The Wildlife Movement pleaded that if eco-friendly felling was to be tried out, as the Government is suggesting, it should be in the commercial woods. Apart from that, the friends of the woods could prove just how in Finland nature was played off against jobs. The example of the small, ecologically important and up to then almost untouched primal forest of Murhijärvi impressively contradicted the same threadbare argument of job loss. The regional Community administrator had pointed to 500 woodcutters who were unemployed. In the event the chief forestry authority after a few months had to concede the opposite: there were not enough woodcutters to do the work. The result was the use of heavy machinery, as in the commercial woods.

That example is not exceptional. The Finnish forestry schools suffer from a great lack of pupils. It becomes ever clearer that in forestry management rationalisation and mechanisation will continue their triumphal progress. It seems all the more dishonest to try and claim primeval forest for jobs that cannot be filled. In sparsely populated districts, however, it makes a splendid debating point, as they do have high unemployment.

While the Finnish Wildlife Movement tirelessly sought to mobilise European public opinion, and Harald Helander travelled all over the Continent to direct attention to 'his' forest gems, the Government stuck to its clearance plans. The European Natural Heritage Fund addressed an urgent appeal to the European Parliament, pointing out that Finland stood, as it were, on the EU's doorstep, seeking entry to the Community, yet they were ruthlessly destroying their own natural heritage, which was also part of Europe's. Therefore, the Foundation said, Parliament should intervene, make representations to the Finnish Government, and point out that the clearance plans accorded neither with EU environmental policy nor with the Bird Protection Directive of 1979.

And indeed, amid strong input from the Finnish media the question was raised in Helsinki, and roused some response. But apparently too late for Kessi and Hammastunturi. The clearance gangs moved in on Kessi in August 1991. The end of the forest seemed to be approaching, despite all the efforts of the Wildlife Movement and its friends in Europe. Harald Helander and a handful of activists, guessing the moment when tree-felling was about to start, reached the place at dawn and chained themselves to the heavy machinery – with the result that further clearances ceased for the time being. However, the law came down on Harald Helander and his friends. A law which, of course, gives economic claims preference above ecological necessities. After some months of tough sessions in court Harald Helander and the other activists were fined in July 1992.

The fines should really have been paid by those who wanted to penalise future generations with the burden of having to do without treasures like Kessi and Hammastunturi. The future of Finland's ancient forests can only be viewed with scepticism. Even the present marginal cutback on the felling in Kessi – due to the brave action of the Wildlife Movement and above all Harald Helander – will not necessarily have far-reaching consequences in other areas. One must continue to fear for the forests near the Arctic Circle. The Eco-Twisters do not stop at the remote regions of our Continent. We ourselves have to act, by our own behaviour as consumers, to help reduce excessive paper consumption and use recycled paper wherever possible. And as Europeans we must insist that a level of protection is achieved for the natural habitats of our Community which allows no country to destroy unique natural features such as primeval forests. For the ancient forests are also threatened in other countries. Thus the Norwegian Society for Nature Protection fears that Norway, that huge country, will place only 0.6% of its woods under protection. Even the abundantly biodiverse coastal woods and the probably most important woodland complex in Norway, Lundsneset with its twenty square kilometres along the Swedish border, are not assured of protected status – although Norway likes to present itself as the 'good citizen' of the environment and was among the first signatories of the Rio Convention on Biodiversity.

The dual morality of the Scandinavian countries becomes most evident in view of those who appeal to the poor countries of the tropical forest belt to preserve their rain forests – although they only show a fraction of their economic performance. It throws a sombre shadow on Finland's handling of its woods. Since 1 January 1995 it has been a member of the European Union. The environmental policy crimes against the forests were not mentioned in the entry negotiations. It must be made clear to all Europeans, and that includes the Finns, that woods must be treated with more care than hitherto. Minimum standards for protection of habitats must be observed, especially when, as with Kessi and Hammastunturi, forests are concerned which, for their ecological value, would also conform to the criteria of the Bird Protection Directive and the Flora-Fauna-Habitat Directive. Europe, whether near the Arctic Circle or along the Mediterranean, must not become an environmental low-level-zone. That goes particularly for the relatively rich and future EU-member countries.

Chapter 4

The lust for adventure

Our European society bears a banner with the strange device 'Self-fulfilment at any cost'. One must get every last bit out of life, every dram of fun, every last drop of excitement. This insensate quest for gratification, which seems to render common sense powerless, must be genetically embedded in us humans. How else to explain that, in the cause of pleasure, nature is being exploited and used up by a veritable leisure machinery, down to the last surf wave – although this involves the destruction of our fellow creatures, and indeed of the basis of our own lives?

I want my fun

No hope for the Elbe beaver

This is the place, far from obscure, lying on what was the border between the two Germanys, whose name has since the late '70s became a synonym for the nuclear industry, and for its opponents: Gorleben. Less well-known is the fact that with its few hundred inhabitants it is one of the most affluent places in Germany. Anyhow, Gorleben seems to have become trendy. That is the only explanation for what is happening on the Elbe ...

It all begins quite innocuously, and you need a vivid imagination to visualise the farcical outcome. The victim is probably nature, and more directly, protected animal species. The case of the 'Gorleben Loop' shows that money can get you hooked on leisure pursuits, to the detriment of nature. It is a tale of pretensions versus reality, in personal as well as public and political behaviour – a divergence that illustrates the blandness of the paper on which EU nature protection rights are written. To understand what it is all about, let us – in thought at least – visit the Elbe.

The traveller now has a wide view to the East, where formerly a wire fence cut off any visual 'insight' into East Germany and Eastern Europe; a fence that was installed on the opposite bank of the Elbe. Only a few houses line the bank of the broad river, and the formerly bricked-up windows of those buildings have been reopened only since the reunification.

The border between the one-time ideological blocks has also opened for an unspectacular immigrant, previously held back by the realities of the Iron Curtain. For the first time in decades the Elbe beaver is resettling on the West Bank of the Elbe.

But it seems that for it the reunification will not work, at least not here in Gorleben: the wealthy enclave is thinking of other things than beavers. However, the beaver, one of the most endangered mammals of Central Europe, is not the only prominent beneficiary of this habitat around Gorleben, on the bank of the wide stream. The Lower Middle Elbe, as it is environmentally classified by the authorities, who are at last considering a National Park there with the co-operation of Federal lands Lower Saxony, Saxony-Anhalt and Brandenburg, demonstrates a full range of spatial and biodiversity: extensive grasslands, periodically flooded low-lying water meadows, the remnants of once prevalent pasture woods marked by high waters, the varied tributaries of the Elbe. All these have qualified for the patronage of the European legislators, and under the EU Bird Protection Directive are highly worthy of preservation. Years of research have shown that this landscape harbours a very special wildlife. Thus you find white storks as well as white-tailed eagles. Other illustrious inhabitants of the flood-prone habitat are waders and meadow birds such as lapwings, redshanks, great curlews and bar-tailed godwits. In view of this exceptional importance for species protected under the EU Directive, the EU Commission has given the area protection status under Article 4. Among the requirements of such reserves the Directive states that special conservation measures are needed for species named under Annex I in the designated areas. Thus under Paragraph 1:

'Member States shall classify in particular the most suitable territories in number and size as special protection areas for the conservation of these species, taking into account their protection requirements in the geographical sea and land area where this Directive applies.'

And specifically, under Paragraph 4:

'In respect of the protection areas referred to in paragraphs 1 and 2 above, Member States shall take appropriate steps to avoid pollution or deterioration of habitats or any disturbances affecting the birds, in so far as these would be significant having regard to the objectives of this Article. Outside these protection areas, Member States shall also strive to avoid pollution or deterioration of habitats.'

In concrete terms this means that the EU Member State Germany (and thus also Lower Saxony) has to protect the habitat of the said highly endangered species. Thus far the document.

That would appear a far-reaching claim on protection. And indeed the EU Directive prescribes the preservation of habitats as comprehensively as can be foreseen. But as so often the reality looks different. Once again the EU Bird Protection Directive turns into one of Brussels' paper tigers – this time, faced with a yachting marina.

On the Gorleben Loop, a tributary of the Elbe, according to plans which have cropped up ever since the late '80s, the mini-community of Gorleben, made rich by its nuclear power station, proposes building a marina, to give fellow citizens the chance of a trip on a 'modest' boat. What had originally been seen as a 'modest' harbour on the tributary, with just 15 berths, swiftly assumed the proportions of a major project, involving a correspondingly major upheaval. The shrewd rural district, which under CDU-rule had always kept a low profile in conservation matters, quickly discovered financial acumen and hinted to the community that the project might be at least partly financed by EU structural funds, always popular with Eco-Twisters. It seemed that a subsidy of up to 40% could flow from the Brussels cornucopia towards the Elbe. However, the precondition was to increase the size of the planned marina: it must provide 60, or at the very least 40, berths.

The planning began to take off. The conservationists reacted not just with dismay but with strong protest. After all, this was no less than a serious violation of the EU Bird Protection Directive. A violation which would encroach on the landscape and press like a mortgage upon the planned National Park. Clearly there could be no compromise solution. Apart from probably putting a stop to the return of the Elbe beaver, a marina would cause massive disruption of a large area of the wetlands between the beautiful old village fringe of Gorleben and the Elbe itself. Not only the beavers would suffer from the destruction of their barely reconquered habitat, but innumerable migrant and breeding birds. And of course the marina would serve as a bridgehead of further destruction of ever greater areas of countryside. The conservationists fear that the leisure activities would get out of hand; through the proliferating visitors' traffic and the infrastructure of ancillary facilities which always follow such initiatives, from car parks to cafeterias, a development would be set in motion which could soon get beyond all control.

The conservationists made their objections abundantly plain in a petition to the European Natural Heritage Fund. The plan should be totally rejected on principle, because a marina on this site would run counter to the provisions of the EU Bird Protection Directive. No EU funds should go to such an enterprise. The petition, presented to the European Parliament, scored an unexpected success. The Lower Saxony Ministry of

Economic Affairs, which was responsible for the distribution of structural funds (Communal promotion concept for Target 5 b regions – rural zone) refused financial aid for the marina. There was great rejoicing, as it seemed that in this case the conservationists had actually succeeded in enforcing the EU Bird Protection Directive. But the apparent eco-triumph was soon diluted by an announcement that there would be an environment-compatibility test for the project. The EU Commission as well as the Regional Government in Luneburg entrenched themselves behind that environmental testing.

Once again we see that the Eco-Twisters do not give up so easily; they pursue their apparently progressive, but environment-damaging, schemes with the utmost perseverance. But the conservationists, nature's champions, have got wise to the tricks of the 'men in grey suits'. With the healthy scepticism of the experienced environmentalist, Dr. Frank Neuschulz, longstanding proponent of a National Park along the Elbe, they began to suspect that an official environment compatibility test might well view the marina favourably. Conservationists feel it is hardly necessary to spend time, money and energy on such testing – an environmentally acceptable realisation of a marina on the Gorleben branch is quite simply impossible.

The European Natural Heritage Fund therefore decided to demand the long-overdue protection of the region as soon as possible. The basis for this, and it seemed a good 'negotiating hand', was once again the Bird Protection Directive of the EU, calling on Member States to designate suitable areas for protection. But no such luck. When the Fund asked the Regional Government to ensure 'temporary safety for the Gorleben area, according to the Lower Saxony Nature Protection Law', and thus put a stop to the plans for a yacht marina, the reply was a curt reference to the current planning assessment procedure – including environment-compatibility tests. At the same time one was well aware of the 'special importance of the area in question, particularly with regard to protection for a habitat valuable to bird life', and could sympathise with the concern of the Fund. It was therefore proposed to designate 'the Elbe Foreland between Vietze and Langendorf' a protected area.

But why should the protection initiative be relegated to the future, while today one of the most valuable parts of this area has to undergo environment compatibility testing for a marina? Once again the scrupulous delayers are at work, noticing their own dual morality as little as that of the pseudo-progressives, who will not stop at the last remaining nature reserve.

Anyhow, the conservationists cannot see the logic of it; they consider marina and wildlife preservation as irreconcilable, and therefore continue to insist on the speediest possible protection. The habitat's safety must be assured, so in view of the EU Bird Protection Directive they demand that no financial aid from EU structural funds be made available for such a nature-destructive project. Otherwise there would be yet another case to be inserted in the chapter of 'Lost Credibility', regarding the EU and its own conservation directives. A case which could mean the end of the line for the first Elbe beavers on the West Bank . . .

Can a boat trip be a bad thing? It all depends on the route . . .

The lust for killing

Making a killing at the sales

They do not seem to think much of Albert Schweitzer's words, 'I am life, that wants to live, in the midst of life that wants to live'. They claim to love nature, yet they line up to kill parts of it. In Italy alone allegedly 150 million songbirds a year fall victim to trigger-happy killers, birds which only get to Italy because somewhere else friends of nature have expended loving care and money to preserve them and their nests. In Greece hunters with their hailstorms of lead shot cause such high concentrations of lead in the soil that these can be traced up the food chain into large game.

Hunting has become a worldwide gigantic environmental problem. In Germany the hunters – who in the past have come mainly from the upper classes – have eliminated entire species. Any attempt to introduce or reintroduce such extinct varieties as wildcat, lynx or wolf have failed against the determined, straight-shooting opposition of the sportsmen in green coats. They fear the competition of nature, which certainly managed the environment better than they ever could.

Some find direct satisfaction in the actual chase and killing of living beings, compounded by bringing home tangible trophies. Another sector, the lessors of hunting grounds, get their satisfaction from the huntsmen who pay good money to keep the upper hand in the unequal fight between man and animals.

Hunting has many environmental facets. In German game 'preserves' – renting which is so expensive that only the privileged get to hold a rifle – certain species are carefully bred and nurtured so that they can end up, perhaps, as a fine pair of antlers on somebody's wall. One result is that there are far too many deer in German woods. Many hunters are not concerned with their ostensible task of regulating stocks. Lust for trophies, not ecological purpose, is their criterion. The natural equilibrium in the woods has long been thrown out of true by this wrong-headed hunting. The owner of the wood – and that is usually the taxpayer – bears the cost. He pays for special enclosures to protect saplings against the depredations of excessive game populations.

Many well-heeled huntsmen began to find their own hunting grounds too confined, and monotonous as well. It was worth the journey to Canada to kill a bear. But excursions have become shorter and cheaper since Eastern Europe opened its doors. Hunters are invading the countries which have nothing of interest to offer them save their stocks of wild animals.

For example in Albania the most important bird sanctuaries have long been a target for Italian sportsmen – who are not sportsmen in any true sense. Entrenched in dugouts 1 metre square and almost as deep, they stand and blaze away with their high-speed guns at anything that moves. It is not clear whether anyone, and if so who, has given permission for this barrage. But then, nobody asks. Nor do they ask whether the birds are protected. In countries like Albania money is the strongest argument of all, certainly stronger than love of nature. And to complete the deal with nature, egg theft is also going on in Albania. No ship sails from Albania to Italy on which an illegal import of eggs from highly endangered bird species could not be found. But nobody bothers to check. After Italy's wildlife has been almost annihilated, the gun-happy riflemen get down to robbing other countries. For the same reason German hunters swarm into foreign hunting grounds.

There are also cases where a State freely offers its natural potential for gunning down wildlife. Latvia is one example: its wildlife is threatened by a grim sell-off. If it were up to the Forestry Ministry, wild animal species would be for it. The tourist brochures praise not only the beauty of 27,000 square kilometres of woodland, 777 Latvian rivers or a mere 2,300 lakes. They also praise the country's game stocks, estimated at 12,800 elks, 86,000 deer, 17,000 beavers, 6,000 badgers, 17,000 black grouse and capercaillies. Good profits can be made from offering these to the guns.

For DM. 190 per day the German hunter, at whom this brochure is directed, is offered all the back-up organisation required for a successful shoot: accommodation, transport, experienced guides, full board. It costs DM 100 for the completing and registration of a licence, DM 25 for registration of the sporting gun. If you left your gun behind in Germany, no problem in Latvia, DM 60 per day will equip you.

If you want to go on a bleak wild boar hunt – which would also be comparatively simple in Germany – you pay about DM 50 licence dues. For the current year a shot boar piglet will cost you DM 20, a boar with tusks above 18cm. in length DM 1,550, and an extra DM 30 for every 10 mm. If an animal is only wounded, it will set you back DM 100 to 300. Elk – obviously – will cost more: licence dues DM 180, a shot at a bull DM 300, at a cow or calf a mere DM 25. Deer, of course, come a lot cheaper.

Rarities have their price. For a wolf hunt, something extremely exotic-erotic for the German sportsman, you will have to put down DM 1000. The lynx, totally extinct in Western Europe after centuries of hunting, is still available in Latvia, at DM 2000 apiece. Capercaillie and black grouse, in danger of extinction in Germany, are all fair game in Latvia, and can be translated into the hunter's foreign currency. Should the more or less experienced shot miss lynx, beaver, capercaillie or black grouse, animals and conservationists can rejoice, but so can the Latvian national purse, for to press your finger on the trigger is worth 50% of the listed price even if you miss.

For every brown bear still found in Western Europe, 100 of his kind can be found in Eastern Europe. The West-East proportion for the otter is 1 to 20. The East European white stork force is 40 times superior to the West European. There is still an incredible abundance of species. For now, owing to the poverty of the countries involved and the trigger happiness of the wealthy tourists, species in the East are threatened with the same fate that has overtaken wildlife in the West: a deplorable decline, in which hunting plays a large part.

Sporting tourists are not interested in such matters. They even believe they are doing good. They defend their hunting of predators with the argument, inter alia, that they are alleviating stress on partridges, because the poor beasts suffer so much from cruel nature. We are never at a loss, are we, when it comes to justifying our passions.

Chapter 5

The illusion of the possible

Do you know what bureaucrats, technocrats, progress fanatics, speculators and ignoramuses have in common? Briefly, they all believe, and act as though we have complete control of nature – as though anything was possible. Whereas it has long been shown that nature has its own laws and will revenge itself on future generations for the violation it has suffered. The progress fanatics (who are in fact yesterday's men) care little for that. Why do we put up with them?

Rules where there is nothing to regulate
The Eurocracy's mania for standardisation

The obligatory trip to the supermarket, a routine thing for John Consumerunit, usually includes a call at the vitamin supplies. As a rule that means putting a few apples in the trolley. Apples in particular have in recent years virtually achieved the status of basic foodstuff; and the pervasive health movement, rightly, supports that view. It is so easy to reach for a Granny Smith, a Golden Delicious, or a Cox. On the other hand, is anyone aware that the apple trees themselves are groaning under the burden of EU bureaucracy?

Experienced EU citizens, hardened by suffering from regulations and adept in dealing with such elementary rulings as minimum weight of rolls or size of toffees, were none the less amazed – at least, the apple-eaters and ecologists among them – when early in 1990 a new regulation came out of the European capital. Commonly known as the 'Apple Minimum Size Rule', it is a model of the official EU's passion for standardisation: a model from which conservation and consumer protection societies do not expect much good.

The regulation provides that apples with less than a minimum diameter of 55 mm. may no longer be sold – assuming they belong to varieties 'other' than the so-called 'large fruited', whose minimum size has been upped by 5 mm. as against previous regulations, to a proud 65 mm. Essentially this means that apples which are smaller and thus have no status under the severe scrutiny of EU interventionists and market controllers, must end up as animal fodder, or juice, or be destroyed.

In 1989 alone, i.e. before the new regulation came into force, the Bonn Consumers' Initiative pointed out that more than 600,000 tonnes of the popular fruit found their way to the rubbish dumps, or were fed to farm animals, or processed into industrial alcohol. 11% of the total apple crop was involved, and this was by no means profitable. The destruction itself cost over £68m in just one year.

But it is not only the anachronism of mass destruction of foodstuff in a world full of hunger which drove the environment – and consumer associations up the wall – or rather, up the apple tree. For behind it the entire agricultural philosophy of the European Union was revealed: you could see what the Common Agricultural Policy is all about – growth, or withdrawal.

If you want to achieve the EU regulation's recommended minimum size, in order to market your wares as dessert apples, experts warn that you must treat your apple orchards with pesticides on an average of twenty times each season. The chemicals used to control pests are anything but harmless, as they can be concentrated in living organisms and get into the ground water. In addition massive quantities of fertilisers have to be applied to produce these 'blown-up' apples – a conception that makes one shudder in view not only of the quality of the apples, but the quality of the environment.

Anyone who has seen the clean-swept plantations of half- and three-quarter-sized trees with the ground between cleared almost to microscopic scrutiny of all vegetation, will know how intensive cultivation is here. As habitats these plantations virtually do not exist. They are foreign bodies in the countryside, labour-intensive and far removed from nature. But the trend is all in that direction. As smaller apples, often local or regional varieties, organically grown – without massive applications of fertilisers and pesticides – cannot compete for size, they are increasingly handicapped in the market. Varieties which have held their own for hundreds of years, and for which not only the experts claim that they have a better flavour than the 'EU-standardised fruit'. One fears that not only the smaller apple species will suffer, but so will a whole profession – the organic growers – and the whole environment. It is precisely the smaller, not artificially blown-up, apples from full-size trees which come out of a cultural landscape of great ecological significance. In old apple trees – as opposed to the commercial plantation dwarfs – numerous animal species find their living space, from the little owl and the hoopoe to hornets and butterflies. They all help to give character to the landscape.

Bavaria and Baden-Württemberg have recognised this: both these Federal Regions are promoting traditional orchard cultivation. These meadows studded with fruit trees and a characteristic species-rich vegetation, which needs neither fertilising nor pesticides, are among the most biodiverse habitats in Central Europe.

Yet now the showy products of fertilisers and pesticides get further boosting on the market. More favouring of the 'blown-up EU apple' to the detriment of environment and consumers? The Federal Government does not see it like that. To a question from the delegate Dietmar Schütz the then Parliamentary

Secretary of State von Geldern replied on 25 May 1990: '... A reduction of traditional orchards due to minimum size specifications for apples to EC standards as extended by EEC Regulation 487/90 is not expected. With expert cultivation procedures (pruning, soil improvement, fertilisation, thinning of fruitlets) the necessary minimum sizes can be achieved regardless of the form and lay-out of husbandry. Apples below the required minimum size are as a rule insufficiently developed. This is shown in shortcomings of quality with regard to flavour and food value, and in their lack of market appeal...'

Does that require a commentary? Perhaps it does, for those who have never eaten 'undersized apples' (they taste delicious). But tastes differ, as we know. The only remaining hope for organic farmers on the EU apple horizon lies in direct marketing, selling straight from the farm. In this way even apples without official status, which would never pass the strict criteria of the Regulation, can be sold as before. That should encourage more people in the future to buy their apples from the farm: they would also get an impression of conditions of work and management on the spot.

Conservation and consumer organisations are not satisfied with the present state of affairs. They demand new criteria for the cultivation of apples and other agricultural produce. The consumers' initiative therefore pressed the EU-Commission to formulate fresh criteria to denote quality. There should be a move away from the previous classification of fruit and vegetables by marketability and EU standards of approval. Assessment, instead of going solely by appearance as hitherto, should also take note of food value, vitamin content, flavour, freedom from extraneous residues and method of cultivation (ecological or conventional). The Consumers' Initiative also calls for the marketing order for apples to be rescinded. Instead of subsidising destruction, there should be support for environment-friendly cultivation of fruit and vegetables. In addition the consumer protection activists asked for a tax to be imposed on the use of artificial fertilisers and pesticides. This has long been the foremost demand of the environment societies, but unfortunately has little in common with the reality of Brussels agricultural policy. Eve would have a hard time nowadays to find the right apple. Unless there are old-style orchards in Paradise . . .

Aid which does not help
Why the woods are burning in Southern Europe

Have you ever wondered why, especially in summer, reports of forest fires in Southern Europe proliferate so greatly? Certainly Greece, Southern Italy, Southern France, Spain and Portugal all experience prolonged dry spells, and dried-up woods do burn faster. Also we have heard various reports that, above all in France and Italy, woods are set alight deliberately. In these countries there are strange legal regulations whereby a wood that has burnt down is no longer a wood; therefore in these areas, where there should actually be no development, speculators then have a free hand.

But all that is only half the truth. In fact we are faced with the desperate situation that measures meant to prevent forest fires ultimately facilitate the burning of the woods. In Greece alone every summer between 50 and 200 forest fires are recorded. Every year an average of 380 square kilometres are burnt to the ground. So it sounds like a good thing when the European Union and the concerned national and regional governments provide funds for preventive protection of the forests. But what actually happens could be part of a grotesque film even Hollywood would hardly dare think up.

This is the set-up: In remote regions of Spain, Italy and Greece they have been constructing so-called firebreaks for some years. Strips 8 or 10 metres wide, or even more, are cleared in the woods so that not a tree or bush is left standing. This is generally linked with the creation of paths. The paths are also supposed to be firebreaks, and prevent the spreading of fires that do break out. But the precise opposite is the case. Along these cleared strips and convenient paths the fire-raisers now have access to remote woodlands which previously were all but impenetrable on account of the thick undergrowth. Who are the people that start the fires? They might be shepherds who burn the woods to create new grazing areas, or anarchic characters setting out to prove that the relevant authorities are incapable of mastering the forest fire danger. Then again there are tourists and other visitors to the woods, who leave Coca Cola tins and bottles lying about, and the hollow at the base of a bottle can act as a burning-glass and start devastating conflagrations.

It would be much better – landscape ecologists and wildlife protectors are agreed about this – to leave extensive woodlands alone as before, and for fires that do break out – perhaps where lightning strikes – to create a preventive unified European firefighting service: a specialised forest fire service, equipped with helicopters and other appropriate appliances, and operating internationally.

Yet further woodland paths and firebreaks continue to be built, even in the most remote regions. And all financed by European taxpayers. So we need not be surprised if next summer more fires break out over Southern Europe. Why will no one learn from experience and past mistakes?

For they know not what they do
Nestos – dammed from Here to Eternity

Goethe talked of 'nations warring in far-off Turkey' – and so it was, in his day. But today that is well and truly out of date: two hours' flying time and we are in Istanbul.

We are all in the same boat, or rather, in the same Spaceship Earth – cheek by jowl ... We get worked up about other people's sins and compose fiery protests against the massacre of forests in Asia or South America, but hardly utter a word against the destruction of forests at home in our very own Europe. On the contrary, we support the destruction with vast sums of money, in a good cause, as they say.

Ah yes, the good cause. We want people in Europe to have a better life. But that is just what the people in Asia and South America also want: a better life. But *there* it is a matter of naked profit; in Europe it is known as carefully thought-out structural policy. Two sides of the same coin and they have the same result.

So we'll go no more a-roving, but Look homeward, angel, to where disaster lies on your very doorstep. That doorstep being the region which until a few decades ago formed an artificial seam between Orient and Occident. The region of the Nestos, the river marking the border between Macedonia and Thracia in Northern Greece, where today the European Union contributes a great deal of money towards destroying what it really wants to preserve.

At this point we must dip into Greek mythology, and remind ourselves that on the banks of the Nestos, in darkest Antiquity, lived the Centaur Nessos, half man and half horse, who was killed in a fight by Heracles, a son of Zeus. Nessos, who gave his name to the river, took a posthumous and perfidious revenge on the Hero, meanly making use of the demi-god's innocent wife to propel him in turn into the Great Beyond.

Nature lovers delight in the Nestos, particularly its Delta. But recently there have been horrific premonitions. The river rises in Bulgaria and carves a narrow course through picturesque rocky gorges across the Rhodope Mountains, finally flowing broad and leisurely into the Aegean Sea. A paradise for fauna and flora, for rare plants and animals threatened with extinction – but a desperately endangered paradise.

'An extensive system of wetlands along the Aegean coast, 20,000 hectares of natural woodland pasture, brackish lagoons, with adjacent saltmarshes, reed beds and an abundance of other wetland habitats give living space over 100 kilometres of coastline to an astonishing variety of animals and plants – from otters and lesser spotted eagle to spur-winged plover and the rare sand narcissus.' That is how Hans Jerrentrup, the European Natural Heritage Fund representative in Northern Greece, describes the region in his book *Der Nestos*; Ein Rastplatz und Uberwinterungsgebiet fur Millionen von Zugvogeln und zahlreiche vom Aussterben bedrohten Vogelarten. (The Nestos: a resting and wintering place for millions of migrant birds and numerous bird species threatened with extinction.)

Until this century the Nestos Delta had very few inhabitants: floods and malaria were the order of the day, swamps permeated the district. The most notable feature of the region was the Kotza Orman, the primeval Nestos forest, which was considered the largest grazing forest in the Southern Balkans. *Was* considered . . .

The Greeks do not care to hear that it was the Turks who maintained this forest particularly well. Under Ottoman rule it was preserved because it was valued as a safeguard against flood water and also as a hunting ground. Felling trees in the Nestos Forest was strictly prohibited. After the break-up of the Ottoman Empire, Macedonia and Thracia became Greek territory. Barely 40 years later began the systematic destruction of the Kotza Orman.

At that time the grazing forest was still 27 kilometres long and up to 7 kilometres wide – all in all 7,200 hectares. After World War Two it was cleared piecemeal during the Greek Civil War because partisans found shelter in the impenetrable depths of the wood. The local population by further clearance turned the wood into arable fields. Altogether 4,500 hectares fell victim to saw and axe; 900,000 cubic metres of timber were burnt, because it could not be transported and processed quickly enough.

By 1952 only 2,700 hectares remained of the original woodland, and today there is only a fraction of that. Hundreds of thousands of sheep and an extensive drainage system with concrete-lined canals to supply an intensive agriculture continued the work of destruction. It spelled ecological disaster from the start, though by taming the high-water flooding of the Nestos and irrigating more than 20,000 hectares of arable land it seemed to make economic sense.

Anyone visiting the remnants of the Kotza Orman today will still be impressed by the biodiversity one encounters. But everywhere the visitor goes he will also find the deep tracks which man has left, and is still daily adding to: the banked-up dams, between which woods have withdrawn on either side of the river, the poplar woods which have displaced the ancient, liana-hung giant trees, the spreading maize plantations, and everywhere the illegally created fields – the days of pastoral wood on the Nestos seem to be numbered.

The mouth of the river presents a peaceful picture. Calmly the river flows into the Aegean, facing the mighty island of Thasos. On the beach a pair of spur-winged plover which conservationists have made the symbol for this bit of land. There are only a few spur-winged plovers left in Europe, and their days too seem numbered. For only a few kilometres away new dangers threaten this idyllic landscape. An army exercise ground in the middle of a protected reserve is hardly what breeding birds desire, so they stay away. And a planned extensive hotel development on the hitherto untouched dune shore may attract tourists, but will scare away all other forms of life.

In a hotel in the small port of Keramoti a little group of German nature lovers is staying, eager to discover what the Nestos Delta still has to offer. It is still quite a bit. But these visitors also feel that time is running out and working against the biosite. 'We are glad to have still seen it all,' says an elderly lady in the small hotel bearing the grand name of *Holiday Inn*. It is run by a Greek who worked for a long time in Germany.

On the way back to Kavalla you feel really sickened. The regional capital here shamelessly relieves itself of its domestic and industrial refuse. Steaming and stinking garbage in the midst of the landscape, rusting barrels bearing the warning skull – 'Poison' – simply dumped here, black puddles of oil slick in the open country, green-iridescing unidentifiable matter in the dead side arms of the Nestos, frogs squatting on plastic bottles, turtles flopping into bubbling poisonous water, a chemical factory right in the countryside. Horror film or nightmare? Unhappily, this is reality.

But the ultimate doom of the Nestos lurks menacingly upstream. About halfway to the Bulgarian border lies the town of Paranestio. Nearby the biggest dam in Europe is under construction. The gigantic project, which also includes two other, smaller dams, is backed by EU funds to the tune of millions, and is meant to supply power to Northern Greece and promote the economic development of this poor region.

The Greeks are proud of this miracle of Western engineering, and they cannot understand all the fuss about the dam's being built in an area prone to earthquakes or that the obligatory environment compatibility tests evidently did not comply with EU standards. The construction of the huge Aswan Dam in Egypt was in its day and from the start a centre of public interest. But until recently not a soul cared about the Nestos Dam, although it has already been several years in the building. The sudden interest is doubtless due to the new European sensitivity to environmental matters, but also to the fact that, as well as the Nestos, Greece's other legendary river the Acheloos is fated to be destroyed. Lord Byron must be turning in his grave!

Though it is situated in the wilderness of the romantic Rhodope Mountains there is a wide road leading to the construction site. There are no secrets; everyone has a clear conscience and nothing to hide and a true Greek-style open information policy. The Nestos Dam is, and is meant to be, a monument.

However, we did not choose to take the comfortable road, but the 'ridgeway'. The journey by Jeep starts at the entrance to the Nestos Gorge – about 30 kilometres from the sea – and leads upstream towards Bulgaria. At this point the Nestos leaves its narrow rocky bed and spreads out on its way to the sea, amid sandbanks and boulders. It is quiet here, eerily silent. Then a distant sound of bells: goats on the steep slope. They are the gravediggers of the region. Denuding the countryside of vegetation is the original sin around here. But worse was to come.

The engine of the vehicle is labouring. It is a steep climb past flocks of sheep and goats. The road soon ceases to be a road and becomes a track, barely two metres wide. Rough gravel and landscape: On one side the unforgettable view of the Delta, the Aegean, Thasos; on the other, the deep gorge – Grand Canyon flashes through the mind. The river, bays, sandbanks – almost a thousand metres below. On, over the roughest terrain, past deserted villages, whose inhabitants used to cultivate tobacco.

A black stork rising on an upward air current – where are the binoculars?

Brake suddenly – scarab beetles on the path, hundreds of scarabs – and surely that was a brown bear in the undergrowth? Truly, one is out of this world in the Rhodope. And then the discordant note: suddenly one is back to reality. No more storks, no more scarabs. Concrete.

We have reached the building site. It is Sunday. No fence, no locked gate, no watchman, no checkpoint. We can move about freely, and we are impressed and horrified at the same time. Impressed by the sheer magnitude of this technical project arising out of previously untouched wilderness. Horrified by the obvious consequences of the dam's completion. Horrified also by how negligently and recklessly the environment is being treated even during the construction work.

The largest of the three dams – the Thissavros Dam – has a height of 180 metres and a length of 700 metres. In a lake 40 kilometres long with a surface area of 25 square kilometres 600 (some data mention 700) million cubic metres of water are to be stored. Water for water supply, but also to generate electricity. The electrical capacity of this dam lies around 300 megawatts, the two smaller dams downstream between them will achieve the same again.

It rains incessantly, and the deserted building site is a waste of mud. The mammoth dam rears up powerfully. Down below the Nestos disappears into a tunnel. The surrounding mountain slopes are denuded, blasting has left its traces everywhere. There is no one in sight to tell us anything or to stop us. Excavators, caterpillar tracks and lorries stand about on the site. Countless old oil barrels are piled up in a dump. The dark contents trickle out, mingle with the rainwater to form filthy puddles, seep into the ground.

The three Nestos dams doubtless have great economic significance for Greece. But the environmental sacrifices are as gigantic as the project itself. Large parts of one of Europe's last original forests will disappear under the waters of the reservoir, and with them numerous rare animal species thus robbed of their habitat. The Nestos Delta because of the new controls will no longer have high tides or sediments – the dam wall will stop them – and will thereby lose the basic conditions of its existence.

At the Nestos site the baby has already gone down the plughole with the bathwater, and can hardly be salvaged. But the lesson could be, never to let such things happen again.

Going for uniformity

All is not nature that is green

If your next holiday takes you to Calabria in Southern Italy, to Portugal or to the Spanish regions of Cantabria, Asturias, Galicia or the Extremadura, have a good look at the landscape. In some areas there are huge woods. And many would think that here all is still right with the world, rich green trees as far as the eye can see.

But appearances are deceptive. For a long time many areas in these regions have not been as nature made them. A closer look reveals that wide stretches have been planted with eucalyptus trees. Now eucalyptus pastilles may be very helpful for a sore throat, and products made from essential oils of eucalyptus can be soothing for the bath or for flu and coughs. But for nature in Europe eucalyptus trees are anything but beneficial. This shows, for instance, in Calabria, where with state funds and additional subsidies from the European Union such eucalyptus plantations were made. Mountains covered with eucalyptus trees only look like woods from a distance. In fact they are death-dealing monocultures for the indigenous flora and fauna.

The Eucalyptus is a native of Australia. It grows very quickly and therefore produces a lot of wood in a short time, but it takes more nutrients from the soil than it gives back. The result is an impoverishment of the soil leading to its complete exhaustion. Also eucalyptus trees have a notably higher water consumption than other tree species which are adapted to the local conditions. They soak up the groundwater like sponges, so that in areas of these plantations the water table goes down very quickly; indeed, wells and springs may dry up near eucalyptus trees. No wonder that in the mid-twentieth century these trees have been used to drain whole stretches of marshland.

One of the strongest points against eucalyptus plantations is their grave effect on the ecosystem. This has been shown in a study by the Spanish conservation organisations FAPAS and *Fondo Patrimonio Natural Europeo*. Anyone walking through the plantations will soon realise that these are regular ghost woods. The eucalyptus, not adapted to the respective regional and local conditions, displace virtually all other vegetation, so that hardly any undergrowth exists between the trunks.

In this way the wildlife of the district is increasingly impoverished. We see this in various parts of Italy, Spain and Portugal with formerly common animal species such as lynx, wildcat, wolf, imperial eagle, Bonelli's eagle and black vulture. The reason being that the animals simply find nothing to eat in these countryside-alien and positively life-hostile plantations.

Who can understand it? We Europeans look anxiously at Africa and other regions of the Earth and deplore the ominous spreading of desert areas, but at the same time permit whole areas of land to be laid waste on our own Continent with our own tax money! And the devastation is swift with eucalyptus trees. When the rain comes in the southern regions, the soil is washed away in unguessed quantities. After only a few years most areas with sparse soil are down to bare rock. Devastation also advances with forest fires. When such an artificial wood catches fire, there is no containing it.

After forest fires the burnt spaces are quasi 'colonised' by eucalyptus saplings – the life-stifling areas thus spread even further. And fires are frequent in eucalyptus woods. Most of these fires are not accidental, for with burning down of the plantations – the wood, even from dead trees, is perfectly good for paper manufacture – the protected period before felling can be splendidly circumvented. So to get at the timber more quickly, simply set the plantations alight.

The worst of it is that despite all these adverse effects, eucalyptus planting continues. In the Spanish Extremadura alone well over 80,000 hectares which were previously indigenous and ecologically valuable mixed woodland, of maquis and oak wood have been sacrificed to the countryside-alien eucalyptus monocultures.

Undoubtedly eucalyptus has short-term economic advantages with its fast growth and its ready adaptation to the Mediterranean climate. Yearly growth in favourable conditions can exceed 30 cubic metres per hectare. Every 10 or 12 years the trees are then 'harvested'. Advocates of eucalyptus argue that the trees thus produce a far greater profit in a few years than do the traditional native species. But this point of view is more than dubious, ignoring the tendency to gloss over facts in the interests of your own pocket. The purely economic calculation is incomplete because it omits the cost of maintenance after the first felling, as well as the enormous social burdens imposed by the loss of jobs which went with traditional methods of agriculture and stock-farming. Again, the negative ecological consequences do not appear on the balance sheets. Even where the planting of eucalyptus has been stopped, the ghost woods are still spreading – so serious is the damage already caused.

But also this kind of ghost wood continues to be planted. Through greed for profit an alliance of diverse Eco-Twisters sees to it that, without regard for scenic, economic, ecological, cultural and traditional values, whole tracts of land are still being transformed into eucalyptus monocultures. In Galicia in North-West Spain, for instance, the actual timber production is to be doubled within the next 40 years. Almost the whole of Galicia will thereby be turned into one single constantly growing paper factory. Two billion Pesetas are earmarked for this purpose. 50% of this is public capital. Around 18% of the whole planned forestry area is to be planted with eucalyptus, and around 53% with no less problematic pines. Meanwhile not only conservationists and genuine forestry experts but a growing section of the Galician population is criticising any further expansion of the already excessive afforestation with landscape-destroying pines and eucalyptus. Deplorably, two multinational paper manufacturers – *Eurogalizia forestal* and *papelega* (partly backed by a Finnish firm) – have shown interest in establishing a branch in the district around Ferrol. Both – is anyone surprised? – have been received with open arms by the Regional Government, concerned only with quick profits.

It should be said that Galicia has been hit by the closure of several shipyards. Many jobs have been lost and the region therefore faces a host of social problems. But eucalyptus planting cannot possibly deal with this unemployment. Once again shortsighted thinking will devastate a countryside. It would be better to use the money to maintain the traditional, landscape-friendly agriculture. Yet while the local peasant farmers can expect virtually nothing, the business investments planned in Galicia will be subsidised with 80 million pesetas by the Regional Government. The firm Eurogalizia plans an additional investment of 105,000 million pesetas to set up one of the largest paper mills in Europe with a capacity for producing 300,000 tonnes of wood pulp to yield 150,000 tonnes of paper. Despite the fact that prices for recycled paper in Europe have dropped right into the basement due to overproduction!

Here again we have a vicious circle. Paper production requires water, a lot of water. And particularly in Spain and Portugal there are many regions with a distinct shortage of water. As a result of paper manufacture and the planned paper mills, water will eventually have to be obtained from somewhere else. This is usually done by building reservoirs and diverting rivers, so that water can be brought long distances. But this results in a further loss of water to the countryside, and more areas being changed for the worse. Whole ecosystems are altered, and with them the foundations of life for future generations.

A possible silver lining on the horizon is the plan of the Spanish Ministry for Agriculture, which in the framework of its *Plan nacional forestal* aims to afforest 100,000 hectares of land per year, but will no longer grant subsidies for planting eucalyptus or poplars. A conflict with the regions crying out for eucalyptus is already foreseeable.

Once again the bureaucrats in Brussels are less far-sighted. An afforestation order issued in July 1992 (No. 2080/92) could be a terrific chance for reafforestation and consequent climate improvement in South European member countries. But again there is a snag. For afforestation with fast-growing eucalyptus 2,000 ECUs per hectare would be paid, and for fast-growing – and in these regions equally landscape-hostile – conifers even 3,000 ECUs per hectare. It is some consolation that the locale-suited deciduous tree species will be subsidised at the higher rate of 4,000 ECUs per hectare. But the deciduous trees grow more slowly, and as people will aim to make money through tree-felling as soon as possible, one can visualise the ghost woods still spreading.

In order to comprehend such disastrous developments,

which ultimately our taxes pay for, we must learn to read the landscape like a book. Nature can only be effectively protected when we realise how it is being attacked. For this it is essential to know which species belong where, what is meaningful and sensible, and what is not. Close scrutiny reveals many grotesque man-made changes in the countryside – in the interests of more effective and profitable agriculture. One example is the orange plantations in Southern Europe.

Orange blossom has an intense and gorgeous scent, and citrus trees somehow seem the very essence of a holiday in the South. It is a glorious sight to see orange trees in flower covering whole valleys, yet these plantations are deadly. Not to us humans as we eat the fruit, but to the landscapes in which they flourish – and that affects us too, in the end.

In Calabria in Southern Italy whole ranges of hills are telescoped and flattened to make room for the planting of intensely cultivated orange and lemon trees. Mature landscape structures, with a diversity of hedges, wild scrub, solitary trees, even centuries-old, carefully tended olive groves, all have to give way to an agriculture of the architectural drawing-board. So hurry to visit Calabria while you may still find corners of the landscape as it has been for thousands of years.

Much of what made a characteristic landscape, gave it individuality and made it unique, will soon no longer exist. It is a scandal, which almost seems to have become an unshakeable official rule, that nothing is ever learned from mistakes that will inevitably occur – to err is human, after all. The dramatic consequences of agricultural clearances such as were carried out in Central Europe in the '60s and '70s have long been known. But short-term devotion to profit, the belief that anything can be done and controlled, and the lack of co-ordination and checks by the European Union lead to ever-growing destruction of landscapes. Thus within the space of one or two decades whole regions have been more drastically altered than in the preceding two centuries. These changes are of advantage only to those who make an immediate profit.

For the people of Europe, however, the elimination of natural scrubland, natural woods and natural meadows means the piecemeal destruction of climate regulators and water storers. Not only the rain forest is dying. The rape of the Amazon country should be in the minds of yesterday's men, the granters of subsidies, the planners, the irresponsible 'responsible' regional politicians, as also the representatives of corrupt businesses and their willing henchmen.

Sweeping your own doorstep
Europe also violates its rivers

Iguacu, Pantanal ... Proposed projects that conjure up horror scenarios in the minds of nature lovers aware of ecological damage in other parts of the world. Gigantic dam projects, blocking off arms of rivers and devastating drainage have cut deep into the face of South America, with the inevitable consequences for ecology and people. And it became ever clearer that this megalomania, to which many thousands of square kilometres of rain forest have been sacrificed, which has destroyed thousands of animal and plant species and brought others to the verge of extinction, and which has made innumerable people homeless, is a global threat. For such a massive contempt for nature is possible not only in South America. Europe, too, stands accused: in this case the finger points to Greece, one-time cradle of democracy.

Slowly the large, sagging net is raised toward the fishing vessel from the clear waters of the lagoon. Dozens of silver-shining fish wriggle in the net until the fisherman shovels them into the boat. There they join several hundred fellow-sufferers waiting to be consumed that evening in scattered restaurants on the outskirts of the coastal villages. An everyday scene in the lagoon landscapes of the South-Western Greek wetland area of Missolonghi – a scene which will, however, in a few years' time be replaced by the remark, 'There used to be a lagoon here ...'

– unless one of the craziest projects of EU-Europe and its nature-ignoramuses can be prevented. This is the planned diversion of the Acheloos, Greece's largest river.

The River Acheloos, 220 km. long from its source-springs, its mossy origins in the Pindus Range to its estuary in the lagoons of Missolonghi, is a vivid presence in the memory of all who have undergone a classical education. It is constantly cropping up in Greek mythology, famously represented as a river-god. Today the river is famous less for its legendary past than as a symbol of the idiocy of turning everything into concrete and the waste of billions of ECU tax monies to the detriment of nature and the people of Europe. Recent events around the Acheloos present the very image of megalomania, contempt for all living things, and investment that is disastrous both financially and ecologically. A story which (unfortunately) once again demonstrates that much apparent aid does not help, but in reality destroys.

A gigantic diversion project would reroute the Acheloos eastwards to the plain of Thessaly. Plenty of reasons are advanced by planners and politicians in Athens, Brussels, and elsewhere. Foremost is the allegedly huge rise in energy demand, necessitating more electricity from water power, and therefore the construction of five gigantic new dams which are to be dug into the deep valleys of the river's upper course. Nor is that all. In order to work the turbines with water from the Acheloos, vast tunnels are to be blasted into the mountains, up to 19 km. in length! Such dimensions, so far only familiar from South American tropical examples, are to be justified by the power performance of the dams, which the planners, a European consortium called TayEuro and the Greek Government, estimate at 680 Megawatts.

However, as so often, someone is putting a spanner in the works – in this case, surprisingly, the Greek national electricity company DEI. The DEI, which already runs four hydroelectric power stations on the middle and lower course and fed by the Acheloos, challenges the beautifully worked-out productivity figures of the Government. According to DEI calculations, there will even be a loss in total power production from the river, because the lower power stations will have a lower output or none at all. The DEI adds another blow, much to the annoyance of the policy officials in smog-ridden Athens. They demand an annual compensation payment of a hefty 140 billion Drachma from the Greek Government for damages. This makes the alleged economic necessity for the mammoth project appear to have feet of clay, and there are doubts regarding the true motives.

A broad phalanx of conservation societies from all over Europe in conjunction with local and regional Greek groups – nearly 70 associations pulling together – has scrutinised the actual motives for the planned diversion and the resulting consequences for people and environment. They have set off an outcry of indignation which so far has gone unheard only in the Athens ministries and the EU. It is obvious that the project, whose costs could lie between £5 and 6 billion, is to serve the shortsighted interests of politicians, who wish to bring in the voters but are the stooges of intensified agriculture. This in a Europe whose grim agrarian situation is characterised by a butter mountain, a beef mountain, an egg mountain and a milk lake. But quite obviously the idea is to compensate for previous mistakes in the Plain of Thessaly.

For in the '60s and '70s nearly every water course that people could lay their hands on was drained. The consequences are all too clear today. Wells run dry and a water table sunk to 15 metres make up the depressing reality. The farmers of Thessaly naturally see themselves as the sufferers, and look for their water-suppliers, literally, among the politicians of Athens. Unfortunately they seem to have found them: the Acheloos project has been in preparation for years, construction work has begun to redirect the water as soon as possible eastwards to Thessaly – even though the financing is not yet secured. Instead of tackling the roots of the problem – beginning a renaturalisation of the waters, drawing up the artificially lowered groundwater level, and translating a nature-friendly agriculture into being – one of the Continent's most unspoilt rivers is to be sacrificed, and with it all that depends on it, human and all other forms of life and landscape.

Ironically this has also focused attention on the Brussels agricultural policy. The worthy policy of the Brussels bounty, according to the Commission, is that no more projects shall be financed by EU funds which would lead in any way to further agricultural overproduction. And there lies the rub, amid the cotton or the root crops. The Acheloos strategists of Athens hope for Brussels money as their main source. EU funds are to contribute substantially to the diversion of the Acheloos, and it is as sure as Jacques Delors' French officialese that without such funds there would be no chance of realising the project. Therefore the Athens politicians had to look swiftly for a good cover story – the abovementioned power supply generated by the dams.

Apart from the ruined mountain valleys, the greatest danger from this idiocy is to the lagoons in the wetlands of Missolonghi. Where for thousands of years the Acheloos has pushed its way to the sea via its Delta, it created one of the most important habitats for endangered birds in the whole of Europe. If any area deserves to be called the supreme bird turnstile of the Mediterranean, the wetland complex of Missolonghi is surely it.

Conservationists have in decades of detailed work ascertained what lives around, by and in the Acheloos Delta region. Ornithologists named dozens of breeding birds, most of them on the Red List of endangered species, and huge numbers of endangered migrant birds, who seek out the 63,000 hectares of the Delta as a resting and feeding place and need it for their survival. For some species, such as the curly-headed pelican, the loss of the Missolonghi wetlands could mean extinction, for with its stock dwindled to near-vanishing point it is wholly dependent on this habitat. There is no similar lagoon-complex left in the whole Mediterranean. It is the specific character of the lagoons, composed of both sweet and brackish water, which makes for their exceptional species-diversity and consequent heightened importance. You see numerous herons standing motionless in the water or strutting about, searching for small fry, and a sizeable stock of the highly endangered otter in the shallow lagoons. There are extensive reed-bed zones with their characteristic biodiversity. Off-shore islands of limestone serve as breeding places for seabirds.

The European Union did not fail to recognise the importance of the Missolonghi lagoons for conservation. The complex was designated a Special Protection Area according to the EU Conservation of Wild Birds Directive of June 1979, the 'highest category of protection' recognised by the Brussels legislation, and recommended to its Member States. But such protective restrictions seem of no interest either to the Greek Government or to the EU-Commission itself. Otherwise how to explain that Brussels is evidently willing to help finance the Acheloos diversion which would lead to the destruction of the Delta wetlands?

All the experts agree, even the collaborators of the EU General Management Committee for the Environment: If the Acheloos is diverted as planned to Thessaly, the wetlands of Missolonghi are doomed. The amount of water then reaching the river mouth would be so meagre that the lagoons will become entirely salt-water – or, worse, the sea will penetrate far into the land, the groundwater far inland will become salty. This would threaten the very existence of agriculture in that part of Greece. Fishermen also, rightly, fear for their livelihood. They will be the first to miss the water from the Acheloos inshore. The extensive spawning grounds, probably the richest in Greece, will be lost forever. And ultimately, less spectacularly, the offshore islands would disappear, because the sea water would have full sway over them.

What now seems the horror scenario of the 'beheading' of a whole river, could soon be grim reality. We see here, with the utmost drastic clarity, how far such reality is removed from the claims of EU environmental policy. On the one hand the Environment Committee of the EU recently commissioned a study regarding the nature-friendly cultivation and development of the lagoons of Missolonghi, on the other there is the fear that EU structural funds will supply the money to kill off those very lagoons. Dual morality is at it again!

It remains doubtful how Greece, which meanwhile has fallen far behind even Portugal in its economy and now represents the EU's taillight, can manage to pay its own share – certainly also a matter of billions. So far Athens politicians have not given a satisfactory answer to that, any more than to the remonstrances of the electricity company DEI, which does not want the 'blessing' of any more power stations, but instead expects them to be a liability. In a recent report the European Audit Office has again forcefully pointed out the basic disaster of European grants policy. One side of the Brussels fountainhead gives out money for conservation, while the other side gives much more toward the destruction of the areas to be preserved . . .

By way of an afterthought, even results of the prescribed environmental compatibility test are doubtful, as a high official actually admitted to conservationists. For reasons connected with the politically explosive 'subsidiarity debate' one would, however, have to accept it. Of course as yet outstanding detailed studies by the Greek Government would still have to be presented before the money could flow from Brussels. Incidentally, this is not a trivial sum, translated into every taxpayer's contribution. The Royal Society for the Protection of Birds (RSPB) pointed out that 'every British taxpayer is contributing £2.29 to the EU subsidy for the Acheloos diversion'. Another reason, surely, to reinforce efforts to avert this insane project.

Add to this that the calculations advanced by the plan's supporters in politics and finance, which form the basis for the economic feasibility of the project, are constantly under fire. Fishermen and electricity company alike cast doubt, for example, on the repeatedly advanced values for the water outflow of the Acheloos. They claim that even today the amount of water is a third less than quoted, and the rainfall in Western Greece lessens from year to year. Moreover – and this also reduces the quantity of water reaching the Missolonghi Delta considerably – diversion of the eastward-flowing River Evinos has already begun, so soon this too will no longer discharge into the lagoons. Conservation societies and the fishermen of the Missolonghi Delta therefore trust the official figures as little as the threadbare promises of the politicians who want to sell the Acheloos for a mess of pottage.

Europe looks on, the official Europe of the EU, which through misguided political considerateness is loath to apply its own environmental rights and block funds for this absurdity. Will this be the final swansong for the Acheloos and the lagoons of Missolonghi? Not yet, as possibly the representatives of the building consortium will overreach: their demands via the estimates for further works – the Mesochora Dam is already virtually finished and has caused great devastation – have risen to the incalculable, even for the Athens Government. Hope remains that the money will give out and the life of the Acheloos will not be extinguished. If the Acheloos does die, so will the last shred of credibility of the EU environment policy.

The terrible onslaught on Greece's largest river throws a telling light on reality as against pretension. On one side the EU indisputably set standards for environmental rights – as with the introduction of environmental compatibility tests, or with the EU Bird Protection Directive – while on the other side it rubbishes its own environmental rights and even finances the violations. An added aggravation is that it means a complete negation of the decisions of the European Parliament. The Parliament postulated that structural funds should only be granted if they do not involve environmental destruction. They have a long way to go. Too far for nature, perhaps – and for European taxpayers.

Chapter 6

Looking after Number One

Everyone has experienced it in one form or another: in a crisis, you have to look after Number One. It is very wrong, however, to exploit such situations entirely for one's own advantage, meaning profit. The East European countries are now threatened in their economic and ecological crisis by a massive application of Western technologies, even those that are known to spell harm to economy and environment. That simply will not pay off.

Exporting your mistakes

From exploitation to sell-off

The house of the European Community, that beautiful villa everyone loves to talk about, has suddenly and unexpectedly landed on the East side with an extension ripe for demolition.

Officially, of course, the owners of the villa are all for this. What could be better than the ending of the old East-West (military) conflict, the East opening up to the West and adopting the market economy? While the villa owners are not quite sure how to cope with the annex, the annex owners have high hopes that the villa owners, after all their kind words, will be a power of help with the renovations. Could they be deluding themselves?

The villa owners can see the cracks in the walls and the defective roof of the annex clearly enough, but nobody dares actually go in, to discover the precise problems, perhaps even learn something new for their own house. There is much talk about the new people in the East, and the services of Western electricians, plumbers and interior decorators are warmly recommended. To be duly invoiced, of course; payment by instalments can be arranged, provided certain rules are obeyed. But one is not keen on lending a hand with the renovation of the annex. Nor are the mistakes one made with one's own building works discussed with the new people. For one's own marble bath has to be fitted with gold taps before one can think about unblocking the drain in that old building. And there is such a damnably long wait for delivery of the gold taps, and they are so hideously expensive, that one has to go slowly. Especially as the vestibule between villa and annex has just been completely restored unfortunately not with environment-friendly materials.

While in Western Europe, thanks to environmental techniques, thanks to sewage works and waste water rates, as well as limitation of inflow, the quality of water has been improved, Eastern Europe faces tasks in this department which it cannot cope with by itself. But at present it is left very much alone with these problems. Only when it is a question of doing business deals in the East does the West wake up. The ailing Western economy can do with new (Eastern) orders. But sharing, exercising restraint, doing without gold taps in order to get the Eastern annex into some sort of shape – the West appears unwilling to do any of that. Yet the key to solving all the problems lies undoubtedly with the West. It must realise that it is the model for global action, therefore it has a duty to be a good model. It must be ecologically aligned. Habitat Earth cannot take marble baths and gold taps in every house.

One small example to show how Communism got things into a mess and what huge problems the present authorities face, is the 'Industrial Lake Kalina' in the grounds of the 'Hadjuki'

Chemical Works in Swiechtolowice near Katowice in Polish Upper Silesia. Chemists reading an analysis of its water will be aware that it is not the place for a refreshing bathe: pH 9.4; soluble oxygen 0.0; (BSBS 2350); Phenols 513 mgm./cu. decimetre. For non-chemists, be it said that this Upper Silesian 'Phenol lake' is a rustcoloured broth with an unbelievably corrosive stench. No board up to signal 'Bathing prohibited', but there is one reading 'Danger to Life'. That should do.

In the heat of summer the exhalations are at their worst. The phenol lake has become a centre of attraction for people studying pollution in Upper Silesia. 'Let's get away quick,' many say, on account of the penetrating smell which very soon causes nausea and dizziness with some. Visitors can indeed get away quickly from the scene; not so the inhabitants of the region. The emanations cause disease among the 20,000 people living around the lake (which is 9.9 hectares in area and up to 15 metres deep) diseases ranging from eczema to skin cancer. 'It's worst for the children,' said one local inhabitant, embittered about those responsible for turning the lake into a hazardous waste dump. 40 years ago it was possible to swim and to catch fish in Lake Kalina. Now at least they want to build a fence round it, to save people from the fate of some dogs who fell in and afterwards died. But a fence cannot keep away the health-endangering effluvia.

What will happen to Kalina? The first thing to note is that the water will go on being fed phenols, even though the process that produced them has been stopped. This is due to the 4 hectares of slag-heap from the chemical works, harbouring 900,000 tonnes of industrial waste, the seeping water tops up the poison in the lake. So the water cannot be detoxified until the dump has gone. An American firm thinks it can do the full job within 2 years for DM 4 million. This offer sounds great to the authorities responsible, because it is cheap, and that is important. But many experts feel it cannot be a serious offer, because so little money could not possibly clear away so much filth.

Those now running the factory have no money for the disposal and disclaim all responsibility; the phenol lake is not their fault. No one has any money in Poland. The Regional Government has none, and the national economy is full of deep holes. So the discussion will continue about Kalina, people will continue to hope for cheap solutions and accept sickness as the price for the past. That is, unless a solution turns up which could make the phenol soup literally disappear. Experts surmise that there will soon be major subsidence in the region with opening of new seams of coal. It is conceivable that Kalina will then drain away, the phenol water will seep into the ground and no longer trouble the population; it might pollute the groundwater, however, or – through being pumped out of the mires – the Oder or the Vistula.

This example is just one case, the Phenol Lake Kalina just one old liability. A very bad one, though, which shows up the full desolation of an East European industrial zone. Altogether there are thousands of old liabilities in Upper Silesia which have not been talked of. It is the acute ecological and health disasters which set off the present discussions. The whole of Silesia stinks from end to end. Polish conservationists call it 'an outsize gas chamber in the middle of Europe'. The Upper Silesian industrial district produces 98% of Poland's bituminous coal. The smelting of Poland's lead and zinc takes place there, half of Poland's electricity and steel are produced there. For size and concentration of industrial structures in the most confined area it must be unique in the world. On this 2% of Polish land area live 4 million people, ca. 10% of the population, and they produce more than a third of the country's entire gross national product.

Clearly therefore this region is vital to the Polish economy. But it makes the inhabitants and the environment sick. The money made there disappears somewhere into the national budget, which after all is only about half the size of the European agrarian budget. Only a minute part is used to clean up the environment or improve the living conditions of the population. Such is the tradition.

Upper Silesia is a region of exceptionally rich mineral resources, zinc and lead ores, coal, even silver. Coal production began in the mid-18th century. By 1770 400 tonnes of coal were produced per year, by 1850, 1.1 million tonnes. In 1913 50 million tonnes of coal were hauled out of the ground, today more than double that amount. A multiplicity of foundries and coking plants sprang up. The first European coke oven was built here in 1796, at Gliwice.

Many have profited from the mineral wealth of the region, but least of all the people who lived there and their environment. Up to World War I the profits were shared out between the Prussian realm, the Austrian Monarchy and the Russian Empire. After the Great War it was German, French, Belgian and American companies which had the say and pocketed the profits. But there was never any money to spare for the economic or social development of Upper Silesia or to remedy the environmental damage, apparent even then. Nor was it any different after World War Two. The proceeds from the State industries – which were only achievable, or at any rate greater, because nothing was spent on protecting the environment – were used for rebuilding shattered Poland and for developing new industrial centres (in the course of which the environment was messed up just as badly as it had been in Upper Silesia). The example of Nova Huta near Cracow is telling.

What remained in and around Katowice was poison-discharging and technically superannuated industrial installations, side by side, all without filters but with broken conduits. Next to them, right by their outside walls, the traditional workers' estates, in which people still have to live today, in almost unimaginable conditions.

The internationally accepted limits for environmental pollution, which critics consider set too high and too tolerant towards industry, are exceeded all the time in virtually every respect, and with lasting effects. In the case of lead by 2.5–50 times, for dust by a factor of 10 to 90, for sulphur dioxide, nitric oxides, hydrogen sulphide or coal tar derivatives roughly three times, for phenols 4–17 times. The consequences are obvious. Bronchial diseases are rife. The expectation of life has fallen rapidly, and lies well below the Polish average, which again lies at the bottom end of the scale for Europe. The expectation of life of an Upper Silesian is ten years less than that of a German. In the district of Katowice 15% more diseases of the circulation, 30% more cases of cancer and 47% more respiratory diseases are recorded than the average for Poland.

The average pregnancy for the women of Katowice lasts only eight months. At half the births the children are born already ill. Infant mortality is around four times as high as in Sweden. It is calculated that in Katowice alone an additional 150 children a year die because of environmental pollution. Horrifying blood-lead values are found in all Upper Silesians. Medical men say the upper limit should be a maximum of 20 micrograms per decilitre. At above 30 micrograms one begins to see symptoms such as epilepsy. Yet figures of 35–40 micrograms are not rare. Every third child has a lead content higher than the acceptable 20 micrograms. A sorry record was set by a child from Rozbark: the 'limit' was exceeded by a factor of 120. In UK the introduction of lead-free petrol was especially promoted to reduce the presence of lead in children, because lead damages brain functioning. It may sound harsh and contemptuous, but it is no exaggeration to say that a whole region will become feeble-minded because of pollution. The sad truth is that the school network for educationally subnormal children in this region is stretched far closer than for the rest of the country.

In the steelworks of Nova Huta near Cracow only 12% of the workers leave their jobs for reasons of age. 8% die while still in the job, 80% leave prematurely for health reasons.

Really no fruit or vegetables should be harvested from the local gardens. The soil is heavily polluted with lead and cadmium, and from the air, too, harmful substances settle on the plants. In lettuces one may find up to 230 mg. of lead per kilo. No one should ever ingest more than 3 mg. per week. In practice some people do grow produce on these 'poison dumps': the economic situation makes it a necessity. The Polish Ecology Club tries desperately to help the children in particular. The idea is to get 'healthy food' from other parts of Poland to the children, to families, nurseries and schools, so that at least the food is clean where the very air is polluted.

And the water... What comes out of the pipes there has little in common with drinking water as defined by European drinking water directive. Again cause is the ubiquitous environment pollution, which naturally involves the water, and on the other hand lack of money to advance the building of sensible water processing plant. Each day the Polish rivers are burdened with over 7,000 tonnes of salt from the coal mines alone. The water of the Vistula is many times more polluted, so that it is no longer even suitable for refrigeration. The pipes would be corroded too quickly. Even ships' hulls are affected by the cargo of filth.

Sewage works are still in short supply in Poland, although to its credit the country has tried hard since the late '80s to redress that. Domestic waste frequently goes straight from the houses to the rivers, if it even gets that far. For because of damage to the mining works there are thousands of bursts in the sewage pipes: they are estimated at 8,000 a year. The waste water seeps into the soil and contaminates the groundwater – a vicious circle.

Since the end of the '80s the State has at last begun to close some of the worst environment-polluting factories. The population is in two minds. On the one hand it naturally suffers under the extreme pollution which surrounds it from birth. On the other it dreads the growing unemployment. In Poland as in other East European states there is no carefully thought-out cushioning to break the fall, as in the Western industrial countries. The conflict between ecology and economy, intensified by the integration of the former East European states into the world economy, has taken a dramatic form in Silesia. Many of the environment-polluting concerns have gone bankrupt because they were simply no longer competitive. This has led to palpable improvements, though not yet enough. The remaining factories lack financial margin for investment in general and conservation investment in particular. If conservationist pressure on these concerns increases – which is urgently needed – it would at the same time increase resistance to an appropriate eco-policy. Jobs are simply more important than clean air to those concerned.

The first aid projects have started. Secretary for the Environment Stroetmann is, for instance, involved with the detoxification of the Phenol Lake Kalina. Though this is to be welcomed, it is no more than the proverbial drop in the ocean. The budget of his Office provides a mere DM 20 million for Eastern Europe. Yet aid for such regions should not be grudging, but immense, to the tune of billions. Fewer roads for us, more environmental protection for them. But Western policy is against this, for the sake of those gold taps.

In Upper Silesia we see the conservationists' warnings of the early '80s coming true – after the woods, human beings will die. And here too the greater part of humanity just looks on, from the windows of the villa with the marble bath.

Don't get it right, don't stop the wrong
Regarding the logic of no aid for Eastern Europe

There is much talk within the EU of the proactive and reactive principles of precaution and causation. Precaution means that environmental problems should really not occur at all; causation implies that at least the one who did cause ecological damage is responsible for making good. But this daft idea is never actually carried through. The operators of nuclear power plants do not take full responsibility for the consequences of a possible accident. The consequences of climatic disaster do not hit hardest at those who use energy most intensively (thus producing CO_2), and the CFC producers and consumers do not pay for the consequences of destroying the ozone layer.

A consequential application of the causation principle is frustrated not only because not all damage is quantifiable and many questions cannot be answered. Do you know anyone who could work out precisely how much the global warming will cost? How much does the extinction of an animal or plant species cost, what compensation do you pay a person with skin cancer? Can all damage be made good by financial settlements? Can one buy oneself free of environmental pollution? But the logical introduction of the causation principle also fails because politicians do not want it: for one thing they would have to admit that we have far too long been a burden on the environment, then again they would have to face the frightening consequences of an appropriate settlement. A petrol price of £2.50 per litre, which would be required if all quantifiable environmental consequences were considered, would put our economy in its present form at risk. That is why there is much talk of the causation principle, but not corresponding action.

The situation in Eastern Europe is very similar. There too one is miles away from a foresight- and causation- principle. The difference is that East European countries have not set their claims on such a policy as high as the West Europeans. Nevertheless the principle of 'paying for environment pollution' seems to provide a way of getting some money into the chronically empty coffers – funds which could be used purposefully to clean up the environment. In some East European states a tax on pollutants has been introduced, still a dream for West European conservationists.

While they have been arguing unsuccessfully for months in the EU conference rooms about taxing CO_2 emission, countries whose environmental policy has been regarded with arrogant superiority by the West have actually acted. For instance, in Poland if you release SO_2, CO_2, other gases or harmful substances such as heavy metals into the environment, you have to pay for it. However, the money collected is not nearly enough to deal adequately with the problems. It cannot be done without Western aid. But this is not yet forthcoming. At a conference of European Environment Ministers in Lucerne, in which some important non-European partners also participated, an 'environment plan for Central and Eastern Europe' was discussed. It did not really get beyond pointers, tips and action guidelines for the East European states. There was no promise of funds, although threats to the environment in the East also endanger the West.

This has been known at least since 1986, when the reactor of the nuclear power station at Chernobyl exploded. The Eastern nuclear reactors with their wretched safety standards, monitored in hit or miss fashion by inadequately trained personnel, pose an acute threat for the West, too. But even after it was revealed what scrap materials were used to produce atomic power in the East, it was a long time before the West agreed on a plan, and financing it was another subject.

One Chernobyl should be enough. Roughly DM 700 million would be needed even for short-term nuclear safety emergency measures, double-figure billions to raise the power stations to Western safety standards. The Eastern states do not have this money. At the Lithuanian nuclear power station Ignalina, which the Federal German Reactor Safety Minister Töpfer visited in Spring 1993, the managing director asked his German visitor to procure a special fire-protective paint costing DM 5 million. Money had run out, but the paint, manufactured by a German firm, was vital to preventing the spread of fires in the graphite reactor of the Chernobyl type. DM 5 million for those Western enterprises which run nuclear reactors would be a small item in their advertising budgets.

Regarding nuclear energy, the alternatives facing Western politicians are: Either put the sums mentioned into aftercare, or shut down. But none of the proponents of nuclear power who at present rule EU countries want to see the reactors shut down. So it has to be back-up safety measures. This is also more likely to achieve consensus because it looks like being fantastically good business. Not only for makers of specialist paints, but for the Western nuclear industry, which is at a low ebb.

Aftercare security measures, where of course Western technicians would have the say, are also reassurance for the West. Our technicians would prove that they can do better than the Easterners: that they can tame the atom, that they can build 'safe' nuclear power stations. At a time when the steel is developing cracks in West German reactors – which for security's sake it should never do – it is great to talk about clapped-out Eastern reactors. But the money has to be found, and here the West, keen as it is on orders, is dragging its feet. Despite the acute nuclear threat, it seems unable to produce appropriate sums quickly and without bureaucracy. We have seen it all before: much is said, little is done, and virtually nothing is paid out. Not even where it is in one's own interest.

The argument as to whether it would not be better to put the 700 million DM and the extra billions into closing the monster reactors and improving local energy efficiency has not arisen.

'Money is always the problem,' as the Polish Ministry of the Environment knows very well. Its former chief official Nowicki has, together with the Government, developed ideas that would kill several birds with one stone. He has approached members of the so-called Paris Club, an association of countries who have lent Poland money, with a suggestion of debt remission earmarked for environmental policy, under the name eco-conversion. The idea is as follows:

In April 1991 the Paris Club granted Poland 50% remission of its debts, amounting to 15 billion US dollars. This of course gave the country 'a real breather', but it is still oppressed by a heavy burden of other debts which must be repaid by the year 2010. This is essential, as non-payment of the outstanding debt would ineluctably lead to the cancelled 50% being put back in full on the negative account.

Every year a certain sum in the Polish budget is set aside for repayments. In 'hard currency', of course, requiring a large part of Poland's remaining foreign currency reserves. As so often, debts and their interest can devour you. Money for other investments which has to be paid in foreign currency, not in Zlotys but in US Dollars, Deutschmark or British Pounds sterling, therefore hardly exists. Yet virtually all environmental technology essential for rehabilitating the decaying installations is of Western origin and has to be paid accordingly.

Poland's idea is very simple and sensible. One should ask the countries to remit a certain amount of the debts again, in this case 10% of the original sum. This money, necessarily no longer part of the Polish budget, should not disappear into the jungle of other expenditures, but should be paid into a newly established Eco-Fund specifically for environment investment. And appropriate environmental investments should then be paid, or at least partly-funded, out of this. Four focal points have been chosen as aims for the Eco-Fund. Air pollution, which transcends borders, and gas emissions which could contribute to the greenhouse effect, are to be reduced. The Eco-Fund should also contribute to cleaning up the Baltic and to maintaining genetic diversity.

Suitable projects can then, on application, be supported by the Eco-Fund. The idea is to start them, not provide 100%. For instance, should the managers of the brown coal power station at Toruw call on the Eco-Fund for a flue-gas cleaning installation, they could not expect more than a 30% subsidy. Nature protection measures would receive the maximum support, up to 80%.

In the USA the idea soon found ready listeners. The Bush administration declared itself willing to agree to this environment-orientated remission of debts. Al Gore in his book described purposeful debt remission as a good possibility, and the European Parliament also asked the EU-Commission for 'Conversion- and debt-remission measures in the interests of environment protection'. Up to 2010 this US consent will bring the Poles a sum of 360 million Dollars. The Federal Republic takes a much tougher stance than the USA, and their position is extremely important for Poland. Many other countries, such as Switzerland, Norway, Sweden and the Netherlands, look on Germany's behaviour as their model.

For Germany the acceptance of Eco-Conversion would mean renouncing DM 38 million a year in repayments – the equivalent of one kilometre of motorway, of which there are still far too many being driven through Germany's already overexploited countryside. But the Ministers of Economics and Finance agree that Germany is too poor for debt remission in a good cause, we cannot afford it.

Yet it would not actually mean the loss of that money to the German economy. Poland offered in the negotiations to conclude separate agreements with the countries joining in Eco-Conversion, regarding preferential shares for indigenous firms in giving orders for investments. The programme even promises to become a business trends service for the Western environmental technology industry, provided the money is made available.

That sounds attractive; nevertheless the Federal ministers concerned with finance do not wish to accede to the Polish request. And they have all sorts of different reasons for that, which they advance separately, successively, or concurrently. At times it is said there is no money; again, there is reference to an already partly remitted credit, its resources at present supplied from a special fund but over whose distribution one no longer has political influence. Then again the model is roundly rejected, because one does not want to establish a precedent. For if one were to grant Poland such remission, one would have to make similar concessions to other countries. And where would we be if we granted everyone part-remission of debts?

In Poland's case an earmarked environment-policy-directed debt reduction would seem totally justified. No other country is as badly affected by air pollution from the Federal Republic as Poland. In 1988 the excess sulphur dioxide drifting across from Germany to Poland amounted to 502,000 tonnes, excess nitrogen, 66,600 tonnes. In 1991 it was still 234,000 tonnes of sulphur dioxide and 55,100 tonnes oxides of nitrogen.

No other country in Europe has such comprehensive rules regarding environmental taxes on pollutants as Poland. While they are still lamenting around the EU conference tables that the EU cannot act in isolation in the matter of a CO_2 tax, Poland long ago opted for such a measure. So if Germany had to pay the Poles a pollution tax on sulphur and nitric oxide emissions which it exports to Poland, it would have had to pay 64 million DM for 1988, 48 million DM for 1991. To repeat: The Eco-Conversion would 'cost' Germany ca. 38 million DM a year for 17 years.

There is no need for lengthy discussions. There is no shortage of ideas for financing the cleaning up of the East European environment. Nor are the Western industrialised countries short of money. What is lacking is political good will. We are much too inconsistent in the West: we want to help, but we don't do it. In the long shadow cast by the hyper-rich nations, initiatives like the Polish Eco-Conversion threaten to fizzle. But it is not so long since that famous quote: 'If the Mark won't come to us, we will go to the Mark.' West Germany should remember that. If the industrialised nations are not willing, or able, to admit that their life-style is chiefly responsible for global environmental problems and that passing on that life-style to Eastern Europe or the Third World could swiftly cause global disaster, they should at least share enough of their wealth to alleviate the worst environmental and social problems. If that does not happen, it will not be surprising if one day not only economic but environmental refugees coming knocking at the door.

You have to have something in the bank, Frank
The Wood in the Gas Chamber

In the West politicians and environment technologists are celebrated jointly. Here an installation to remove a few percent more pollutants from the air, there a process that will make the car a bit more environmentally-friendly.

Environmental technology has become a lucrative economic branch of our growth society. But it has its drawbacks, being well suited to divert attention from our real problem, continued economic growth. Environmental technology does not question our economic arrangements, it positively helps to preserve mistaken developments like our excessive use of motor vehicles. The successes of environmental technology must therefore be regarded critically, though the limitation and removal of pollutants is a positive step. All-round growth, e.g. increased density of vehicles, more traffic and longer journeys, will swallow up the successes of pollutant reduction. In other words: our Planet could die of too much clean technology.

Technology alone cannot solve our environmental problems. Neither, on the other hand, can they be solved without it, so it is absolutely right for politicians in industrialised countries to describe anti-pollution regulations as an advantage. For the environmental technology sector, which makes its living from the existence of strict rules, will be one of the most important export-orientated growth industries of the future.

However, environmental technology comes expensive, often too expensive for countries that have no such know-how of their own. While in Germany millions and billions are spent on reducing SO_2 by 98 instead of 95%, other countries may not even have filtration plants. People and environment in those countries undergo extreme suffering – so extreme that one must consider whether money should not be invested there rather than here. Again one needs to look at the East.

In the mountains of the Riesen-, Sudeten- and Iser-Ranges there is hardly a tree that is not sick. In Czech North Bohemia and in the Polish regions of Jeliena Gora and Walbrzych things are particularly bad. In the Western Sudeten-Gebirge 85% of the wood are "heavily damaged", 13,000 hectares have no trees left at all. In some places a few stumps are left standing because they bear the markings of former footpaths. But nobody cares to go rambling in this landscape of death. No birdsong, no shade, no fragrance of spring. The whole of nature, not only the woods, has suffered a cruel death by gas.

In other parts, too, of the so-called Black Triangle – a region of some 32,000 sq. km. at the junction of Germany, the Czech Republic and Poland – it looks no better. Altogether 20% of the forests once covering 10,000 sq. km. (200,000 hectares, in other words) have already gone. An unimaginably great area poisoned by the fumes from thousands of filthy chimneys.

The Black Triangle is simply the essence of pollution by power stations. 6.4 million people live here in an area the size of Belgium and Luxembourg combined, corresponding to 1.5% of the European Community of Twelve. The region breaks all conceivable records for emanations of the classic pollutants, sulphur dixoide and dust. The inhabitants suffer 12 times as much dust, 7 times the sulphur dixoide, and twice as much nitric oxide per head as the average EU citizen. In bare figures: 2 million tonnes sulphur dioxide, 600,000 tonnes of dust and 350,000 tonnes of nitric oxide are blasted into the air. That corresponds, to give some idea, to 13% of the sulphur dioxide and as much as a third of the total dust emissions for the whole of the EU – all on to 1.5% of the EU's total area! The chief contribution of SO_2 is from the German area (50%), followed by the Czech (40%) and the Polish (10%).

The greatest single cause of pollution is the large power stations. In this region much dirty brown coal is used, e.g. in 42 power station complexes producing over 200 Megawatts. In the Czech region it is the power stations Prunerov II (5 x 210 MW), Tusimice (4 x 200 MW), Pocerady (6 x 200 MW), and Ledvice

I/II (1 X 200 MW). In the Polish sector there is only the Turow Plant (10 x 200 MW). On the German side it is chiefly the power stations Boxberg (12 x 210 MW and 2 x 500 MW) and Hagenwerder (2 x 520 MW) which poison the atmosphere. Some of these monsters have old, inefficient electrofilters for dust reduction. Smoke purification plans for CO_2 reduction do not exist. In addition there are the smaller power stations, industrial plants, domestic fuel, and cars.

Of course it is not only the woods that suffer from this extreme pollution, but the people. Respiratory tract diseases are found to increase above a concentration of 150 micrograms of sulphur dioxide per cubic metre. The mortality figure rises from 260 micrograms per cubic metre. In February 1993 peak values of 2,400 micrograms per cu. m. were recorded. Two thousand four hundred! Over 6000 children were evacuated from the Teplice area during the day, but were returned to the smog in the evenings.

Now there is at least a hint of improvement. After reunification, there is stricter control of the emissions with time allowed for transition, in the former DDR as well. The German power stations in the Black Triangle are either being refurbished to the most recent technical standards, or closed down. And on the Polish side a lot is being done. Turow is to be modernised, some plants shut down, others improved. By 2005 or 2010 the action should be completed. It cannot be done more quickly – as always it is a question of money.

A study has shown that within a space of three years with a financial expenditure of less than 200 million DM (£91 m) in Czech and Polish regions alone the SO_2 emission could be reduced by 340,000 tonnes a year, the dust emission by 75,000 tonnes. For that sum you could just about afford 400 owner-occupied houses in, say, Munich or Stuttgart. It would at any rate mean a reduction of 35–40%. And this, from a Western point of view comparatively cheap, solution would still be economic if the plants concerned were only operational until the year 2000.

One can only hope that this rapid reduction will take place. But at the same time the invasion of Eastern Europe by the Western Nuclear Mafia is being prepared, praising the advantages of the nuclear industry as against filthy fumes. In Slovakia billions are being pumped into the nuclear industry in order to switch off the Bohemian electric power stations. You can work it out: A nuclear plant of 1,200 MW will today cost at least 5 billion DM (£2.3 bn). Money which will not be available for sanitising the environment. How clean could one make the brown coal power stations with such sums?

Yet even if the 200 million DM (£91 m) for first-aid rehabilitation could be raised, further reserves would be needed. The measures necessary for further reduction would be much more expensive. But the money to bring even the big power stations completely up to Western level is not available. And then, beside these big power station blocks, there are the smaller units, industrial plants, and heating in the homes. The latter especially will doubtless be run on the polluting coal for many years yet, because the people cannot afford to install modern heating systems and initiate energy-saving measures. Most certainly traffic will increase for the next few years and make for a new, greater source of pollution.

Even if the acute threat to human beings will lessen, perhaps even rapidly, the woods will probably continue to die. Woods are more vulnerable than people. In speaking of woods, we mean more than just an accumulation of trees. While people can just about stand 140 mg. SO_2 per cu. m., a wood in extreme cases already suffers from a continued exposure to 20 microgram per cu. m.

The processes that damage a wood are complex; it is not ony the actual concentration of a certain pollutant which is decisive. One has to consider the cumulative effect of two substances which singly may not cause damage. One knows about that effect from the combination of medicines and alcohol. The products of chemical reactions can be utterly destructive; for instance, the acid formed from nitric oxide, which turns the soil so strongly acid that nutriments are leached out and plant-harmful aluminium ions set free. All this has a devastating effect on the ecological chain. In the Netherlands it was found, over a research period of six years, that in half the breeding pairs of great tits the eggshell was very thin, porous and fragile. Even where the eggs did not break, many chicks died still inside the egg, because so much water evaporated through the excessively thin shells that the embryos dried up. The cause was not that acid rain dripped on the shell and dissolved the calcium. Rather it was found that the leaching out of calcium from the soil reduced the calcium in the leaves or needles of the trees. This reduced the calcium intake of caterpillars and insects generally, and thus of the birds (such as tits, greater spotted woodpeckers and nuthatches) feeding on the insects. The end result is the thin eggshells.

Air pollution not only causes deficiency phenomena, but also overproduction, as of nitrogen. We are now getting as much nitrogen from the air as farmers used to scatter for fertilising their fields. Moors as nutrient-starved biotopes no longer stand a chance, and in the sick but still existing woods the biological balance has also changed. It is a vicious circle.

But it is not these biological-ecological realities, it is the well-being of an ordinary person of average body-weight which determines permissible values of pollution and the limits of noxious gas emissions. The ecological long-term changes are a taboo subject for our politicians. So woods will continue to die, not only in the Black Triangle, but everywhere in Europe, with diminished speed perhaps, but what is the good of that? New planting will stand little chance on the soils where the woods have already died once because the ground is contaminated.

Well, research will go on and make itself the useful stooge of politics, for a strategy of doing nothing, to go on researching – what exactly? 360 million DM (£163.6 m) have already been researched away. That will do, we know enough! Or do we want to go on researching until we have the ultimate emission-resistant, industry-adapted, cloned, pollution-friendly wood?

Going on to breed the pollution-resistant human being? Great tasks beckon for gene technology.

No – we must act, and act at once. Desulphurate instead of sulphurating. Research money will be better spent on phasing out politicians who cannot or will not understand that it is their economic policies which are killing off European woods. Politicians who – rightly – get excited about the felling of tropical rain forests, but who have gone in for this global-ecologically necessary debate at least partly to divert attention from our own wood problems. Conservationists, watch out!

Chapter 7

Everyone longs for the Land of Cockayne

We can literally never get enough. What is offered on our tables in the way of food and drink no longer has anything to do with the basic human need called hunger. It is not an unmitigated blessing to live in a society of gluttons. Our addiction to consumption and gratification at any price relentlessly destroys nature and environment – not only in Europe, but globally. Hardly anybody seems to care that we ourselves will perish through that. 'After us the Deluge ...'

Don't look beyond your own plate

Asparagus – from wherever

Early April – asparagus time. Well, maybe not quite yet. Harvesting in areas of cultivation in Germany, Austria and Switzerland begins – depending on the weather – only in two weeks' time. But in Shoppingland, the big supermarket out there on the greensward, the asparagus season has already started.

Asparagus time – written in great fat luminous colours on the equally eyecatching price tag. And below it says: Greek whole Asparagus. Only £1.36 per lb. The price-conscious housewife reaches out and puts three bunches straight into the trolley. *Nestos*, it says on the paper collars around those far-travelled asparagus spears.

What the asparagus lovers, who particularly appreciate this import-advanced asparagus season, cannot know is the tragedy of concentrated nature destruction hidden behind almost every pound of the royal vegetable imported from Southern Europe. Moreover, it involves both a multiple destruction of nature and pollution. Firstly, there are the asparagus cultivation areas newly opened up with the aid of subsidies from the European Union – mostly in ecologically highly sensitive regions. Then there is the added environmental pollution due to increased HGV traffic. In order to reach the markets as fresh as possible, the asparagus has to be swiftly carted right across Europe. To understand the full lunacy symbolised by virtually every bunch of imported asparagus, it is worth taking a closer look at one of these regions.

Let us stay with the Greek asparagus. A large part of this is harvested in North Eastern Greece, where the regions of Macedonia and Thracia meet. Here the River Nestos, coming from Bulgaria and cutting across the Rhodope Mountains, flows slowly towards the sea. (For other incredible stories regarding the River Nestos and how it is treated, see elsewhere in this book.) Over the millennia it has deposited great masses of sediment, and because of these deposits again and again altered its course. Gradually a huge delta of fertile alluvial plain was created, harbouring an almost unimaginable diversity of wildlife. Near-impenetrable forests, swamp areas, and, where the river discharges its waters into the Aegean, a chain of lagoons and dune lakes, where rare seagulls breed, as well as the last 30 or 40 pairs of spur-winged plover in Europe. Flamingoes stand in the shallow water, and at the edge of the reed-bed zones of some wetlands small groups of pelicans swim. The lower side of the triangle measures a good 100 kilometres, forming the coastline of the Nestos Delta. But the chain of wetlands is only the last remnant of the former natural biodiversity.

The fertile soil of the alluvial plain has long been in agricultural use. What is the connection with the housewife in the Central or North European supermarket? We are back to the asparagus. Since Greece joined the European Union nature has been pushed back further and further to increase the area of agricultural productivity. With the aid of grants from the various agricultural support funds of the EU, radical land clearing has been carried out; lagoons, swamps and other wetlands have been filled and levelled.

Again with the financial assistance of the Union, giant tractors have been acquired and a hydrating system set up which is really more of a 'dehydrating' system. To secure harvests in the Delta – now degraded to a vast agricultural production belt – more and more water has been withdrawn from the Nestos and used to water the large area of fields by means of irrigation plants. Asparagus is the least of it. Wheat and maize are grown here, agricultural produce which is already a surplus in Europe.

As yet there are pockets of wildlife paradise along the river and on the coastline either side of the estuary. They are not only important for the Greek pelicans, flamingoes and spur-winged plover, but also for the preservation of North- and North-East European waterfowl. White-fronted geese, several varieties of ducks, geese and diving birds – more than 200,000 aquatic birds rest and overwinter in the floodplains of the Nestos Delta. The exotic-looking golden oriole, a songbird of the Central European meadowlands, crosses this region on the way to its East- and South-African winter quarters, as does the red-backed shrike we so carefully protect.

A sensible amount of agriculture would be quite feasible in the Delta if the existing nature sanctuaries were preserved. And at first it looked quite good. Greece signed the RAMSAR-Convention in 1975 and undertook to place the wetlands so vital for migrant birds under protection. The RAMSAR-Convention is in fact 'Convention for the Protection of Wetlands of International Importance, especially as Habitat for Aquatic Birds', and was the first international agreement for nature conservation and also the only one primarily directed at preserving habitats. It is named after the place of its origin, the town of Ramsar in Iran.

Don't worry, we are still with the asparagus. For nothing has been done. On the contrary: Greece did commission the demarcation of areas preliminary to placing them under protection, but there the matter rested, for years. Then it got worse. With unbelievable ecological carelessness, and quite unhindered by the European Union, Greece mistreats this piece of European heritage. There is renewed talk of marking out the areas, but much more narrowly so that new stretches can be brought under the plough. For the last few years this threat has been hanging like the sword of Damocles over these unique landscapes.

The necessary measures for soil enrichment are once again paid for by the taxpayers of EU member states. The upshot: We will be able to go on buying asparagus, perhaps even more cost-effectively, two or three weeks before our home-grown asparagus crop – at two or three times the price – comes into shops and supermarkets. If our local farmers can manage to keep their prices up. For already the price of home-grown asparagus is tumbling. Is that really good news for the consumer?

Only short-term. If the price of home-grown asparagus falls, our farmers will be forced by the lower income to intensify production. This chain of cause and effect demonstrates how subsidies in one region of Europe have repercussions in other regions. To sum up, wrong-headed investments have a nasty habit of rebounding.

To return to the Nestos Delta. Wheat is also grown there, further increasing its overproduction in the European Union. Its guaranteed price in the EU is now barely 27 DM. 20 years ago it was still 45 DM. Add to that the billions which have to be laid out in subsidies to accommodate the wheat on the world market. With such subsidised produce we drag the Third World countries into a merciless competition. Those countries can then no longer sell their agricultural products on the world market. And the roundabout of subsidy, poverty and giveaway wheat as food aid goes on turning, yet another vicious circle.

Considering merely the prices takes no account of the destruction of our natural resources. To us in other parts of Europe it does matter how nature is treated in the South-East of the Continent. We pay for it all with devastated nature, but also in cash. This is money which the European Union pumps into so called underdeveloped regions, for subsidies and structural programmes which kill off nature and our own quality of life.

If Greece fails to put its wetlands of the Nestos under protection (long overdue), but actually reduces their extent, the government officials responsible are not only Eco-Twisters but criminals against nature. Yet such crimes are committed quite legally. The men with responsibility in the Brussels offices do not carry out environment compatibility tests and do not care a scrap about the last remaining pelicans and spur-winged plovers of Greece. With incredible ecological ignorance, the destruction of nature in Greece – long known to the EU's official conservationists – is simply overlooked.

But strictly we are all small-time Eco-Twisters – whenever we thoughtlessly buy what is on offer – at bargain prices and outside the natural season. Ultimately we are helping the greater Eco-Twisters in Athens and Brussels to continue their destructive work. We must ask ourselves what is the value of a bird – perhaps one of the last few rare species of pelican in Greece.

It is not that our greek fellow-citizens of the EU should not receive grant aid. The problem lies solely in the how and what for. Asparagus and the spur-winged plover are only two very small aspects of the conglomerate of environmental scandals which take place legally or under the infinitely tolerant eyes of the EU officials.

Yet the alternatives are well-known. The EU should grant aid and subsidies for indigenous wares characteristic of a region and produced by environmentally friendly methods. Have you ever bought a genuine Greek ewe's milk cheese, as found in a Greek salad, on your recent holiday or from the 'Greek delicatessen' round the corner? Even the so called *Feta* you get somewhere in Greece often hails from Denmark and is made from cow's milk.

Try tackling your local MP about these problems. Usually these ladies and gentlemen know nothing about the scandals, and are quick to point to the difficult situation in Brussels. If you talk to the officials in Brussels, they reply, with some justice: 'What are you on about? The departmental ministers from your country sit in on the decisions of the Council of Ministers . . .' And so ad infinitum, everyone puts the blame on someone else, and the subsidy roundabout goes on turning. Powered by the taxes of European citizens, whose democratic rights simply do not go far enough, they elect a European Parliament that exercises no influence.

Never mind what I said yesterday
The suffering of the marine giants

The sale of whale products is now prohibited in many countries, but the killing of these sensitive marine mammals has not ceased. And a few uncaring countries are just now painfully reminding us of this fact. Whaling is more in the news than ever, even in Europe.

Most of us must have seen, all but physically experienced, that last great fight of Moby Dick with Captain Ahab, which introduced whole generations – at least on the screen or in the book – to those marine giants, the whales. Another drama is being enacted with equal force, worthy of any Hollywood director: the battle for survival of most whale species, performed on the stages of diplomacy, parliaments, press conferences and gatherings of experts. All this after the centuries-long sufferings of the marine mammals appeared to be reaching a Happy Ending when in 1982 a 'Moratorium' for the protection of whales was passed by the International Whaling Commission (IWC).

The IWC, originally purely representative of the interests of whaling nations, had since the late '70s, under international public pressure, increasingly turned into a forum considering the maintenance of whale stocks. Several countries – and this is among the pleasanter aspects of the otherwise gory history of whaling – joined the IWC to persuade it to turn away from whaling altogether. This included inland states without maritime involvement.

Whaling has gone on ever since people have been able to penetrate far enough in their boats to reach and kill the giants of the seas. However, it was done with such limited technical means as hand-held harpoons and lances. Later technology led to a worldwide boom in whaling. Even two hundred years ago fleets from many countries were prepared to sail for months over all the oceans of the world to return with their valuable freight. Sea shanties, souvenirs such as engraved whale's teeth, and harpoons preserved in the museums of countries with a sea coast still tell of the long epoch of whaling from sailing ships.

Then in 1864 came the great turning point, which not only multiplied the suffering of the highly intelligent creatures (they are actually capable of communicating), but put their very survival in serious jeopardy: the invention of the harpoon gun. Henceforth it was possible to reduce the populations on a positively industrial scale. The species mainly affected were the blue whale, fin whale, sei whale, byte whale, and humpback whales of the impressive dimensions. At the same time there was a great upsurge in shipping. The steam engine was introduced into seafaring, increasing the speed of whaling boats. While previously the sailing ships could hardly pursue the swifter whales (a sei whale when fleeing can attain a speed of up to 30 knots), now with the help of fast engines the whalers could pursue the animals over great distances. Also the whalers' sphere of action was extended. Stations were set up on the remotest archipelagos, such as the famous Grytviken Station on South Georgia. Even the Antarctic waters, among the richest in the world for whale populations. But then stocks began to fall. The constantly increasing intensity of the chase meant that merely between 1948 and 1985 more than 1.7 million large whales met their death.

1961 and 1962 were particularly black years for the marine mammals. In that whaling season no less than 70,000 whales were slaughtered. In addition, since the immediate post-War years there has been increasingly comprehensive utilisation of the whales. In the 18th century it was lamp oil that was needed, in the 19th, whalebone for corsets, umbrellas, etc.; then, from the beginning of our century, oil for margarine and finally the meat itself were in great demand.

The technique of the chase continued to improve, leaving the animals less and less chance of escape. Meanwhile the whalers are able to target their prey with such accuracy that they no longer have to spend a long time searching: the depth sounder gives the whales no chance at all. Even when they dive they can be located by this method, and chased until they have to surface again. The ways of killing have also become more cruel: high explosive shells shot into the bodies tear the internal organs to pieces until the animal finally dies.

So there was great rejoicing when, after the years of intensive whaling, in 1982 the longed-for Moratorium decision of the International Whaling Commission was passed, to take effect from 1985. It was a glimmer of hope on the horizon, and surely also a consequence of the failure of the previous system. That ruling had made a classification of whales, and under the designation 'NMP – New Management Procedure' had been applied by the IWC since 1975. It distinguished between legitimate prey and whale stocks to be protected. Reality turned out somewhat different. The stocks of the endangered species continued to dwindle dramatically. Through the refinement of techniques and the opening up of further whaling grounds ever more populations could be found and hunted down.

And as so often in life, in the case of the IWC Moratorium joy was soon succeeded by disappointment. By 1985 it was clear that the then Soviet Union, as well as Norway, Japan and Iceland, would not honour the Moratorium. The particular perfidy lay in the claim by these countries – especially Norway, Japan and Iceland – that continued whaling was 'necessary for scientific reasons'. But the countries in question would not even keep to the hastily drawn up basic criteria of the IWC for that purpose.

At the moment Iceland is merely 'pausing' in the pursuit, but continued to see itself as a whaling nation. The true reasons for continued whaling are frequently exposed, as for instance when Japanese restaurants openly advertised 'Whale titbits', or it emerged that whalemeat was used as fodder on mink farms. Just recently there has been an extensive campaign in the Land of the Rising Sun to eat more whalemeat again in restaurants, canteens and private homes. Business firms en masse are urged to eat whalemeat, amid grandiloquent effusions of chauvinism in which 'whaling' is equated with 'Japan'. So the consumption of whalemeat becomes a patriotic duty, and the nation thereby elevates the extermination of several species to a question of national pride.

The scam of 'whaling for science' soon showed results. It is estimated that no less than 15,000 whales have died since 1985, despite the Moratorium. It is not only the larger whales, which naturally arouse the greatest public interest, but also the smaller species which are still falling victim to barbarism on the high seas. One cause of this is that the stocks of giant whales have shrunk so drastically that hunting them is no longer financially profitable – so there is more call for the smaller species. This involves chiefly minke whales, but also dolphins.

Norway in particular did not cover itself in glory when, despite the disapproval of the IWC and public opinion, it allowed nearly a hundred minke whales to be killed in Summer 1992. Political observers scented a clever strategic move behind this, to enable the Norwegian Government to buy its population's consent to joining the European Economic scene. Norwegian conservationist observers also interpreted the unhappy decision to resume whaling and the threat to leave the IWC as the Brundtland Government's sacrifice of the minke whales to a sombre public mood which wanted to give 'national self-interest' more power again, and which consisted of an indefinable conglomerate of national pride and desire to make an impression. Certainly there are no economic advantages worth mentioning connected with Norwegian whaling – unless Norway wants to blast the fishing policy and Iceland off their equilibrium. This would result both in the IWC losing face and in achieving higher fishing quotas. International conflict duly escalated around Norway's whaling, and the Norwegian Prime Minister's insensitivity in lobbying for the massacre of marine mammals has happily failed to get the wider public to acquiesce.

The call for Norway to renounce whaling will not go away. Anyhow, 15 member states of the IWC protested against Oslo's attitude. The European Parliament, too, took action. In a decision of the Strasbourg Chamber it stated surprisingly plainly that continued whaling did not accord with a country's aspiring to join the EU. Even the then EU-Commissioner responsible for Fishing, Manuel Marin, agreed with the Euro-MPs on this.

One must remember that practically no one in Norway is financially dependent on whaling; but there is a strong negative streak, a clinging to symbolism celebrating the independence of the Norwegian Government, and the minke whale fell victim to this.

This symbolism resurfaced at the most recent IWC Conference in the Japanese city of Kyoto. Norway again had the knives out against the whales and opposed the majority view with shocking obduracy – cheered on, as one might expect, by the aggressive Japanese delegation and its subservient press. The Norwegian attitude was also commended, again as one might expect, by Iceland, which however only participated in the Conference as an 'observer'.

By this behaviour Norway placed itself outside the community of nations who had long outlawed whaling as a deadly anachronism, and as a whaling nation it should not be given the chance to join the EU. The theme remains topical, as Norway is still aiming to join the Brussels Club. It is up to the Community to make it plain that the door will remain closed while there is whale blood on the Norwegian flensing knives.

So is there no hope?

In addition to the depressing news and developments in the realm of commercial whaling, there are further frightening reports which make it hard to feel optimistic regarding the fate of marine mammals. One would guess that Japan will carry on its intensive Pro-Whaling campaign, with the unfortunate result that at the very least ostracism of the slaughter will lessen in Japan itself. With the acceptance of whale products on the home market there is also the danger that whaling territory will spread further. The Japanese whale hunters do not even stop at 'Whale Protection Zone Antarctica' – requested by France, planned to be operational soon, and again rejected by Kyoto. Every year the Japanese whalers' 'Great voyage' is celebrated as a national event. It is only thanks to the courageous action of Greenpeace and certain other organisations that world opinion is kept informed about all this.

The situation is doubtless similar in the European whaling nations. Unless the countries of the European Union follow the example of the USA, which does not hesitate to apply trade sanctions against nations who ignore IWC decisions, we must expect an expansion of whaling. Of course ultimately that means that even the grudging 'Self-limitations' of the two nations concerned to certain species of small whale will not be kept – perhaps cannot be kept. For the danger of confusion between species – genuine or pretended – is so great that virtually all species of whale are liable to get caught. Nobody can keep an effective watch on the activities of the slaughter ships. Endangered species will once again be the first to suffer, because their stocks cannot recover. The population density has become too small for regeneration.

A further threat is the pollution of the high seas, which leads to diseases of the animals' skin and internal organs, and often to infertility. The dragging progress of international agreements for keeping the seas clean can hardly make one euphoric about any quick improvement. On the contrary: as long as industrial growth and indifference allow discharges of waste into the seas to go on increasing, the time bomb of 'species extinction' in the seas will tick ever faster.

The fishing industry, highly industrialised and marked by driftnets and trawling net combines, contributes yet another factor to the death of the whales. Thousands of animals die entangled in the nets of the fishing fleets, in company with seabirds, marine turtles and other fellow sufferers. It is calculated that in the Indian Ocean thousands of sperm whales a year suffer a cruel death in trawler nets. If Saving the Whales – with whom humans have for centuries felt such a close bond – is to succeed. there must be a fundamental ecological change in fishing policy. A change which the major fishing nations of the world, especially within the European Union, must fill with guidelines: as for instance renunciation of driftnets, the reduction of industrial fishing according to the advice of monitoring scientists,who demand a larger mesh size and a decrease in catch capacity, as well as the extension of regeneration zones. And of course the hunting down of whale populations must stop altogether – even where it is said to serve 'ancient traditions', like the annual massacre of whales in the Faroes. These plausible arguments should no longer be misused as a charter for the ruthless killing of whales. Economic sanctions must be applied: the barbarism of whaling must be outlawed.

And of course we should ask ourselves, the declared friends of the whales and, as we hope, a majority, what we ourselves can do to put a stop to whaling. Protests should be made clear to the country involved – who would care to take a holiday in a country, or give it economic support, when it will not leave the marine mammals in peace? The bell has gone for the last round in the fight for the whale: we have to find out whether we can avert the final gong.

The instant feast
Yes, we have no bananas

Why is the banana curved? This question has engaged European minds ever since the discovery of America. For some time now the yellow tropical fruit has again been causing confusion and dismay and with long-term effects.

The coup was successful, and nobody noticed. Within the next few years banana plantations like those in Latin America will start up in Southern Europe, protected and financially supported monocultures to the detriment of the environment. A coup forging unholy alliances between North and South, not even sparing the sacred cow of free trade. A typical European tale. Once upon a time . . .

. . . there was a banana war, and reports from the theatre of war sounded anything but reassuring. The tactical situation was confused, progress at the front impenetrable and certainly not straightforward. The combatants were well-camouflaged, and the daily bulletin spoke of shifting fortunes among the contracting parties. There were spies and deserters, small skirmishes with winners and losers, gains and losses of territory – it was just like a real war. On one side was the alliance of Euro-States and Colonial Banana-States, with their battalions from the twelve EU countries besides reinforcements from Africa and the Caribbean. On the other side, the united troops of South- and Central-American Dollar-Banana republics with their well-concealed North American multi-counsellors. Above all the battle cry: The banana belongs to us!

The first preliminary skirmish of this confrontation lies several years back. It is on record at the discussions around the

EEC agreements of the Treaty of Rome. The signing of the Treaty was delayed for several days because of this tropical fruit. Then the German delegation at the behest of Federal Chancellor Konrad Adenauer had successfully forced through the unrestricted and duty-free import of 'Dollar bananas' into the Federal Republic, and anchored it in the so-called 'Banana Protocol'. Gritting their teeth, the other EU founding members had assented.

One still wonders why Konrad Adenauer was so unyielding at that time. Was it that the banana was a symbol of affluence, to the old Federal States, as now to the new? Was Adenauer himself passionately fond of bananas? Or was there a little pressure from the Americans, in the shape of the United Fruit Company, that multinational producer of bananas, to help things along?

Be that as it may . . . For 35 years, at any rate, the Germans consumed, with relish and without regrets, those curvy things from Latin-American plantations: not too sweet, of consistent quality, and thanks to duty remission considerably cheaper than fruit grown in the European Union itself.

After cars, television and holidays, the banana has remained the Germans' special favourite. Every year each citizen of the Federal Republic consumes an average of 17 kilos thereof, twice as much as the inhabitant of any other EU country. And in the new Federal lands it is as much as 27 kilos: 'The banana as the symbol of reunification,' according to a commentary in the *Neue Züricher Zeitung*. In 1992 altogether 1.4 million tonnes of dollar-bananas, to a value of 1.2 million DM, were imported.

The curse followed upon the deed. The Brussels EU-Empire struck back. The Common Market of all things, in whose sane and beautiful world freedom was supposed to be unrestricted, became the scene of the Europeans v. Tropics banana war. The starter's pistol for the long-desired market without frontiers also fired the first shot on this battle front. It was fired on 13 February 1993 at the Brussels Council of Ministers by a majority of EU Ministers of Agriculture against the German Minister of

Agriculture. The latter had anticipated the attack, because Bonn had agreed to the 'Banana Deal' in principle as early as December 1992, and he stuck all the more bravely to his lost post – at the head of a small 'band of European men of honour'.

Ammunition was supplied by a new banana market regulation, which the German EU-Commissioner Martin Bangemann had long ago termed 'pure lunacy'. The consequences could be foreseen: a case for the European Court of Justice in Luxembourg. The Federal Government complained, but the complaint was, as expected, soon crushed.

Swiftly the theatre of war is transformed into a Theatre of the Absurd. The scene becomes a tribunal. The actors in the exotic setting are Ministers of Agriculture and EU-Commissioners, political and other travelling salesmen, importers and exporters, lobbyists and sombrero-wearers. They argue heatedly, haggle about contingencies and percentages, act and inform, juggle figures and quotas, utter fears about unemployment, rural exodus and recourse to the drug subculture, threaten reprisals and invoke the sanctity of free trade – and above all, guard their own interests. Markets, sales, prices, jobs are at risk. Fears are aroused, and nothing is created but discomfort and peevishness. And below in the stalls the public wonders ... The consumer is, as ever, only the onlooker – the one who pays. But the problem is subtler. What is it all about?

No doubt about it, we live in a banana world. The Federal Republic is not itself a banana republic, but the European Union by its banana policy has become a Banana Community which has withdrawn into its banana-stronghold. Its citizens ate nearly 4 million tonnes of this particular fruit in 1992. Around 1.5 million tonnes of this were produced either in the cultivation areas of EU member countries or their former colonial dependencies in Africa or the Caribbean and were treated like European bananas, i.e. imported duty-free. The greater part of the remainder, over 2 million tonnes of dollar-bananas, came from Latin America: since Adenauer's day, as aforesaid, imported duty-free into Germany, but carrying 20% tax for other EU countries.

Up to the end of 1992 the situation was largely plain. Now it is to become plainer still. Or, again, the opposite could be the case. With the abolition of borders within Europe, the cheap dollar-bananas would inevitably also come duty-free through Germany into the other countries of the Community. This is what the European banana growers feared. It endangers the European and Colonial plantations on which a worker could earn as much in a day as his Latin-American colleague in two weeks.

For this reason a complicated system of quotas, tolls and import limitations was invented, and importers were landed with a mixed system for the import of Colonial- or Dollar-bananas. Result: bananas will become more expensive, at least for the German consumer. How much more expensive remains to be seen. The suggestion for the future is a tax of 20% on 2 million Dollar-bananas. Imports exceeding that number are to carry a tax of 180%.

The public outcry was enormous, the subject grist for the mill of politicians, associations and journalists, for beside the economic it also had an ideological component: the Dollar-Banana in a Post-Colonial Age. But the picture is still pretty confused, the consequences not wholly foreseeable.

The present production quotas for Euro- and Colonial-bananas have been firmly laid down in the new market regulations. But we do know that money breeds – and bananas proliferate. It is hard to believe that the banana cultivation areas will stay at the present level. It is to be feared that the Dollar-bananas will gradually disappear from the European scene, making way for new plantations and ever more mono-cultures in the European Union. The plans are doubtless already on file. That is the real coup of the 'Banana War' – and nobody noticed.

We are onlookers in a Theatre of the Absurd, in which the

play about permanent protectionism is given a new production with a new fruit. Of course for Europeans one's own banana skin is a closer concern than the Latin-American banana shirt. Who cares about GATT or the fate of plantation workers and their families in the Banana Republics?

Anyhow, one can cushion that to the tune of millions spent on EU aid for developing countries. Further advice is apparently not desired, but retaliation measures have already been announced. Cocaine in place of bananas. But such an unsolicited gift from Santa Claus may only be the anxiety nightmare of the lobbyists.

Better look this gift horse in the mouth
Death freight gives humanitarian aid – Pesticides for Albania

Radu Schmidt-Cretan cares about people. Not only do the board games and playing cards he manufactures cheer up the dullness of everyday life. He also thinks as a European, he helps the poorest of the poor.

Around the middle of 1991 he was staying in Albania and negotiating a nice present. Radu Schmidt-Cretan knew that in the pesticide stores of former DDR concerns there were stock piles of old plant-protecting chemicals. Plant protectors whose shelf life was limited, in some cases had already run out, and which therefore under the new law were no longer allowed to be used on German agricultural land. These substances would therefore involve expensive specialised waste disposal for their owners. But German Federal law has left beautiful loopholes for such cases, and Radu Schmidt-Cretan knew them better than anyone. Such hazardous garbage can be wondrously transformed into exportable assets. That is, if you can find someone who will take the stuff for further commercial use.

Schmidt-Cretan's deal with Neyton Kodra, then Plant

Preservation Inspector in the Albanian Ministry of Agriculture, was presumably quickly concluded. Whether the negotiations were accompanied by a certain flow of palm-grease is an interesting subject for conjecture. Anyhow, it was fascinating to note what Kodra – against whom meanwhile preliminary investigation proceedings are pending in Albania – ordered from Schmidt-Cretan, moreover, against the advice of his own experts. The exact amounts which were lying around in certain farm chemical stores in East Germany appeared on Kodra's order forms. He even ordered chemicals which could have no possible use in Albanian agriculture, e.g. *Melipax Aero*, which can only be disseminated by special aeroplanes. But there are no such aeroplanes (fortunately, one should add) in Albania. Was all this ordering of useless stuff – which at the same time meant the cheapest form of disposal for the German former owners – merely Kodra's 'Thanks a lot' for the fact that Schmidt-Cretan delivered the whole load of junk for zero tariff, as 'humanitarian aid' to Albania? Or did the odd Dollar bill or two ease the passage of that order form, irrelevant to Albania's actual needs but very important for Schmidt-Cretan to get hold of? That order form worth 7 million DM, because the old chemicals would not have to be sent for expensive disposal. . . . We do not know the answer. What is certain is that it was only Kodra's order that made Schmidt-Cretan's pesticide transaction legal.

In the period from the end of 1991 to the middle of 1992 a total of 785 tonnes of pesticide made the train journey to Albania. Dubious as the order was in itself, and the fact that all this came as a free gift to desperately poor Albania, equally dubious were the accompanying circumstances of the way the chemicals came to Albania. Here again the full truth may never be known. Of the four trains we know about, one was swiftly unloaded in Albania, and two were sent back from there to Germany because the new Government already in power became suspicious and 'refused acceptance'; the chemicals were returned to their places of origin,

Mecklenburg/Pomerania and Brandenburg respectively. In the Brandenburg case the return delivery was only discovered by chance by Customs which then organised 'appropriate disposal' at the taxpayers' expense.

However, the fourth train was still standing under the fierce Albanian sun in the Summer of 1994, and this one was not to become a symbol of German legal toxic waste disposal. Instead it proved that Schmidt-Cretan definitely acted on the principle 'Out of sight, out of mind'.

From 30 August to 6 September 1993 a team of experts from the Federal Ministry of Agriculture and the Federal Ministry of the Environment examined this train which stood at Bajze on the border of Montenegro. A train with 17 goods trucks, property of German Railways, which demanded a daily rental per truck. By now Albania owed the *Deutsche Reichsbahn* well over 100,000 US Dollars for what is surely the most unsafe of all pesticide stores in the world. The report (Confidential, for official use only) of the expert group reads like a horror novel. The team discovered, inter alia, that 40% of the chemicals no longer had effective action, or were unfit for use for other reasons. They found leakages, dripping from the trucks on to the ground. The train stood near a lake, whose water was especially threatened by the chemical *Camphachlor*. One litre of this *Camphachlor* in the water would kill all the fish in the 2 million cu. metres of the lake. There were 5.85 tonnes of it stored on the train. Because *Camphechlor* is so dangerous, it must, by international transport regulations, be kept in steel-walled containers when on the move. On this train the chemical was stored in glass carboys! The cheapest non-protection for the poisonous gift, and a clear contravention of valid transport rules. But to violate transport rules is not a crime, only an irregularity. In addition one would have to prove that when the train started out the substance was already packed in glass carboys in contravention of regulations. Thus saith the law. No one was called to account.

'The trucks – in their present condition in the station at

Bajze – cannot be moved on.' That was the conclusion reached by the German experts, who had also found false documentation entries and criticised the transport conditions. Quote: 'These regulations [transport of hazardous goods] were not observed either in the packing of the substances or in the loading of the trucks. If the relevant rules had been followed, this train with its dangerous load and inadequate packaging of the latter would never have been permitted to leave Germany.' The customs officials, inter alia part-responsible for monitoring the observance of declaration and transportation rules, belatedly let fall that it was not in fact possible to inspect all deliveries to ensure that they accorded with regulations. There was simply not the manpower. That was precisely what Schmidt-Cretan had gambled on. It was proved that one train had been certified by the Chief Customs Office in Hanover although it had been dispatched in Walddrhena in Brandenburg and had never crossed Lower Saxony at all. An actual inspection had therefore not been possible. 'Only in suspicious circumstances would spot checks be carried out,' a ZDP investigatory team was told, which together with the European Natural Heritage Fund (EURONATURE) was subsequently tracing the course of a train. Might one think there were suspicious circumstances when a playing-card manufacturer gives away pesticides past their use-by dates to Albania?

In Albania further frightening facts emerged about the train. For example 96 canisters each containing 25 litres of damp-corrosion treatment, the mercury-compound *Falisan* (Universal Damp Corrosion Treatment) 1.2, had been stolen. Not that the peasants wanted to get at the chemicals tax-free, no, the local population simply needed the containers. The corrosive chemicals were presumably just dumped in the countryside (the official report would say 'improperly disposed of'), the containers roughly rinsed out. This alone caused at least 70 litres of pure mercury to get into the environment! But, said the reports which reached the German Press, to reassure worried citizens, there was no actual danger to people or environment.

Nevertheless – and this is thanks to the commitment of the Federal Ministry of the Environment – the Federal Government did eventually retrieve the pesticides at the expense of the German taxpayer. Environment Minister Töpfer and his Secretary of State Stroetmann, although their department was not in fact responsible, were the only ones in the Federal Government who showed any feeling for the catastrophic situation in Albania.

The Federal Minister of Agriculture, Borchert, the Cabinet member responsible for pesticides, remained wrapped in silence, as did the Minister for Aid to Developing Countries, Spranger, into whose department contacts with Albania would fall. Minister of Finance Waigel, whose Head Finance Officials would have control of the Chief Customs Offices – which totally failed in this case – took no action and even delayed Töpfer for some time with regard to funding.

Radu Schmidt-Cretan's 'humanitarian action' created many losers, and a few winners. The former owners of the out-of-date chemicals saved millions because they did not have to dispose of toxic waste. Some of the money saved could well have gone to Schmidt-Cretan. The German taxpayer has had to fork out several times over, e.g. for the expensive retrieval – costing 10 million DM – of the chemicals from Albania, as well as for the destruction of the chemicals which the Albanians had sent back directly. The senders had refused to take the goods back, on the grounds that they could show an official order. The returned pesticides thus came into State ownership without the public's knowledge. The transaction represented no aid of any kind for Albania. On the contrary, problems of health and environment resulted. The only ones who profited were Schmidt-Cretan and his backers.

But he is not the only Eco-Twister and wicked business man. The politicians who make such morally indefensible transactions possible, by transmuting hazardous waste into valuable assets by a stroke of the pen, are equally to blame.

By the way, did you notice that in this chapter for once the EU-Commission was not at the centre of our criticism? Unhappily we now have to make up for that. For the 785 tonnes of pesticides from Germany was not the end of it for Albania. The EU in conjunction with the World Bank delivered a further 3,644 tonnes of fungicide, 212 tonnes of herbicide, etc. Out of all that, well over 500 tonnes were unusable even at time of delivery; they probably originated from old DDR stocks.

You should also know that Albania used to chuck plant protection chemicals about in no uncertain manner. 8,000–10,000 tonnes were scattered on the fields every year – per unit of area, twice as much as in the former DDR, and three times as much as in the old Federal Republic. After the Change in Albania, consumption dropped to 66 tonnes per year. Albania needs no pesticide advisers and no aid deliveries. Albania needs counsellors to show the country how agriculture can be carried on without pesticide: but how many such counsellors exist in official EU Europe?

I could eat you up

From the smallholding to the agrarian factory

In a free market economy, and all the more in the areas where the state or the community of nations legislates for order, meaning the order of the market, it should be the primary task of policy to set up a framework for the economy by laws, regulations and decrees, establishing the rights of people, animals and environment. The right to live with dignity, according to one's species, not to be tortured, and to know the basis of one's life preserved.

Politics has not only the duty, but the power, to do that, unquestionably. But it does not carry out that duty, when it comes to the environment or animal farming; it does not use its power. On the contrary, it plays along with an economy whose lobby is much more powerful than that of environment and animals.

In the realm of agriculture, policy is concerned with two principles. One: Areas of agricultural use are meant for fodder plants and domestic cattle. Anything interfering with that is economically unacceptable and must go. This principle has in recent decades led to the sell-off of wild flora and fauna. The second principle states: Exploit your useful plants and animals for all they are worth, to maximise profits.

This policy is not simply incapable of doing justice to the various species of farm animals, it actually makes for the utmost proliferation of animal suffering. Pigs are kept in large numbers packed into the smallest possible space, on slatted cement floors, imprisoned in darkness. The complete darkness is meant to ensure immobility; the light is only put on for feeding. The reason is not just that movement would counteract weight gain and therefore harm the profits, but that the animals are so stressed by the tormenting conditions that they could not stand up to the added stress of more light.

The animals' excreta fall through slits in the concrete into the ground on which they stand. There is no straw in which the animals could burrow. That would be labour-intensive and too expensive. So one lets faeces and urine fall into the slurry pit under the floor. The ammonia concentration within reach of the animals' snouts is extremely high – sometimes so high that the nasal membranes corrode. Well, they are not meant to sniff out truffles any more, they are meant to get fat for slaughter. Cannibalism is no rarity among the beasts, which in compassionate conditions would exhibit peaceable herd behaviour.

Mass factory farming involves calves which are fed against their natural requirements, merely to keep the meat white. The animals are deprived of all roughage, such as straw or hay, and fed only a liquid diet. Factory farming involves hens who can lay claim to less space apiece than the book in front of you. And factory farming additionally means infringements of the already far too lax rules, hardly any supervision, and far too mild penalties, if any. All that in order to get cheap food to our tables.

Over 100 million pigs, 80 million cattle, 100 million sheep and 13 million goats are kept in the 12 Member States of the EU. We love eating them, but that is the limit of our love. They are not evenly distributed across individual countries. 25% of the cattle are in France, 27% of all the pigs are fattened in Germany, Britain and Spain are in the lead for sheep and goats (29% and 24% respectively).

Of course there are still some traditional methods of farming where one can observe a symbiosis between animal, man and nature. Thus in the oak woods of the Spanish Extremadura free-living pigs roam at will and eat themselves fat as they please, and this extensive, species-adapted and environment-friendly form of stock farming is a precondition for the preservation of the unique oak landscapes, which are of the greatest value as wildlife habitats. Yet such forms of management are by EU standards uneconomic and therefore politically undesirable. Productivity, meaning profitability, determines the way animals are kept – not their own needs, nor consideration for the environment.

Regional as well as factory-style concentration of animal farming is recommended, as in the industrial sector. In other words, factory farming, which started about 30 years ago, is coming on strong and to a large extent has already completed its triumphal progress. That agriculture, unlike industry, is dealing with living things seems to be of no interest. The animals have been degraded to the status of production factors like screws, tinplate or valves.

Methods cruel to animals are more profitable and they have been legitimised by the current laws. Only Switzerland sets an example of justice to animals. Keeping them in cages, for example, is prohibited there. But Switzerland is not in the EU. If it were, and attempted to stop the marketing of factory-farmed meat or eggs, the European Court of Justice would soon punish such 'interference with trade'.

The official statistics do not even wholly express the silent revolution that has overtaken the land and the stables. Were it not for the odd hormone scare or a report on the transport of disgusting, festering masses of flesh, we would scarcely register all the horrors that take place.

In Portugal or Greece even today the average farm unit has barely four dairy cows, in Spain less than seven. But European policy is determined by the interests of Dutch and British dairy farmers, who will have 40 to 60 animals at their disposal. And the Greek, Portuguese and Spanish peasant farmers will soon be overrun by this lobby. Politics, the EU billions and the economy, working together, will see to that.

In Germany so far 'only' 20% of all fatstock pigs are kept in units of more than 400. The tendency is still rising.

Holland, and also Britain, point to the future. There changes of structure have meant that already 50 to 75% of pigs have to vegetate in purpose-built sties, in bays too narrow to move about, so that they do not waste energy in movement which should go to growth (which equals profit). When needed, which arises more often than one would think, the pharmaceutical industry will help the stressed animals. A flourishing, often illegal business.

The concentration of factory farming has advanced furthest with regard to poultry. But here too statistics do not always make it plain that concentration is almost total in some sectors. Thus in Germany over 90% of chicken farms are small units with up to 50 laying hens. Fine, one might think, smallholding agriculture, where only 10% of all farms have more than 50 hens. But the 90% of small units contain only about 9% of all the birds; 90% of the (often featherless) birds are held in the barns of only 6% of large-scale concerns. And the number of large factory farms does not reveal the number of egg tycoons.

The biggest name in the German egg business, Anton Pohlmann (of Nelling-Hof), has turned nearly every one of his barns into an independent, autonomous concern. That means, for instance, that he can evade such trade union requirements as works councils. Pohlmann, who apparently controls more than 5 million laying hens in Germany alone, and is now trying to get footholds in other EU States (such as Marne in France), is happy with an egg price of 0.11 DM. He still makes a profit of 1 Pfennig per egg. But his competitors go bust.

Pohlmann would call this market economy, and he would be right. This policy may also help the aim of the EU, to fix 'appropriate' prices for the consumer. But such prices tell us nothing about the endless suffering experienced by the animals, nothing about the gigantic environmental problems arising out of factory farming, nothing about the social problems of the workers, the farmers, or the Third World which produces the animal fodder. The prices merely reveal some of the shortcomings of the policy. But the market economy, which claims to be both ecological and social, is not interested; nor are the politicians, or things would have changed long ago.

The regional concentration of factory farming is worst where cheap feeding stuffs from the Third World can be landed, which, unecologically grown and causing great social problems, displace locally grown grain from the feeding troughs; but also where there are large outlets. One such region is the district around South Oldenburg/Cloppenburg, including the Munsterland with its market outlet in the Ruhr territory. Animal feed for the area comes in at the Lower Weser port of Brake. The rural district of Veshta, for example, which makes up a mere 0.5% of the West German area of agricultural use, contains 20% of the egg-laying hens, 14% of the cockerels, and 5% of all the fatstock pigs in German. There, too, you find the worst ecological damage. 60% of the cockerels are kept in factory farms which have no agricultural land of their own; they have to buy 100% of the fodder, and also they have to arrange for the disposal of the animals' excreta.

The excrement is in the form of so-called slurry, a mixture of water and faeces. The old farmyard dungheaps, which were better than slurry for fixing nitrogen, are not available for factory farms. They would of course be ecologically better, and better for the animals, but they would require labour and that makes them too expensive. It is far cheaper to keep pigs and cattle on bare concrete floors with slits. Of course it is also too expensive to transport the huge quantities of slurry over long distances to where the nutriments could actually be utilised, in regions where there is hardly any livestock but where the plants in the fields need fertilising. In effect all the slurry is unloaded on the areas where the animals are massed. There is far too much slurry, as evidenced by the catastrophic pollution of the groundwater.

The EU limits for nitrates are in many cases heavily exceeded, the water for the whole area is poisoned by the slurry, totally unfit for human consumption. Slurry here is not manure, but the waste of factory farming. The fields become a garbage dump – and the politicians look on.

In addition the factory farms pollute the air with ammonia compounds. Experts tend to believe that some of the forest damage in North Germany as well as the excess nitrates in the North Sea and the Baltic are partly due to factory farming.

What would you expect from the politicians? Of course, that they would try to remedy these wrongs. One may hope for that, but it is an unrealistic hope, as the excesses described are the inevitable outcome of the agricultural development policy. Even the hormone scandals, another logical consequence of the growth policy, do not lead to doubts about factory farming. Instead of prohibiting it, instead of setting limits for numbers of stock or suiting the animal management to the area, instead of setting up rules for stock-keeping which are fair to the animals, things proceed in a purely technocratic manner. The water supply is centralised in the polluted regions, getting water from distant, pollution-free places, in order to go on polluting the contaminated site. And one sees off slurry regulations which try to control when and how much slurry is discharged. These get no further, as the Council of Experts for Environment Problems found in 1985: 'The ... agreed upper limit of three dung units per hectare is in the Council's opinion too high, and not acceptable even where a time- and crop-linked discharge is guaranteed...' But that cannot be guaranteed, for as we know animals do not necessarily do their 'business' where the useful crops need their supply of nutriments. The pronouncements of the Federal Government's appointed experts had no results whatsoever.

Agrarian industrialists and barn farmers now think they have found the solution. One simply needs to dry the excreta (energy-intensively!), and then their cheap transport to other regions is no longer a problem, but 'big business' in every sense. And the politicians rejoice. They see this as a proof that a market economy can always come up with imaginative solutions. You can actually make money out of shit. In the minds of politicians, administrators and technocrats that may be plausible. But it is not the shit that stinks to high heaven – the real stink is from this method of animal farming and the agricultural policy which permits it.

All those who truly want to change such structures – hostile alike to environment, animals, small farmers and the Third World – who do not look for a partial solution which will itself cause new problems elsewhere and leave other questions unanswered, know that one must combat factory farming in particular and agricultural policy in general. It is simply wrong that billions of our tax money go to enrich the few, while environment, farmers, consumers and animals are increasingly impoverished.

More, more, more – means less
Agricultural policy which is no policy

Why is there a Common Agricultural Policy? To help the farmers? If you believe that, you are on the wrong track. The EU agricultural policy these days serves to use our tax pennies to abolish farmers and build up an agrarian industry instead. That sounds brutal, and it is brutal, happening as it does against the will of those concerned, including taxpayers. Or do you approve of factory farming, agriculture that pollutes the countryside, and the end result of these developments – the shrinking cutlet in the frying pan? Agricultural policy and the many Eco-Twisters involved in it do not care. The sole concern is to cover it all up. Every effort is directed towards persuading us that smallholder farming is particularly dear to all their hearts. Yet what the policy actually promotes is the chemical-intensive, overrationalised and totally mechanised agro-industry. The prospectus may show poppies and cornflowers with an idyllic horse-drawn plough in the foreground, the reality is a hard policy of chemicals and intensification.

Politicians like to point out that they have created an ingenious system to protect our agriculture against non-European competition. A competition that works, among other things, with extremely high subsidies and a radical exploitation of people and environment to flood our market with cheap produce. Yet does the EU system really protect our farmers? To grasp the full extent of eco-twisting, it pays to look closely at EU agricultural policy, which is not really a policy at all.

EU agricultural policy is based on three principles: The first is known as *siphoning off*. It represents the official demarcation of the EU market from outside markets. Cheap goods from outside Europe are fixed up with a tariff (the siphoning off) when they reach the EU market. This raises the prices of the products to bring them level with existing prices – not only for agricultural produce – inside the EU. This is to protect EU products against undercutting by the competition.

The second pillar of agricultural policy is meant to boost the sale of EU produce outside the Union. But as EU products are indeed somewhat more expensive, the price difference between the higher EU level and the lower world market level must be evened out, otherwise nobody would buy. So the exporters of EU goods are given *reimbursement*, i.e. the produce is subsidised to make it cheaper when it is sold outside Europe.

The third prop, beside siphoning off and reimbursement, is *price bolstering* of certain agricultural products inside Europe.

For tinned beef (a product of the abattoir), for sugar (a factory product), for butter or skimmed milk powder (produce of the dairies), prices are fixed. For the farmers, the only guaranteed price is for such produce as wheat. But that guaranteed price is now so low that farmers cannot grow their wheat to meet it. So it is no use to them.

That these divers regulations cannot be entirely cheap to run is understandable. But have you any idea how much the EU's agricultural policy costs us altogether? Right, we will tell you. In 1975 the agrarian budget of the EU comprised £4 billion, in 1981 it was already three times as much – £12 million. After £16 billion (1983) and £28 billion (1989) it had meanwhile risen to £32 billion, and the trend is still rising. What one could do with such sums!

There is no evidence that the high outlay helps farmers or farmyards who work traditionally in harmony with animals and environment. The billions spent are no indication that a 'mixed farming' policy is being encouraged. The fact is that the EU goes on pumping more and more (tax-fed) billions into its agrarian budget, while at the same time the farmers are getting less and becoming, by comparison, progressively poorer. There is probably no other part of EU policy inside Europe which costs so much and is so far from fulfilling the needs of those for whom it is supposedly meant. That is the real snag of agricultural policy; it is the greatest of lies and deceptions. Together with the structural funds, the agricultural policy is the biggest job killer and Eco-Twister on our Continent. Profits are for the exporters, storers and distributors, dealers, the processing industry, and all kinds of dubious characters. The agrarian budget has become the farmers' nightmare and the money conjurors' Eldorado, a self-service superstore for obscure money-coiners. But more of that later.

The fact that the remaining small farmers demonstrably have not, or only marginally, increased their average income, indeed, that many owners of farms have even had to register great losses, shows that the goblet of generous subsidies has largely passed by the farming fraternity. In fact the flood of money that swept over Europe did not halt the 'structural change in agriculture', a.k.a. the demise of farmers, but deliberately speeded it up. Ever more farmers are going bankrupt, others juggle with set-aside grants and other subsidies. Those that remain have to produce more and more intensively and therefore environmentally-damaging in order to survive.

In Germany the number of farm businesses has decreased by almost two-thirds since 1950: more than 1.4 million farms have been abandoned. Every day 40 more farmers are made bankrupt. 84% of the jobs in agriculture after World War Two have, with tax money, been knowingly and deliberately rationalised away, not only in Germany. Inside the EU every two minutes a farmyard goes bust. Would you have expected such a costly policy to produce such a heap of ruins: engineered unemployment, environment destruction, cruelty to animals, as well as poor quality food?

Politicians are silent on the point that this is not just an occupational hazard, but deliberate aim. 'Growth, or go to the wall' is the principle. Smallholding agriculture, that branch of the economy which for centuries shaped our cultural landscape and resultant biodiversity, is to be wiped out. It is not modern enough for politicians and economists, insufficiently profitable or productive. Farmers will be abolished by what calls itself an agricultural policy, but is clearly an industrial policy. In the minds of Ministers of Agriculture and Eurocrats the farmyard, the mixed use smallholding of perhaps 30 hectares, with a few cows, pigs and chickens, has long ceased to exist. The surviving examples are surplus stock, end of range – at best museum pieces of a bygone age, an entertainment for Holidays on a Farm. With social programmes and ecologically virtuous alms one can just about keep them going until the manager retires. That also keeps rural discontent off your back. Successors to take over farms are virtually non-existent. In some agricultural colleges there will soon be more teachers than students. The farmyard has been sacrificed to the agrarian factory.

In the Western industrial countries rural agriculture with its minimal share of the gross national product (in the EU less than 5%) is not only not valued, it has become an encumbrance. Every Mark, Dollar or Franc which is not spent on food today is freed in the consumer's purse for the products of the industrial sector or the service industries; and our economy is far more dependent on these than on agriculture. In other words, every Pound we spend on farm products rather than on the mass-produced rubbish of the agrarian industry is unavailable for investment in manufacturing or service industries. The EU knows that.

If the raw materials the food industry needs are still to come from local producers, they will have to become even cheaper and agriculture will have to become even more productive. Otherwise the economy will have to get those raw materials elsewhere. There is an incredible pressure on prices, powered by the agrarian industry, accelerated by the EU's agricultural policy, and rounded off by the GATT-negotiations. Large-scale structures are deliberately encouraged, and have prevailed; prices are geared to these, not to an ecological and hence more expensive method of production. Prices again fixed by the EU and the Council of Ministers, with the necessary impetus given by industry.

Politicians have ruthlessly streamlined agriculture in the interests of industrial growth and the general economy. The decisive criteria governing agricultural policy have long ceased to be of an agricultural or ecological nature. It is not the guidelines of environmentally-friendly farming, but the demands of a purely quantitative-growth-directed economic policy which matter. Cheapest mass production is the motto, in the fields as in the barns.

This ever more productive agriculture not only exacts the sacrifice of farmers, it is also environment-hostile, mounting a vast campaign of destruction against wildlife, countryside and people. The groundwater is polluted with nitrates due to excess fertilisation, an offshoot of factory farming. There is an attempt to solve this problem by blocking off wells and springs, and organising expensive centralised water supplies, which in turn cause fresh environment problems. The idea of tackling the roots of the problem does not occur to the policy makers. It cannot occur to them, because it would question their basic aim, the industrialisation of agriculture. They accept the fact that pesticides make farm workers ill. Agrarian policy is also responsible for grubbing up hedges, asphalting roads, merging fields, draining wetlands, losing grasslands; for billions being squandered, finding their way into pockets where citizens would not care to see them; for a huge decrease in biodiversity of crops, and farmers being urged to tolerate no companion plants (also knows as weeds). Progress comes at a price.

Industry itself was both interested and helpful in all this, finding in industrialised agriculture the cheapest supplies of basic and raw materials as well as a market for its own products; tractors and sheds, fertilisers and pesticides, seeds and embryos. Gene technology also scents a huge potential market in agriculture. Ketchup tomatoes, which can be gathered by combine harvester and are easiest of all to process, already exist. Super-turnips and turbo-cows are on the drawing board and only waiting to be let loose on the consumer. Agriculture without farmers is a good little earner.

Politicians prefer to keep quiet about all this. The involvement of the multinationals remains under covers, for it does not accord with the consumer's image of agriculture. That is still conditioned by nostalgia, by received ideas, by fairy tales and our children's picture books. The agrarian industry uses this state of affairs very skilfully. 'Country Eggs from XY Farm' is what one reads on the box, which also shows a picture of the appropriate farmhouse, with or without dungheap. But of course such pictures do not correspond with the real-life sterility of mass factory farms, from which the eggs usually come, and which have as much connection with a farmyard as a Formula One racing car with a bicycle.

You should test your own conception of agriculture. When

did you last see a farmyard? When did you last speak to a farmer? When did you last see a pig grubbing about in the straw? Bet you have never been inside a shed packed with 600 or 1000 pigs, several thousand chickens, or 200 calves. Society is alienated from agriculture, it retains a positive, romanticised picture of the farmer and his farm, and the politicians would like to preserve that, come what may.

So it is more useful for a politician to be photographed with a piglet in his arms, in front of a compost heap with a cock scratching about on it, and to breathe the usual promises to preserve mixed use smallholdings into a microphone than to broadcast the true aims and consequences of the policy. For if the consumer knew that the money never reaches the small farmers, that agrarian industry creams off his tax contribution, that his tax pennies go to destroy the environment, and that his vision of agriculture is all wrong – then his revulsion against that expensive policy would grow and flourish exceedingly.

Chapter 8

Driving out the Devil with Beelzebub

Every day all over the world programmes, projects and actions are started which are supposed to help people. However, the opposite is often the case. Instead of bringing help, billions are spent on destroying nature, culture and regional identity. But as the damage is not noticed until later, nobody will admit it. Let us stop accepting alibis for destruction.

Planning with blinkers on
Why Attica is so bare

We are standing in front of the majestic columns of the Parthenon. Like so many others who have been here before us, we admire the remains of vanished epochs high above the rooftops of presentday Athens, stone witnesses testifying to the skill and the highly developed culture of the Ancient Greeks. And like so many others in the age of mass tourism, we look down on a town covered with a thick yellowish smog of car exhaust gases, industrial grime and other pollutants.

Despite this smog – beside the miasma hanging over Los Angeles or Mexico City, one of the worst clouds of pollution in the world – one can still just see the chain of hills at the other end of Athens. It is a bleak, bare hill landscape; no tree seems to break the monotony. A drive out beyond the gates of the exhaust-tormented city confirms the impression. Treeless hills and hollows as far as the eye can see. Only a maquis-type vegetation which straggling scrub covers some slopes. The chirping of crickets, locusts and cicadas blends with the sight of a flock of goats calmly grazing against the sunset to make up an idyllic picture of Attica.

The idyll is deceptive. It is no more authentic than the landscape in which we set it. You may be surprised: this is not a typical Mediterranean chalk landscape.

You may remember we learnt at school that the Ancient Greeks, the Romans and later the Byzantines, by cutting down trees to build their ships, denuded many areas of the Mediterranean of their woods. You can still read it in many textbooks today. But that is wrong, or only half the truth.

Attica – the much praised and poeticised landscape around the new Athens, which was fairly recently laid out again – could today be green over wide areas. The reason why tourists as well as the native population find only a chalky, pretty monotonous landscape is simple, if not always realised: this region, like many other parts of Greece, gets systematically eaten away.

Thousands of guzzling goats and sheep prevent nature from returning. Huge flocks, often of several hundred animals, are driven to and fro by their herders, constantly searching for edible green shoots. Wherever a little sapling tries to grow into a young shrub or tree, sooner or later some sheep or goat with a well-aimed bite puts a swift end to the attempt at reafforestation. Together with the young sprig all hope of regenerating the once-varied vegetation disappears.

Yet for the inhabitants a rewooding of the hills – which are not in any case arable land – would be of great importance. Woods and woody vegetation generate moisture, and more moisture would improve the climatic situation. More rainfall would make life more tolerable again for both natives and tourists in this region regularly afflicted with water shortage. More woodland would also help to clean up the intolerably polluted air. Meanwhile hundreds of thousands of goats and sheep continue to graze on relentlessly under the burning – or setting – sun of Attica. And wherever young green cranes towards the sky, they and their herders are instantly on the spot.

It is not the sheep or goats in themselves that are the scandal, but the fact that there are so many of them. There is a simple, but almost incredible, reason for this: per animal per year the European Union in Brussels pays 2000 Drachmas, roughly £6. So the mere ownership of sheep and goats brings an income. If this programme were solely to help small peasant farmers it would not be so bad. Many people in remote parts of Greece urgently need such support. But the Brussels bounty comes pouring indiscriminately out of the watering-can. Anyone who owns sheep and can thereby prove agricultural activity – even if he otherwise functions as a government official, banker or whatever – can share in the money.

Now £6 per animal is not exactly the earth. But the owner of 1000 sheep, in passing and without much toil, collects £6,000 odd. Without doing any work. For minders to look after the flocks come pretty cheap. Labour costs are virtually negligible. Often it is unemployed Albanians who, seeing the catastrophically impoverished state of their own country, are grateful to work even for a pittance. As they are often illegally in Greece, they keep their mouths shut and thus guarantee their wealthy employers additional profits. Incidentally, the sheep and goats graze on common land, so they do not cost much to feed. When these animals, kept for virtually nothing, are slaughtered, the sale of their meat once again means fat profits for the rich owners.

Nearly all the sheep and goats in the Athens area belong to a few wealthy families. Very few animals are kept by peasant farmers. The rich pseudo-farmers, by dint of their oversized flocks which are anything but landscape-friendly, go on getting richer: at the expense of the European Union's taxpayers, at the expense of one of the most culturally valuable regions of Europe, and at the expense of the quality of life and the environment in and around Athens. Indeed, at the expense of all Europeans, who through the insane subsidy practices of an inflated agrarian bureaucracy in Brussels and an even less penetrable bureaucracy in Greece are being robbed of a piece of their natural heritage.

Next summer will certainly come, and with it the next shortage of drinking water emergency, and the next smog alarm in Athens. But hundreds of thousands of goats and sheep are allowed to go on grazing, keeping public land bare and preventing reafforestation, subsidised by the EU, under the sun of Attica. Sum total: The European Union by its subsidy practice for sheep and goat farming contributes to the fact that Attica, like some other regions of Europe, will stay denuded.

Refusing to learn from one's mistakes
Super-Power in the Rhodope Mountains

Everyone knows what a drama is – a play, with actors taking various parts: we all did Shakespeare at school. And yet the word 'drama' carries a tinge of something more, a breath of tragedy, perhaps. Such a one possibly threatens wide tracts of Northern Greece, possibly the whole Eastern Mediterranean area, if something happens that so far is only simmering at the planning stage. Can you imagine that, only a few years after the traumatic experience of Chernobyl, a new super power station is being assembled more or less do-it-yourself – a grand project without parallel, having nothing in common with a nuclear plant except emission of power? In Greece, it would seem, nothing is impossible . . . It is a tale of ecological ignorance, mistaken belief in progress, and sheer human stupidity.

In the plain of Drama in Northern Greece, not far from the old port of Kavala, for centuries there has been a town of that same name. Drama has known many regimes, it has survived Ottoman rule, the Greek Civil War, and economic slump. Even today this region remote from the tourist routes lacks structural amenities. Unemployment is high, chances to avoid poverty are rare.

Against this background, normal enough in many parts of Europe, bad advisers are not usually far away. Prophets promising quick solutions – solutions which do tend to benefit themselves. The planning of the Greek State Electricity Company (DEI), first announced in 1991, is surely one such 'solution': a gigantic turning of browncoal peat into power. Right there in the Plain of Drama it is to be cut and burnt. At first two, later six, blocks of power plant with a capacity of 300 MW each are to be erected. They are to burn the lignite of the whole Plain.

Huge stores of browncoal peat have accumulated here. On an area of almost 10,000 hectares there are about 2 billion tonnes, to a depth of about 200 metres. If the plans were carried out, what would happen inspired the local newspaper to run the headline: 'The Drama of Drama'.

For the consequences would be disastrous, on an ecological Mega-Power scale. The entire plain, which at present provides the best arable land, would be devastated. A moon landscape would result, slashing deep wounds into the landscape. The mere depth of the deposits of the comparatively young lignite suggests what upheavals and excavations would be necessary. Per tonne of extracted browncoal peat, it has been calculated that there would be no less than 11 tonnes of rubble – huge amounts of debris would be left behind, and so far no politician has been able to say what could be done with it. Again, the browncoal peat contains 60% of water, but a removal of the wet subsoil would be completely uneconomic. Consequently there has already been a suggestion to pump out the water – which would destroy the groundwater system of the whole area.

No one can foretell what that would mean for countryside and people. The only certainty is that the acute shortage of drinking water, which across wide areas of Greece is already a sad reality every summer, would be greatly increased by it. 'A horror', according to the representative of the Activists Against Browncoal Peat in Drama, 'the mere thought of it, that almost every summer in Greece we have to ration water, and on the other hand here a great groundwater reservoir is to be destroyed. That would finally kill off agriculture.'

In this connection one has to ask what site value and credibility the financial programmes and directives of the EU can have for the preservation of vital water resources. The excavations would also destroy 10,000 hectares of fertile arable land. Land, moreover, harbouring treasures we can as yet only guess at. Archaeologists say that with the digging up of the browncoal peat at least twenty archaeological sites of inestimable value will be lost for good.

That is not all. The drama of Drama will continue into the next Act, if the Government and DEI proceed with their absurd project. The burning of the browncoal peat, which has a sulphur content averaging 3.6% – otherwise only found in East European brown coal, and the consequences there are well known – would also release sizeable emissions of the climate killer CO_2 : over 30,000 tonnes a day! This in spite of the EU's having just carried through a voluntary reduction of carbon dioxide emissions. Environment summits become a farce in the face of such plans.

And even this is not enough. Where the Eco-Twisters are at work, they do the job thoroughly. Acid rain would disperse the browncoal sulphur, not only over the plain, but far over land and sea. According to the direction of the wind, the valleys of the adjacent Rhodope Range or the wetlands and towns along the coast would be hit by acid rain. In the Rhodope Mountains and also along the coast there are habitats whose unique character and importance to endangered species led to their designation for special protection under the EU Bird Protection Directive and various international conservation conventions. Besides the Bird Protection Directive, the RAMSAR-Agreement for protection of internationally important wetlands, the Bonn Agreement for protection of migrant wild animal species, and the Berne Convention regarding wetlands such as the Nestos Delta, the mouth of the Aliakmon, and Lake Terkini, all apply. They are all of particular importance for migrant birds, but also to secure the habitats of many endangered species such as the curly-headed pelican and the spur-winged plover, whose strength in Europe is now estimated at only 35 breeding pairs.

A similar situation exists regarding the unique remnant of primeval forest in the High Rhodopes near Zakardenia, where a luxuriant forest vegetation survives such as no one would now expect to find in Greece. Mossy giants of the ancient forests rear towards the sky, collapsed old trees cover the ground, and liana-type creepers obscure the view. Scientists have often regretted being unable to explore the primeval forest because of the then proximity of the Iron Curtain to Bulgaria. Now that the Iron Curtain is a thing of the past, we are threatened with the loss of that treasure, watched over though it is by special keepers: acid rain from the Plain of Drama could spell the end of the primeval forest.

But not only the forest should occupy our attention, nor even the abovementioned 14 "Important Bird Areas' of the internationally significant wetlands. The Rhodope even today offer a varied wooded landscape, a home for species such as the brown bear, lynx, wolf and vultures, which it is vital to preserve. It marks the southern boundary of fir trees, and the woods form a rich mosaic, aspects varying from reminders of Black Forest valleys to gorges in Galilee. All this is now at risk. If the lunacy of Drama is carried out, it will mark the beginning of the end for the Rhodope woods.

Worse and worse: Large amounts of radioactivity will escape from the chimneys of the power stations, because for millennia radioactive water – natural radioactivity from the ancient Thracian rocks – has flowed from the Rhodopes into the browncoal peat. The peat has become radioactively enriched. Radiation values up to 80 Becquerel, according to research, have been recorded. If that peat is burnt, the radioactivity will spread over the whole of Northern Greece, and unfavourable winds will carry it right to the Aegean, to Albania and North Italy. No one can predict how that would affect the health of people in that area, and no one can calculate today the possible effect on agriculture. Again, after the removal of the browncoal peat from the Plain of Drama, a sizeable 'reservoir' of radioactively polluted water from sources in the Rhodope would be released. The polluted water would discharge directly into the river and thence to the sea.

There is considerable resistance to the project in the region itself as in Europe in general. The social and ecological consequences could amount to one of the worst disasters for people in Northern Greece and far beyond, unless there is still a decisive rejection of the plan by the DEI and the Greek Government. Both have kept remarkably quiet in response to the fierce protests since 1991, well organised by the local activists' society, backed by a petition with nearly 40,000 signatures and by all the local mayors; but there are constant rumours that the project has only been put in cold storage. The protests reached as far as Brussels; the European Parliament was approached as well as the EU-Commission, because realization of the project would entail multiple violation of EU regulations, especially with regard to 'Important Bird Areas'. It is a worrying fact that the power stations still figures on the Greek national 10-year plan for the time up to 1999. Yet Greece, like many other countries, could easily end its energy shortfall. A more efficient transmission of power, reduction of losses along the line by improved technology, but also the promotion of wind- and solar power and a more thorough utilisation of solar energy by means of photoelectric equipment – highly feasible on many sites around the Mediterranean – could help to achieve a definite plus in available energy.

The European Union is obliged, both in view of the expected damage and by reason of its own commitment, to undertake everything possible to reduce carbon dioxide. It is now in the position of having to discharge a specific debt by ensuring that the proposed end-of-century folly of Drama will never become a reality: by insisting on the observance of EU nature protection regulations, but also by financial aid to the furtherance of wind- and solar energy in Greece.

Big, cheap and cheerful
Peasant farmers on the Danger List

Peasant farming has been almost entirely destroyed in those EU countries where industry has developed full dominance. Factory farming has taken over, as can be seen from the small number of workers still engaged in agriculture: 2.2% in Britain, 2.8% in Belgium, 3.9% in Germany (the former Federal States), 6% in Denmark and 6.4% in France. Ask the politicians what was so desirable about that, and they will reply that agriculture has become more productive, and food cheaper. Productivity per acre today is twice what it was in 1950. An agricultural worker today is eight times as productive as 40 years ago. But there is a price to pay: £32 billion EU-budget, vast sums from the national budgets, destruction of nature, contamination of water, agriculture's contribution to the death of the woods...

The policy has broken down, but who cares? Agrarian policy-makers and all who profited from the development to date are now trying to do business in those countries which still have peasant structures, and to transfer the policy to them. Inside the EU this means Portugal and Greece. There respectively 19% and 24% of the gainfully employed are still working on the land, as peasants and farmers, in harmony with nature. For how long? The competition is already in place. In North Germany industry produces a Feta cheese from cow's milk – though actually it should be made by Greek shepherds from ewe's milk. Does it matter? What counts is to sell a good name in the market as advantageously as possible. The consumer will swallow it all right.

Forcefully to conquer new markets and pass on ideologies, that is the task now facing the agrarian industry. And it can count on the support of the EU policy. Now the creamers-off and Eco-Twisters have discovered a new battlefield for their campaign of demolition against small farmers and the environment: Eastern Europe. In the former Soviet Union, in Bulgaria and Hungary, almost 20% of the people are still working on the land, in Bulgaria as many as 22%. Your hair will stand on end when you look at Poland: there it is 30% of the working population who again make some sort of living out of agriculture, after industry went in for mass dismissals.

If it is up to the Western agrarian industry and Western policy advisers on the spot, it must not stay like that. No lengthy deliberations about social and ecological conditions, action is the thing.

Eastern Europe is a lucrative export market not only for our agrarian ideology but for our agrarian industry. The chemical giants scent a new dawn, after the sale of pesticides and fertilisers has slowed down in the West and is even partly in decline. The managers realised that it could not go on, our farmers scattering as much nitrate fertiliser on their fields as all the African peasants put together. And therefore the chemicals- and manure-caravan is moving East, without, of course, striking its tents in the West.

What does it mean for those countries? In simple terms, expect an exploitation of resources, countryside and peasantry such as we have had in the rest of Europe. Politics and industry are all set to transport the mistakes of the West to the East, and, it seems, successfully.

An Agro-Peepshow like the *Grüne Woche* (Green Week, Agricultural Fair) in Berlin also takes place very year in Poznan in West Poland: the *Polagrar*. Germany too is always represented with a hall to itself. What is on show is Agro-High-Tech Western style, adapted to an EU agricultural structure which gives neither peasant farmers nor the environment a chance. It is presented in glowing colours by the politicians who will be responsible for the ensuing chaos, and by businesses who will make a lot of money at the farmers' and environment's expense: the chemical industry, builders of sheds, manufacturers of machinery. These concerns already have well-appointed offices in Warsaw and other East European capitals, for there is money to be made there. Their collaborators deploy purposefully. In the Polish Ministry of Agriculture use is already made of advertising films by the fertiliser manufacturers '*Kali und Salz*' (Potash and Salt) to help the argument along. The blotting pads come courtesy of *Bayer*, the calendars from *BASF*.

You will search in vain at the *Polagrar* for a critical confrontation of Western agrarian policy. The beneficiaries of that policy have it all to themselves. The losers, farmers and environment, are simply not present. What would they do there? They have nothing to sell but experience. If one hopes to find out something about the social and ecological consequences of Western agricultural policy, or at least what it would mean if the exhibitors' dreams were to come true – i.e. the transferring of Western structures to the East – one will be disappointed. Anyone trying to start discussions on that subject gets treated like an alien from another planet. The Western exhibitors do not want such trouble-makers, while the Eastern visitors are instantly captivated by the glittering wonder-world of the West.

To the policy makers of the West it is obvious that East European agriculture is out of date, especially the Polish. For after World War Two something untypical of the Socialist system developed in Poland. Over large parts of the country roughly 80% of the agricultural-use area was farmed by private individuals. Agricultural collectives on the GDR-model or state farm complexes were only found on 20% of the land until the collapse of the system at the beginning of the '90s.

The private smallholders, who today on an average own only about 5 hectares each, came into being after World War Two with the expropriation of the large estates. The land was distributed among the agricultural workers. Of course there were attempts in Poland too to combine these new farmers into co-operatives on GDR lines. But they did not succeed; the small farmer structure remains to this day. There are about 2.5 million farms in this country, in which almost a third of the population works on the land, partly in very poor but still land-adapted conditions.

Farming in Poland is hard work. Many farmers have no tractor, they work with horse-drawn vehicles. The extensive husbandry is evident from the landscape. Compared with Western agricultural areas Poland's peasant farming is a nature paradise. That there are still 30,000 white storks is due to the methods of agricultural production. Nevertheless the rural exodus, or rather the attempted exodus, is considerable, for the hard work gives only a meagre income. Young people see less and less of a future in farming. They try to get into other spheres and to move to the towns. Often in vain, however, for there too jobs are scarce. Agriculture, in fact, is taking on new manpower. Many factory workers who have lost their jobs but still own a bit of land return more or less compulsorily to farming. This safety net is better than none. At least the farmer does not starve.

Western advisers consider Poland's agriculture out-of-date, unproductive and poor. It must be developed and made to give higher yields. Western agricultural policy has shown how: the technical aids are ready for export. They can be seen every year in Poznan. Western 'aid programmes' are planned to bring Poland's superannuated agriculture into line.

For a start the EU handed out 100 million DM from the PHARE programme: for pesticides. The relevant programme was aimed at the small- and medium-scale farmers, who so far had used practically no pesticides because they were too expensive. Bad for pesticide manufacturers, but good for the environment. The programme started just at the time when the Polish state farms, which had been using Western agricultural chemicals, were going bankrupt on their 20% of the land. This meant that Western agricultural products were not selling; the EU very willingly helped to get the flow going again. Nobody asked about environmental or social-political consequences.

The World Bank also helps. Poland, which itself produces agricultural surpluses, is to be sent 100 million Dollars' worth of feeding stuff imports. Excess is already produced without imported feed, and, moreover, by these 'reactionary' farmers using 'outdated' methods. 'Agriculture in Poland must become more productive' is nevertheless what one hears from the World Bank in Washington. if one asks why, or where productivity growth is to end – perhaps at the level of the Dutch agrarian industry? – one gets no reply. If one goes on to ask what is to be done with the ever greater surpluses, the answer is a shrug of the shoulders.

Polish agriculture with its smallholding structure does not fit the vision of those who consider themselves chosen to develop agriculture world wide. They set to work with a breathtaking arrogance and high-handedness. They have already ruined Western agriculture, they are responsible for killing off farmers and destroying cultural landscapes, but without any doubts or self-criticism they are now going to work on the East. Nobody seems able to stop them, for they find the ground is ideologically prepared for them. Everything that was typical of the East is now reversed. Especially where it is non-profit-making – like small-scale farming at this time. Everything Western, highly-coloured, big and new, 'modern', is seen as positive, the desired solution. Why stick to horses when the latest tractors are available?

So how does the situation look now in Poland? What consequences will the imposition of Western structures have on an agricultural country like Poland? Unquestionably, Poland with its outdated agriculture has a more than adequate food supply at present, despite lower productivity and smaller crops. Where in the former German Federal Republic five people have to be fed from one hectare of arable land, in Poland it is only two.

Poland's former agricultural export markets in the East have collapsed with the break-up of the Soviet Union. States such as the Ukraine are even beginning to export agricultural produce to Poland! From the West, too, come export-subsidised goods. Poland's citizens, when they can afford it, go for Western goods, from which they expect a better quality, higher standards.

Sometimes the goods are even cheaper. EU butter undercuts Polish butter, although EU farmers get four times as high prices for their milk. Agrarian export subsidies from the EU make it possible. As a result, surplus is beginning to be a problem in Poland.

Polish exports prospects, on the other hand – especially as regards the desirable West – are poor. The (partly protected) West European produce market is overflowing, like the world market. Agricultural export countries only have a chance there if either climatic conditions favour lowest-price production or else the produce receives a high subsidy (as in the case of the USA and the EU). As an exporter, then, Poland can only expect relatively small segments of the market, especially when agriculture in Eastern Europe is considered as one total complex and one brings to mind the development and productivity potentials of agriculture in other East European countries with better soil conditions. Export hopes are set far too high. It is not clear whether these hopes were caused by sheer desire for foreign currency or by ignorance of the market situation. The fact is that in Germany, for instance, the 'organic market' is saturated. It makes up only 1 – 1.5% of the food market and this is covered by ca. 5000 organic growers. If – purely theoretical, this – Polish farmers were to take over this segment of the market, which would not delight German organic farmers, it would be an opportunity for 25,000, perhaps 30,000, or even 40,000 Polish smallholdings. In the face of 2.5 million such farms in Poland, not an enormous amount. This means, in concrete terms: Considering the market situation, demand and supply, and the chances of selling Polish produce, any growth in productivity of Polish agriculture is neither necessary nor even sensible.

An appropriate development of productivity could, so its proponents argue, certainly improve the income of some (growth) farms. This is doubtless true. What is not mentioned is that it would have catastrophic consequences for the great majority of farmers, as pressure on prices would increase, and their income drop once more. The EU merry-go-round for Poland?

If Polish agriculture were brought to the structural and productive level of the West German, it would 'liberate' more than 4–5 million workers at present employed on the land. In addition, again as shown by Western experiences, aggravated ecological consequences would ensue, for intensifying productivity leaves its marks on the land: clearing vegetation, drainage, higher levels of fertilisers and pesticides, etc. Farmers would be on the 'Red List', the Danger List, like many of the free-ranging animal and plant species dependent on the dispersed nature of Polish agriculture.

The starting situation in Poland differs in one crucial way from that within the EU when agrarian policy was being decided. In the EU at that time there was a shortage of food on the one hand, and a need for workers in industry on the other. It made sense, then, to make agriculture more productive, to produce sufficient food and to free workers for industry. But the Polish economy shows no shortage of workers; due to the currently developing, profound structural changes there is immense unemployment. Also there is enough food. So the workers leaving the land would immediately mean another 4–5 million unemployed. Where these people would find work, or how the State could give them social security, are problems excluded from the present Western-dominated discussions on agricultural policy – as is the environmental question.

There are sound ecological and social reasons for not developing Polish agriculture on the Western model, not equipping it technologically for brutal competition on the world market, even if the West can see great profits in doing just that. There is genuine hope that a 'structural change' in Poland along Western lines will not happen so quickly. The Polish State does not have the kind of money the EU pumped into intensifying agriculture. Indeed, many elements of the EU's schizophrenic agricultural policy cannot be transferred to Poland for lack of money. There are no budgets in Poland for ecological performance, setting land aside, or paying farmers to retire; that is a good thing, and probably will not change in the near future.

A structural change in agriculture should not be forced on that country, as there are no prospects outside agriculture. Western advisers should take that into consideration and instead deal with the real problems of Polish agriculture: too quick succession of crops, in places too few landscape amenities, etc. Even more necessary would be advances in the realm of processing and marketing. For what did not succeed with the farmers – centralisation – does function in the follow-on sector. But dairies of partly EU-standard size do not fit in with small-scale farming. It is doubtful whether advisers used to planning for just one dairy in the whole of Schleswig-Holstein or for strict centralisation of abattoirs could come up with ideas for an autonomous, agriculture-adapted regional policy for Poland. So one fears that the market economy will accomplish what Communism failed to achieve: the destruction of peasant farming.

Chapter 9

The battle against one's own inertia

Why do we not deal with urgent matters at once? Why do we postpone problems? Why do we keep giving ourselves further leeway? One thing is certain: if we do not speedily build up a considerate relationship to our environment and nature, the branch on which we are sitting will not need to be sawn off. Our inaction will see to it that the branch rots away and breaks of its own accord. Then it will be too late.

The beam in one's own eye
Can Brussels create an environmental State?

It is not very long, it is not very famous, and so far it has not found its way into world literature, the small river that winds its way through a 'vale' in Flanders, or, more accurately, through various pipes and tunnels. This is the River Senne, regarding which the annals of the Belgian and Flemish capital record that in its valley the later capital city of Europe was founded. The little river, of which the visitor to Brussels scarcely catches a metre-long glimpse, bears a melancholy superlative, that of being one of the most polluted watercourses in the Old World. So there is every reason to conceal the Senne from observation.

Incredible as it may sound, the fact is that the seat of the EU Commission, second seat of the European Parliament –

THE BATTLE AGAINST ONE'S OWN INERTIA

Brussels – to this day does not have a functioning sewage system. A circumstance which, in the face of the constantly reiterated role of the EU as outrider of environmental protection, as manifested in almost two hundred directives and regulations to that effect, seems unbelievable. Yet Brussels appears to have come to terms with consigning its effluent to the Senne, thence to the Scheldt, and then into the North Sea: this despite a round million inhabitants, whose faeces and other water-polluting discharges would not seem exactly negligible.

The scandal, once again, lies in the dual morality of indifference towards environmental policy. One should remind oneself: while the EU-Commission is pondering stricter limits for the protection of drinking water, while guidelines are set for working out a groundwater directive for the EU and in some parts of Europe water supply services are tearing their hair about how to reduce the nitrate content of the water, while numerous communities take up millions' worth of loans to construct third or fourth stages of waste water treatment to keep the rivers clean, the 'Capital of Europe' possesses nothing that could even deserve the name of 'Sewage treatment plant'. Not a tale of the bad old times, but sad reality on the brink of the Third Millennium.

This notorious scandal has surfaced again and again, and environmentalists as well as Euro-MPs raised their voices to change this unworthy state of affairs. At the time when Belgium was divided into regions, the increasing break-up of former Napoleonic central administration down to the smallest details with the greatest relevance, these cries faded away largely unheeded. And Brussels, amid the constant financial squabbles among the 19(!) policy-making authorities of the town, had other things to worry about than its own – literal as well as figurative – mess.

So the environmental societies still face the future with scepticism, although the EU Commission encouraged them, saying that a clean-up was on the way, in the shape of two treatment plants for Brussels and its environs. In response to a petition from the European Natural Heritage Fund to the European Parliament in Summer 1991, the latter passed on this information to the EU Commission, whereupon in accordance with the new Directive 91/271/EEC 'concerning urban waste water treatment' the City of Brussels 'at the latest by 31 December 1998 resp. 31 December 2000' shall be provided with such installations. In reply to a question from Euro-MP Green this was confirmed. More specific, indeed positively 'promising', was the Commission's reply to a question from Delegate Schleicher: Two treatment plants are now being built, one to serve 360,000 inhabitants in the South of the town, and one of 'three times greater capacity' for North Brussels. While the Northern plant was due to come into operation in 1994, the Southern was not to become operational until the year 2000.

The environment societies treat the information with some scepticism. The regionalisation disputes still dominate Belgian daily policy too much; any day you can see plainly that in the country which hosts the EU environment protection is a low priority – one look at the streets and parks of the capital suffices. Brussels is too much imprisoned in the cage of financial needs to give priority to the realization of sewage treatment plant. Also the transition period seems very long; up to the year 2000 a lot of sewage will continue to flow into the North Sea.

Yet Brussels does not seem to be an isolated case, either in Belgium or in Europe at large. The most famous example, however, is also in Belgium. In Charleroi – which, with its 600,000 inhabitants, is also hardly a village – metre-high birch trees are growing out of the long ago completed filter beds – the installation has never been put into operation. The filter beds now serve mainly as a media-effective eyecatcher demonstrating environmental incompetence and indifference.

On top of this the environmentalists received amazing news from the fair hand of the EU Commission. European reality may be suffused with environmental good will, but action is not yet much in evidence. For thus spoke the EU Commission in response to the Fund's petition to the European Parliament: '... The Commission hopes that this situation (which is not unique for a town of this size) will soon change, as construction work on two treatment plants, which will receive and treat the waste water of the whole town, is now in progress.'

It is hard to comment further as to the gist of this. Paper will accept anything, including EU directives.

To sum up: One must continue to view the sewage works for the 'Capital of Europe' with scepticism. Too often a progressive EU measure has been ignored or openly flouted, and too often, particularly in the realm of the environment, have the fine-sounding pronouncements of politicians not been followed by actions. Thus the time limit set by the EU Directive for the Brussels treatment plants offers no guarantee that the new century will indeed be ushered in by filtered effluent. Examples of such disregard of environmental directives make up piles of valuable experience in the repositories of both Commission and environmentalists. We must wait and see whether Brussels really feels able to combine the dignity of a 'Capital of Europe' with the evil of archaic sewage disposal. North Sea mussels may no longer taste so marvellous to some of us, even when consumed in the ambience of the Brussels Gourmet-Quarter.

None so blind...

Data graveyards save no forests

One really hates to believe all one reads. Unimaginable figures record the extent of destruction of much unspoilt paradise. Every day huge tracts of woodland vanish from our map; with the connivance of the State, or even on the orders of the State, they are sold down the river and hacked to pieces. In Amazonia every day an area of forest the size of 15,000 football pitches is destroyed by ruthless felling. The forests are burnt down, to make new settlements for the milling, land-hungry crowds of people; or they get into the sawmills to be made into costly veneers.

In the United States and Canada, too, centuries-old giant trees are felled by chainsaws in a matter of minutes, then hacked up, and they finally land as wood chippings in the cellulose factories of multinational paper-manufacturing combines. In the Canadian province of British Columbia alone an area of primeval forest the size of the Saar region vanishes every year. Chile sells off its forests to restock its exhausted State finances, and on the island of Tasmania, south of Australia, whole regions of rare tree species are sacrificed to the Japanese paper industry.

For a long time Europeans were in the comfortable position of being able to point a finger at others and get worked-up about the razing of tropical rain forests. In fact they were rather pleased that international discussion about the rape of virgin forest diverted attention from the problems in Europe itself.

Since 1987 when environmental conservation became part of the Treaty of Rome with the United Europe document, and thus a concern of the Community, Europeans must increasingly exercise self-criticism and ask themselves how they are dealing with their own woodlands. The amount of destruction is considerable in Europe, too, though it does not reach the dimensions of destruction in America and the Third World. The reasons also tend to be different in Europe. The chief causes for the loss of European woodland are infrastructure initiatives and agricultural projects for development and raising of living standards in underdeveloped parts of the European Union.

That the last remaining idyllic sanctuaries will be especially hit by this seems obvious, and inherent in the logic of the development philosophy. These are regions previously all but untouched by industrialisation and lying away from economic centres. In nearly every case experience shows that regions of outstanding beauty are especially poor regions. The equality principle of the European Union, which guarantees all its inhabitants a comparable standard of living, now aims to change that with the aid of structural funds and the new Cohesion Fund. This raises the threat of scenic destruction to a fixed principle, although the Cohesion Fund itself incorporates a strong conservation component.

The danger inherent in the principle has meanwhile been recognised. Protests by conservation associations, the involvement of the European Parliament in environment matters, stronger control by the European Audit Office, and not least the judgments of the European Court of Justice have in recent years led to a rethinking process among the Member States of the European Union, although in Southern EU countries protection of the natural environment is still seen as a sort of luxury which should receive correspondingly high remuneration from Brussels.

Though in some individual nations efforts to save European woodlands may still resemble a fight against windmills, in one respect a lowest common denominator has been found. Since 1987 the Commission of the European Union annually presents a damage to forests report, summarising the results of national assessment reports and forest damage assessment in the European Union. The incentive for this communal action to protect the forests was the growing forest degradation diagnosed in the early '80s, generally ascribed to air pollution, and spreading rapidly.

The decision was made easier because with the damage caused by air pollution the industrial countries were exposed as bearing the chief blame, and after years of assessment they also had the most accurate data. The findings are depressing, though not particularly surprising. The reports on forest damage presented to the European Union since 1987 largely confirm the results of ten years' research in the German Federal Republic: the state of the forests is getting steadily worse.

The communal forest damage assessment is the first large-scale cross-border conception of this kind on a common methodical basis, using a unified system of assessment and central data processing. It is to deliver every year an up-to-date survey of the current state of health of European woodlands. Subsidies will be granted for carrying out pilot projects and field experiments to extend knowledge in depth regarding air pollution and its effects on woodland, as well as improving methods of observing and measuring damage to forests and working out programmes for preservation and rehabilitation of those woods.

To get the most exact data possible, the total area of EU woodland – roughly 537,000 sq. km. – was covered by a so-called area test network, consisting of 2,005 spot check sites. On each of these test areas 20 to 30 different tree species were selected according to a definite fixed procedure of assessment.

The most important pointers to the woodland's state of health are loss of leaves or needles and discolouration of individual trees. They are assessed by comparison with a suitable reference tree for the region which must be growing nearby and healthy. In this way in 1990 exactly 48,402 spot check trees were assessed. In 1990, too, for the first time five non-EU countries were drawn into the European forest damage report, namely Austria, the former Czechoslovakia, Hungary, Poland and Switzerland. In those countries a total of 18,933 spot check trees on 878 sites were examined by the same common procedure.

The upshot of the inquiry is that a notable proportion of the forests in the Community show needle- or leaf-loss and/or discolouration. Although the health of woodlands undergoes great swings from one year to another, for certain species a noticeable worsening of condition was recorded.

Altogether 5.1% of the trees showed a distinct leaf- or needle-loss of over 25%. Exactly 14.4% of the spot checks showed more than 10% leaf or needle discolouration. Unambiguously, it is clear that in 1990 the state of the forests in the Community had deteriorated as against 1989. In addition the inquiry showed that the damage rises with increasing height of the land and age of the trees. In 1990 for the first time the soils on which the trees were growing were included in the assessment. First analyses proved that the extent of leaf- or needle-loss could vary greatly on different types of soil.

It is interesting to compare the state of the woods in the European Union with their state in non-EU countries. 85% of the EU trees are damaged up to 25%, and 13% up to 60%, while in the five non-EU countries 65% of the trees are less damaged, but 31% are badly affected.

Taking the affected countries one by one, the medium damaged test areas – up to 60% needle- or leaf-loss – were chiefly in Britain, in Germany, in Portugal and in the North West of Italy. Greece, too, had a pretty high number of damaged test areas. Needle- or leaf-loss of the spot check trees was particularly high in Poland and the former Czechoslovakia. The percentage of trees with slight discolouration is relatively high in Portugal, Belgium, Greece, France and North West Italy. In the South of the former Czechoslovakia and in Hungary the occurrence of discoloured trees is very marked.

A total of 109 species were involved in the spot checks during the investigation, the commonest species making up more than 70% of the trees examined. The proportion of broadleaved trees to conifers was fairly even among the data material. Observation of all the EU Member Countries showed that as regards leaf-or needle-loss broadleaved trees are healthier than deciduous trees. For both test values bearing on tree condition, the differences between deciduous trees and conifers were more marked in non-EU countries than inside the European Union.

Though the discussion about the causes of 'forest depletion' – air pollution or 'acid rain' – has not ended and the European report on forest damage will not definitely commit itself for lack of unambiguous data, experts tend more and more to believe that air pollution is the chief cause.

The art of waiting

The silent death of the frogs

Has it struck you that all around us nature is becoming impoverished, slowly but surely? For a long time nobody noticed anything wrong. But now, when on a Sunday picnic we come to a spot where a year or two ago we could still find frogs, or maybe a certain species of butterfly, it suddenly hits us like a blow. At the edge of the wood, where formerly in April and May the brown frogs used to hop about in droves among last year's leaves, fresh green undergrowth and old wood, not a froglet can be seen. And over there, too, where we wanted to show the children the colourful orchids on the limestone slope in June, now there is only monotonous, anonymous greenery.

Almost everywhere in Europe nature is in retreat. It is not always great, sensational scandals of environment destruction which cause our landscapes and with them our conditions of life to decline. The recent history of wildlife destruction by man is full of thousands of individual chapters regarding the insidious death of animals and plants, of whole wildlife communities. Often these are minimal events which, viewed individually and in isolation, only represent a local or regional tragedy – many will think so, and console themselves with it. But that is just where the danger lies, because all those little scandals contribute to the sell-off of our quality of life just as surely as the more noticeable and dramatic attacks on the environment. Because of its apparently purely local significance, the creeping destruction attracts far too little attention.

The decline of our wildlife is also due to the many small-time Eco-Twisters who cumulatively play such a devastating and decisive role. That means responsible officials and decision takers in local authorities, advisory boards and institutions, classic Eco-Twisters playing their part in the sell-off of nature, whether consciously, out of naïveté, through ecological indifference, pleading pressure of affairs (no time to think), or simple indolence: they could fill many separate chapters in this criminal dossier of the European environment. Let us look more closely at just one of these cases, such as occur many thousand times in many thousand sites in Europe.

It is a scandal how, through ten years of official delay and only half-hearted action, the amphibian population of a whole region has been brought to the verge of extinction: one of those little scandals known to only a few, but adding up through force of numbers to the wasting away of our natural world. It all began in 1983. In the course of a *Save the Frogs* campaign, conservationists around the idyllic small town of Bretten in North Baden discovered on one main road innumerable frogs, toads and salamanders squashed flat by cars. To put a stop to this massacre of amphibians, an instant action was organised to protect the salamanders migrating to their breeding waters. Throughout several nights the helpers collected frogs and toads on the busy road and carried them safely to the other side. A few days later – again for several nights on end – the animals on their way back to the nearby wood, separated from the breeding places by the road, were again gathered up and transported.

So far so good. However, at the same time the conservationists asked the relevant road construction authorities to create so-called amphibian tunnels with fixed 'guide structures' to direct the animals into tunnels laid under the road. But that costs money. And so would the purchase of fields on the other side of the road which are regularly flooded at high water in the adjacent brook: fields which, with official approval, could long have been permanent amphibian habitats. A sum of 300,000 DM would be ample, according to Gerhard Dittes, Chair of the local League for Environment and Conservation, to save the amphibian population and preserve wildlife in all its diversity. But here too the Eco-Twisters are at work – and, as usual, they apply the brakes on progress very thoroughly.

A spokesman for the Ministry of Transport in Baden-Würtemberg answered a query by conservationists about guide structures ('toad fences') for a population of roughly 400 mountain- and pond-salamanders as well as numerous frogs and toads thus: 'We only start to consider upwards of 500 animals.' Tough luck on salamanders and toads! And once again, tough luck on one small piece in the mosaic of nature. As the authorities are not prepared to consider structures, the population continues to decline. Simply gathering up amphibians by hand is not enough by itself.

After ten years of dedicated voluntary work the conservationists had to note that the original number of 400 migrating salamanders had shrunk to 100. No wonder then that the road construction department, subordinate to the Ministry of Transport, is powerless to act. It does nothing, thereby logically obeying orders. It is another vicious circle. Above 500 animals the department is prepared to take action – but numbers can never rise to that, as the population is constantly declining because nothing is done to avert the dangers which constantly reduce the stocks ... Does it not sound like a prize Gothamite exploit?

So meanwhile, despite the ten-year voluntary commitment of all those helpers, the time is foreseeable when the population will be totally wiped out by highway traffic. In spite of knowing what should be done. Tree frogs, ground frogs, all kinds of toads, mountain- and pond-salamanders – they all die, in silence. And where you find one Eco-Twister, another is not far away. Even His Honour the Mayor, Paul Metzger, representing the 25,000 inhabitants of Bretten, who boasts of having mounted an 'ecological offensive', to date, in conjunction with the Municipal Council, has successfully prevented the necessary protective action by simply doing nothing.

The League's local group in Bretten years ago presented plans for the protection of amphibians, plans which are still resting in a drawer somewhere. For a whole decade this situation, fatal for amphibians, has been tolerated.

That is just one small instance of the endless, piecemeal destruction of our wildlife. A story that is repeated with similar cases everywhere in Germany, in Europe, and all over the world. So we cannot be surprised if within a few years our natural heritage is completely impoverished, through inaction, hesitation and procrastination. No wonder that many young people, in view of this situation, feel more and more disillusioned with the State and all authorities. The Eco-Twisters are just around the next corner. Don't make it too easy for them.

Chapter 10

Even what the eye does see, the heart doesn't grieve about

It is like an addiction problem. One knows about it, but one does nothing against it. The way we deal with the matrix of our existence, we could all be described as addicts. With our ecological negligence – doing nothing, not wanting to do anything, despite long-recognised dangers – we are heading for a collapse that may well prove lethal.

Two minds in one body
The question of birdcatching

In Germany almost every other household keeps a bird. Unlike dogs, cats, ornamental fish and birds are not taxed. Consequently there are no precise statistics about who in Germany does own a bird. But at a guess some bird twitters or pipes in every second or third home. Canaries and budgerigars are the most popular. Eagles are only found in special reserves.

'Fly away, Peter, fly away, Paul,' crows the young grey parrot belonging to my friends. But no way can he, or did he, fly here, or away. He was caught wild in Africa, and it was years before he recovered from that trauma. Therefore, rightly, the import of exotic birds into the Federal Republic has been stopped.

But of course forbidden fruit is always especially tempting. Along the Straits of Messina and on Malta the shooting of large birds remains a cult action for superstitious Southern Italians. Songbirds are considered gourmet food and are sold under the counter for a tidy sum.

Scene of action: Brussels. On the Grande Place, the Main Square, there is a large market every Sunday morning. And at this market every week the prohibited thing occurs. Underhand and under the counter, but also right under the otherwise stern eye of the law, singing birds are sold, singing birds that were wild caught, among other provenances, in the German-Belgian nature park Eifel-Ardennes.

In Mozart's *Magic Flute*, in the guise of Papageno, the birdcatcher is still introduced as an honourable member of a trade with a centuries-long tradition. In the meantime, however, the attitude of civilised society towards this profession has fundamentally changed. The commercial trapping of songbirds has been outlawed, particularly in Central Europe. Conservationists and politicians are of one mind in this.

The Council of Europe in Strasbourg passed a Convention to that effect many years ago, and all Member States joined, including Belgium. The European Union also issued a Directive in 1979, 'on the conservation of wild birds,' ending in a supplement listing all the bird species occurring naturally within the EU, with a note regarding their claim to protection. The supplement falls into two parts. The first lists a total of 74 species with a special claim to protection in the whole of the EU. Part Two contains 72 species of which 24 may be hunted anywhere. This comprises most species of wild goose, wild duck and game birds. The remaining 48 species are subject to varying national game laws, i.e. they can be hunted or caught if the member Country permits it and when certain rules regarding the method of hunting or trapping are obeyed, in the interests of preserving the species. This holds especially for migrant birds. So for instance in the Federal Republic seagulls may be shot, in France lapwings and song thrushes, in Italy blackbirds and skylarks.

In general, what is protected in one country may well be 'fair game' in another. In the Belgian-German border country that goes for a whole range of songbirds, above all for the bullfinch. By means of decoys it is lured into traps by roughly 4,000 officially licensed Walloon birdcatchers. In this way an estimated 50,000 songbirds fall victim to the birdcatchers, who are supposed to keep accurate records of their doings, and are actually not supposed to sell bullfinches. They do it nevertheless: either under the counter at the markets, or privately, where controls are hardly possible.

But for every licensed catcher there are about five 'illegal' ones, hunting with large nets, which could raise the quota of birds caught to half a million a year. The European Court of Justice in Luxembourg warned Belgium years ago to obey the EU-Directive, but in vain.

Talking to the birdcatchers one can discover no sense of wrongdoing. They argue that singing birds actually have a better life in a cage than outside in chemicals-polluted nature. Besides which, hundreds of thousands of birds would break their necks every year against the glass facades of the affluent society – an argument hard to counter. Yet the situation remains unsatisfactory.

What can one do? The Convention of the Strasbourg Council of Europe is not binding in law. And the European Court of Justice has no power resources to give effect to its rulings. The only recourse is to members of the European Parliament, who for the purpose of animal protection have formed a united *Intergroup* and could set up a parliamentary initiative.

It would also be feasible for Nordrhein-Westphalia, which borders on Belgium, to exert pressure in the interests of good-neighbourly relations. As trapping songbirds is no longer a means of livelihood in Belgium but purely a hobby, it should be possible, with a little good will, to end this scandal.

Then why does nothing happen?

Sweeping it under the Carpet
The North Sea – a patient with no future?

The North Sea actually epitomises the permanent scandal which is made up of all the wrongheaded, ruthless policies which take no account of ecology. Who thinks of overfishing, pollution, agricultural waste discharged in billions of tonnes, or oil disasters, when buying cod on Fridays or the first shrimp of the season? Yet the North Sea, 'the EU's very own sea', makes it plain that a change of direction is essential – in economics, agriculture, transport and environment policy. Even for pure self-interest, the selfishness of wanting to survive.

They died spectacularly in their thousands, the seals who were washed up on to the North Sea beaches in the summer of 1988, and whose corpses so interested the media. Cynically, one should be grateful to the seals, that it was they who died, and not some small creatures whose demise could easily have passed unnoticed. The dying seals voiced, as it were, the cry for help of an entire sea whose survival is balanced on a knife edge.

Though with a maximum depth of ca. 80 metres and an extent of barely 520,000 square kilometres it is a fairly small sea with a relatively low mass of water, the North Sea is among the ecologically most productive regions of the world. At any rate this marginal sea contains an almost unparalleled abundance of fish. And with the coastal waters as the nursery of numerous species of fish, conditions seem ideal for replenishment of stocks. So far an average of ca. 3.5 million tonnes of fish can be caught every year in the North Sea – the only question is, how much longer . . .

The geographical location of the North Sea and the composition of its bed condition a very slow water exchange. Interchange with the Atlantic, only possible north of the British Isles or through the Channel, takes about three years. A heavy burden on that marginal sea, the North Sea. For the inflow of fresh water from the Baltic Sea, from the rivers or from rainfall is comparatively meagre – and usually polluted. The lingering of water masses in the North Sea has therefore become a serious problem with regard to pollutants, which can stay unchanged for a long time. Also they are continually deposited in the sediment. The unique sea with its mudflats and sandbanks washed by the tide offers ideal conditions for that. Conditions which may, however, prove the doom of the organisms living in it, because the pollutants become exponentially concentrated in them.

The chief causes of the threat to the North Sea habitat are contaminants from the air, the rivers, and shipping, but also attacks on the ecosystem such as overfishing in all its variations, industrial settlements, tourism, and dykes.

The North Sea protection conferences of the coastal countries, held with beautiful regularity, have done little to alter that. With a few exceptions – such as putting a stop to the discharging of dilute acid by Germany and the burning of toxic waste at sea – it has remained a matter of announcements. There were, of course, sound economic reasons to facilitate the happy ending of those two problems, which, together with the politicians at last seeing sense, led to a good outcome. The dilute acid discharge became unnecessary not least for economic reasons, after all there were, as environmental experts could report, long-standing installations in the USA for recycling the dilute acid. It had simply been cheaper so far to dump the dilute acid in the North Sea rather than recondition it. A prohibition, if it had come earlier, would merely have meant a more expensive processing for the firms, not the collapse of the whole procedure, as one heard over and over again.

That the burning of toxic waste on the high seas at last came to an end is largely due to the fact that the permitted amounts, for example of chlorinated solvents, were drastically reduced. Nevertheless there is still the danger that burning at sea will start up again, because to date there is no internationally binding prohibition. This danger grows against the background of the pleasing farsightedness with which committed journalists in alliance with conservationists have clearly exposed the mainly illegal sell-off of hazardous waste. So amid all the euphoria about a temporary stop to high seas burning one should not overlook that it remains obscure what the firms are actually doing with the hazardous waste. Nobody knows whether they are now sending it abroad, perhaps to Eastern Europe, where in this economically difficult period practically everything is accepted for payment, stored or buried, or whether they are stashing away the residues until Doomsday. One thing is certain: without a change in the production processes and without a definitive abandonment, say, of chlorine compounds these problems cannot be solved completely. Nobody can exclude the possibility that one day the North Sea will again be the sufferer – when burning once more 'pays'.

However, the worst load of pollution that is discharged into the North Sea comes via the river estuaries. Besides the sewage of settlements, the floods of excrement from the often inadequate or even non-existent sewage plants for over 100 million people dwelling around the sea coast, the shallow marginal sea also has to swallow the residues from our industrialised agriculture. 1.5 million tonnes of nitrates alone go into the sea. 1 million of that through the rivers. In fact the amount of nitrates originating from agriculture accounts for more than half the total input.

Chief responsibility lies with mass factory farming, which has led to animal production of a concentration unparalleled anywhere on earth – packing millions of chickens into batteries in one single shed, thousands of pigs on slatted cement floors, and thousands of calves reflect the grim reality of the EU agrarian industry. And all that at the expense of the environment, the consumers, and the small farmers. Anyone who has seen – and smelt – mass stock farming as practised in Oldenburg-Münster can work out what agricultural policy will lead to.

No less horrible are the residues from the artificial fertilisers and pesticides used in our agriculture around the North Sea: nitrates, phosphorus compounds and heavy metals are swilled in by three rivers. More than 100,000 tonnes of phosphorus compounds reach the sea in this way every year, also more than 10,000 tonnes of lead, 25,000 tonnes of zinc, and over 250,000 tonnes of hydrocarbons and oil residues. In this connection, here is an astonishing fact which will be unknown to most contemporaries, especially passionate motorists. Almost a third of the nitrogen input – around 500,000 tonnes – is transported to the North Sea by air. Motor traffic is easily overlooked as a source of nitrogen, although it plays a decisive role in the fact that roughly 60 kg. nitrogen per hectare per year pours from the air a quantity of 'fertiliser' that would have been used for a full manuring of fields in the '20s.

All these components do not fail to produce ecological *and* economic effects. Ever more frequently we hear reports of crippled, deformed catches in the fishing nets, and ever more species are affected. However, so far the reliable figures only apply to economically useful species of fish. High in the food chain, they concentrate the harmful substances. The next link up – seals, or it could be people – will bear the brunt. Scientists puzzled for years about the chronic diseases occurring in seals, e.g. wounds that would not heal. In the course of time evidence accumulated that the cause must be sought in the pollutant content of food chain animals and water, and it became terrifyingly plain that man could not remain immune to the North Sea cocktail of pollutants. Ecologists point out uncompromisingly that the great dying of the seals in 1988, which was ascribed to a virus, was also partly due to a general weakening of the animals.

How much man should regard himself as the final link in the food chain is clear to every gourmet who worries whether the *mussels provençale* are still safe to eat. Mussels, which act as a filter system, are special accumulators of pollutants . . .

A particularly large item on the debit side of the North Sea's contamination account is the enormous filth due to oil and oil residues. The tanks of tankers great and small are more easily illegally cleaned out at sea, rather than seeking out appropriate cleaning facilities in specially equipped harbours. But also, sailors and shipping firms point out, such facilities are far from general in all ports. It is not only the spectacular disasters of supertankers like the *Braer* in the Shetlands in Winter 1993 which cause oil pollution; as regards the North Sea, there is in any case an unbelievably large mount of oil going in every year. Over 250,000 tonnes of oil enter the North Sea every year – as much as the total load of a supertanker. The rivers alone discharge more than 50,000 tonnes of oil into the sea. The liquid waste of oil production makes up another 50,000 tonnes. Add to this a further 60,000 tonnes due to the above mentioned illegal discharges from ships.

Not the least serious of pollution menaces is one the experts are constantly warning us about: radioactive substances also leak into the misused and exploited North Sea in sizeable quantities, from the nuclear plants at Sellafield (Britain) and Le Hague (France). And it is certain that radioactivity can accumulate and be stored in living organisms . . .

Further debilitation of the North Sea ecosystem is caused by increasing encroachment on an area vital to achieving even some self-cleansing effect – the *Wattenmeer*. This unique habitat, shaped by the tides and lying between the Netherlands Den Helder and the Danish Esjberg, is continually described by politicians of all parties and the often equally influential administrating officials as 'worthy of protection'. Numerous international conservation agreements relate to it. Apart from which the *Wattenmeer*, the largest continuous tide-marked habitat on earth, comes under the EU Bird Protection Directive.

But in fact an enormous spread of destruction and dangers bombards the *Wattenmeer*, although its vital ecological function has long been appreciated. It is a resting place for more than 10 million birds a year. Many species depend on this large rest and feeding area during migration, and as with specialised food needs they cannot diverge. Add to this over 25 breeding species, and a huge number of mudflat-dwelling small organisms, from fan-worms to mussels. Thus the *Wattenmeer* produces a biomass greater than the tropical rain forest. Again, among these flats many flatfish and other species important to the fishing industry have their nursery.

So there is no shortage of evidence for protected status. Yet instead of the promised protection, the exact opposite tends to happen. Looking at Germany with its two National Parks in the *Wattenmeer* gives us an insight into the reality of *Wattenmeer* preservation and its deficiencies.

The ancient exhortation to 'Build dykes or give way' still seems to haunt officials in politics and administration and to motivate their actions. Until far into the '80s large-scale dyke-building was going ahead, as on the west coast of Schleswig-Holstein: such concepts as the Rodenäs Bay, Nordstrander Bay, and the like. Despite strong resistance from the population and the conservation societies, who tried to fight off the grandiose schemes with a hundred thousand objections, the ambitious projects were carried out – pleading ostensible 'protection of the coastline'. In fact, as the conservationists suspected from the start, it was about something quite different: gaining new land for agricultural use – this at a time of butter mountains, milk lakes and meat pyramids, a time when the over-the-top EU agricultural policy had keeled over into the ridiculous.

The conservationists referred to the warnings of biologists, who had pointed out the irreplaceable nature of the ecologically most important forelands, especially the salt marshes which would be lost and which could not be reconstituted simply by compensatory measures. It could lead to a worldwide weakening of stocks of those species who on their migrations depend on mudflats, such as the pink-footed goose with its Spitzbergen population which is dependent on the Rodenäs area. But what do politicians care for pink-footed geese from

Spitzbergen? As we know, geese do not vote, nor can they be fitted into archaic arguments on the Hauke-Haien principle that there must be a constant battle with the sea to reclaim more land from it. The inevitable happened, the dykes were constructed, and the call for more of them rings ever louder along the coast.

That is not all. Now tourism is invading the *Wattenmeer* over a wide front. Of course no one would dispute that the coastal landscape has great restorative powers, and the economic factor of that non-polluting industry is not inconsiderable. More than 100,000 jobs on the German North Sea coast alone depend on tourism, whole communities are defined by it. Unfortunately the industry's managers have not sufficiently grasped that only environment-friendly 'soft tourism' can give hope of permanent success. Large-scale projects like the hard-to-credit Center-Parc-Enterprise in the Lower Saxon Weser marshes can hardly be put in that category. Also the conservation societies have long criticised the way visitors are led through the National Parks. Educational work should be better supported by the countries' public funds, for it alone can raise the necessary understanding for the *Wattenmeer* habitat, and by that understanding prevent damage. When, as in the National Park *Niedersächsisches Wattenmeer*, not even the restricted zones of the Park are adequately marked out – allegedly because there is not enough money for proper signposting(!) – and visitors in their ignorance take the sign *Ruhezone* for an invitation to bask on the beach, it does throw a revealing light on the environment education work of the State authorities. Exemplary work here is only done by the environmentalists, with great enterprise, but unfortunately very limited means.

Naturally it must strike tourists as strange when they are restricted from entering certain zones of the National Park, yet immediately next to Protected Zone One in the Park an advertisement for oil from a multinational firm is permitted, complete with its own stand. Such an anomaly cannot raise people's understanding. One can only hope that even the politicians will see reason and quickly put a stop to this contradiction.

It seems similarly strange and sad that arms testing concerns based near the Schleswig-Holstein National Park of Meldorf Bay can continue to shoot their missiles into the mudflats. A particularly problematic aspect from the ecological viewpoint is the 'searching' for the projectiles by helicopter! A lasting disturbance for wildlife in the shallows. Conservationists are rightly concerned that all these dubious activities, which have absolutely nothing to do with protecting the *Wattenmeer* habitat, are barely compatible with the demands and restrictions of the EU's Bird Protection Directive.

Danger also threatens from the hulls of ships. A hotly disputed subject along the coast for years, besides hunting on the sandbanks, an archaic pursuit for which happily no new licences are being issued in Lower Saxony or Schleswig-Holstein, has been the question of when and into which parts of the National Park sailing ships may enter. The 'Sailing Regulations' issued by the appropriate Federal Transport Ministry in Bonn could not really satisfy the conservation experts, as they provide that the entry permit is not regionally restricted but depends on the water tables. Conservationists object that this does not create any genuine 'quiet zone', and for example seals, which retreat to the sandbanks, are still subject to disturbances, causing 'permanent stress' which badly affects the health of the animals.

Animals as Merchandise
Europe's way with living creatures

Not only potatoes or prawns are carted right across the Community, because division of labour and exchange of goods are so profitable, and transport is so cheap. Live animals, too, are desirable goods for transport, and here too there are huge profits to be made. Usually the slaughter house is their destination, but not always.

Polish horses – supplied non-stop – are sought-after in France. Live, for continued work use, or for slaughter. And it is not rare for German cattle to be sent to the Arab countries for final fattening or for breeding. Perhaps the most perverse traffic is the transport of sheep from New Zealand or Australia to the Arab world. Because people there eat only halal meat, but that method of slaughter, cutting the throat and letting the animal bleed to death without previous stunning, is prohibited in the Western world, the live animals are sent on a journey of many thousand kilometres. The Western world sticks to its principles (no halal killing), the Arab world receives its beasts (for halal killing), and all this is at the expense of the animals. Business is business. The transport on enormous ships is about the most brutal and terrifying thing one can imagine. Many animals die, insiders calculate up to 10%, some would say more. One may never know the exact figures. The dead animals are brought up from the hold into the open on a conveyer belt and automatically tipped over the side, to feed the fish. Which is actually more cruel – halal slaughter or this kind of transport, with halal slaughter at the end?

In Europe there are several levels regarding transport of people. For instance there are coach tourists, who are also carried across Europe for a song. Hardly anyone keeps to limited numbers, hours of driving, speed limits, for competition is extremely tough. Anyhow, the traveller wants to get to his destination quickly, for even on holiday he has no time for the travelling itself, only for the stay.

But unlike animal transport, the manner of tourist transport, despite some spectacular accidents with fatal results, is relatively harmless. People are good customers, they pay for the journey, for drinks when they are thirsty, they give tips for decent service and complain when service is bad. Animals do not pay for their thirst. And with animal transport there is no need to consider sensibilities. All that counts in the entrepreneur's purse. The lorries must be utilised to capacity. That means, drive a bit longer, pack in a few more animals, no pausing on the way.

Animals are only transported the once, nobody asks about their needs. They are treated accordingly.

Of course there are rules to regulate transport. There is a ruling for Europe, though it must be said the German Society for Prevention of Cruelty to Animals has criticised it severely. For the aim of this EU-Directive is not to minimise animal suffering or to treat the animals fairly, but to realize "free traffic of animals within the Common Market". There are no binding limitations on transport times. The Animal Protection Society considers the way from the pen to the butcher should be no further than the way from the farmyard to the nearest slaughterhouse. Quite wrong: there is free choice. There is a free European market. Fatten them in the North, slaughter in the South – or vice versa, entirely up to you. Why should transport be conducted more compassionately than stock-raising?

The unbelievable conditions in which animals are kept on the factory farms are something else again. But what is done to the creatures before they die, on the way to the abattoir or to a distant "new home", is a prize scandal. Domestic animals, they are kept and fed in order that they may feed others: but in between, on the roads of Europe, they are exposed to the most horrifying cruelty, Hell on wheels.

The time of fattening the animals becomes ever shorter, according to the motto: Time is money – and money is short. Yet the way from Scene of Action One (the fattening factory) to Scene of Action Two (the slaughterhouse, or else a new fattening factory) becomes ever longer. The abattoirs should conform to EU rules, but the EU is not concerned with animal rights but with purely economic and technological considerations. The slaughterhouse system must above all be large and centralised, not species-friendly. The old communal abattoirs, where slaughter took place only once or twice a week and which were comparatively calm and decent, have long ceased to exist, at least in the minds of Europe's market economists. Money for extending slaughterhouse structures goes to the large-scale concerns, where up to 600 pigs may be "processed" per hour.

Instead of arranging by the maintenance, or even the creation, of many decentralised abattoirs for keeping jobs in the region and letting the animals have a short and relatively painless journey to their death, in this most sensitive of areas it is all organised by mass industrial standards. Butchery degenerates into a massacre.

The Animal Protection Society demands that the way to the butcher should not take longer than four hours or be further than 200 km. For the animals are torn out of their accustomed surroundings and suffer terrible stress on their last journey. But the realization of that demand would be nothing less than interference with the free market economy. Unthinkable in economy-first Europe.

Taking in water after four hours. The experts consider that animals transported for breeding or further fattening should not be moved for more than 15 hours per day (including three hours rest period). After that there should be a rest of 24 hours. For poultry even more compassion should be practised; they need a rest after a maxium of five hours. But these demands fall on deaf politicians' ears, and of course no one dreams of keeping to them voluntarily. Why should compassion be exercised in the transport of trade commodities? The rights of a chicken, a pig or a horse? Who is supposed to pay for that?

One example: On 22.5.92 some bulls were loaded on to a cattle transport in Mecklenburg. Not an unusual event. The destination was interesting, though – the Croatian port of Rasa. There the animals were to be transferred to ships that would carry them to the Middle East, where our beef cattle are valued. The transporter was discovered in Rasa on 25.5.92, more or less by chance, by a conscientious vet who took his responsibilities seriously and wanted to test for himself whether the permits for animal transport which he made out every day were justified. What he found was dire. Four of the bulls loaded in Mecklenburg were already to weak that they had to be slaughtered on the spot. 72 hours without water – no man or beast could stand that.

Limitation of transport time, intervals for feeding and watering, rest periods, adequate bedding and condition of transport vehicle: these demands are right and proper, but the real state of affairs is very different. Animals are of no value, "shortfall" – that means animals dying on the way – are allowed for in the calculations. Scandals come to light more by chance than purposefully exposed. Enforced slaughter, ordered after inspection or accidents, may be spectacular, but the large number of animals who simply die on the journey gets no official acknowledgement, not even an appearance in statistics.

Polish horses for France, Belgian animals for Italy, Baden-Württemberg piglets for the slurry triangle of Rotterdam-Munster-Bremen. To and fro, hither and yon. Every month 300 dead animals just at the border crossing into Italy at Prosecco. Sheep lead the casualty list, followed by horses, then calves and cattle. There are no records of dead pigs, as pig transports seem to take a different route.

The losses pose no financial problems for the entrepreneur, as the usual profit margins are generous. Buying a Polish horse for slaughter you pay a maximum of 1000 DM, in France it is 3000 DM for a dead animal, 6000 DM for a live one. The losses are within bounds, but business and profit virtually unlimited. Who has an interest in preventing business?

Albert Schweitzer once said: "I am life, that wants to live, amid other life that wants to live." Why cannot one grant to animals, who one only keep alive in order to kill them later on, a reasonably bearable existence? The contempt for animals shown in the way they are kept, transported and slaughtered, is almost unbearable. One would not treat one's worst enemy like that.

Out of Sight, Out of Mind
The avalanche of waste goes rolling on

Herr Lehmann is a decent chap, a good citizen and a successful businessman. For some time now a little problem has been bothering him a lot: the problem of waste disposal. Not on a communal scale, just his own. He is seriously considering whether to install a new secretary to deal with it. The new way of rubbish disposal – the "Green site" – is also a way of creating jobs, or so he had read.

Meanwhile four rubbish bins of varying size and colour stand behind his house: one for "normal domestic" waste; one for biodegradables – such as onion peelings and grass cuttings; one for waste paper – yesterday's newspapers, and all advertising junk; and finally one for the debris of shopping – the packaging. Empty bottles he takes direct to the container bin round the cornor; and sensitive waste – batteries etc. – he stores in the garage until collected. The same with discarded furniture etc., such as the old sofa: the so-called waste of affluence, known to the Town Hall as "large objects".

But then the little problem starts. For Herr Lehmann is supposed to keep a log – like all his neighbours – of what is called for and taken away, when and in what way. Beside business appointments and birthdays of wife and children, the dates of waste collection take up even more space on his already crammed-full wall calendar. And the waste collection dates are almost more important than the business ones, for if the wrong bin is put out on the street at the wrong time he is in big trouble. It is like certain board and dice games: you have to miss your turn – indeed, you might have to wait for a month.

Herr Lehmann is angered, above all, by what he reads in the morning paper. There are reports of gigantic waste scams; of deadly waste transports all over Europe; of toxic waste deals with Eastern Europe and the Third World; scandals that trip up ministers. Millions and billions are at stake. Big business with waste instead of trading with glass beads! Garbage and broken shards as an earnest of good business to come . . .

Waste, garbage: no end to it. The Germans are travel champions of Europe, perhaps even the world. There is no doubt about that. Tourism, even at a time of recession, remains a booming growth industry in the Federal Republic. That does not apply purely to holiday times, but all the year round, for the seamy side. For the Germans are also champions, of Europe if not the world, in waste-tourism.

Everyone knows the scandalous stories around the wanderings on the high seas of toxic waste ships which try in vain to unload their cargo, the dangerous waste of affluence from the industrial countries, somewhere on a Third World country. Reports about the voyages of these ghost ships signal only the tip of the iceberg: how many poison transports have been able to land and unload "successfully"? How great is environmental damage already in Asia, Africa and Latin American from this toxic Euro-waste? There is hardly likely to be reliable information, nor even approximately realistic estimates.

The same holds for land transports into the numerous toxic waste dumps in Western and Eastern Europe – whether officially sanctioned or not – which also represent an incalculable potential for catastrophe. Not to mention discharge into the sea. What is certain is that not only the unscrupulous entrepreneurs are coining money with their poison transports, but that some high up in authority are mixed up in these obscene transactions. The deal is simple, it benefits all those involved, and works according to the formula: Waste disposal for hard currency equals high transport yield.

The following figures released by the OECD (Organisation for Economic Co-operation and Development) late in 1992 give some hint of the gigantic dimensions of the business in Western waste-tourism. Every year a round 2.1 million tonnes of hazardous waste cross the borders towards dumps on the Continent itself, overseas, or into the sea. The Organisation estimates this at over 100,000 border-crossing transports, of which up to 30,000 could be classified as highly dangerous.

By far the greatest share comes from the former Federal lands, with 1.1 million tonnes, led by Nordrhein-Westphalia. After this come, to give a few more examples: Holland (190,000 tonnes), Switzerland (110,000 t.), Finland (65,000 t.), France (43,000 t.), Ireland (14,000 t.), Denmark (9,000 t.), Luxembourg (4,000 t.).

According to the OECD, 400,000 tonnes of waste classed as hazardous are taken across border for recycling; 700,000 tonnes land on foreign dumps; and a million tonnes are simply dumped in the sea by the recipients. Again, these data do not come from nature – and environment protection associations, but from the top overall organisation of the 24 leading industrial nations of the world, which has all the relevant statistical sources at its disposal and whose experts have a deep insight into the economic behaviour of its member countries.

What is today known as waste-tourism was first documented for public awareness in the scandel of the Seveso toxic material containers which in 1983 could be transported without hindrance right across Europe, and according to rumours ended up partly on the Schönberg Tip in what is now Mecklenburg-Pomerania. Since then the succession of greater and lesser scandals of this kind has never ceased.

The reason is that Europe is drowning in its own garbage. Every year around 2.2 billion tonnes are produced, in the Federal regions alone well over 250 million tonnes. There is a "waste emergency", due to progress and affluence, belief in packaging, and sheer thoughtlessness. For far too long the problem has been put on the back burner, politicians and society have addressed themselves to it far too late – the horse had bolted! At least the administrative solution emerged. Now there are waste bins and sacks for the new recycling concept termed "green disposal", where packing of every sort, in accordance with new regulations, is to be channelled towards a future of limited re-use.

Roughly 50 million tonnes of packaging materials are produced every year in the European Union, and have to be disposed of. More trade in the free Common Market will produce even more packaging waste, in the wealthier countries as well as in the poorer Southern states, once the latter have caught up chasing the "EU-Supermarket".

The tightened-up waste laws in countries such as Germany, Denmark and France have put pressure on the EU-Commission in Brussels. The result is a Packaging Directive, which, however, allows for lengthy transition periods and does not go far enough for the conservationists. Also, in view of resistance from some Member States, it can never be more than the "lowest common denominator". If "green disposal" were to succeed, it could be a model for Europe. France is already participating. As yet the Southern countries consider the system too expensive. Despite some euphoria, scepticism is advisable. Time will show how seriously the idea will be put into practice.

In this dilemma "waste avoidance" has become the new magic slogan, key concept for a patent recipe to rid ourselves of the mountains of waste. It is flanked by other magic words like Recycling and Composting. However, on burning the rubbish – especially synthetic materials – opinions are divided.

Anyhow, everyone has become aware of the problem. The sick patient is getting treatment, probably too late, for the rubbish dumps are still growing in spite of all efforts, and new ones have constantly to be opened up. Refuse keeps increasing, despite a shrinking population. And still the old principle of Not In My Backyard holds sway: please, no tips in our own neighbourhood, our own community, our own country!

That goes even more for the ugly remainder, the specialised waste: batteries, old medicines, used oil, the dangerous residues of burning, the poisonous by-products of industry. A toxic dump on their own territory is the horror scenario of every parish council.

That also hold for incinerator plant. But here there has obviously been some misinformation and playing on the fears of the population. Euro-Delegate Karl-Heinz Florenz has worked out that on a motorway section 5 km. long there are more emissions of pollutants than from the chimneys of a modern incineration plant

The logical alternative to this dilemma seems to be: Away

with the filth! Export it. Long live waste-tourism! About 5% of its hazardous waste the Federal Republic disposes of "legitimately" over the borders; the amount exported illegally is unknown. But the good times seem to be over. There is a threat of export bottlenecks and a disposal crisis.

For decades it had been so easy and comfortable. The desolate former DDR needed money, and environment protection was an alien concept in the Communist economy. So one unburdened oneself against currency, and the environmental damage that caused there yesterday has to be undone today at a cost of billions. What an absurd world we live in.

This tragedy will probably be repeated a few more times, because in the footsteps of the former DDR and after the collapse of the Soviet Union some of the new Reformed States of Central Europe have followed suit – Poland and Romania, for instance. The sombre figures for waste transports to those countries are not even approximately known. Dumping, followed by the necessary rehabilitation of the environment: these are business deals worth millions and billions, with varying prognostications. And the retrieval actions so far revealed are anything but a glorious chapter.

And then there is the Third World. Here, in addition to "waste tourism", we find a peculiarly macabre variant: Waste Colonialism. Whether in Asia, Aftrica, Latin America or the Caribbean – waste exports rouse greed for more, because the pay is so good: up to 200 Dollars. With such lucrative terms, no poor country can resist the blandishments of the waste unloaders, let the environment go to the devil. For the developing countries lack the technology for appropriate storage of the dangerous substances. The stuff is simply dumped in the lagoons or the primeval forests, or on remote tips on faraway farms. Despite the high prices paid, this is still a cheaper way of disposal for the industrial states than the heavily taxed disposal at home.

In principle this will not have been changed by the Basel Convention, which in 1989 within the framework of the United

Nations Environment Programme achieved a minimum consensus regarding cross-border waste transports. Numerous crocodile tears were expended on this occasion by the representatives of the 116 participating states, which included 93 developing countries. There was talk of "Rubbish Tip Africa", of "Poison Terrorism" and "Toxic Waste Colonialism". In the end it was agreed that waste transports must be registered and their import officially approved. Since then the ships have frequently sailed under false colours, so to speak. Their cargo is registered in the documents as "building materials", "raw materials", or "Material for recycling". More jobs and new infrastructures are supposed to be created by this. And of course bribery is part of the game.

Apart from serious efforts to solve the problem, there have been frequent cynical and absurd suggestions for disposal. American scientists had already discovered by late 1991 that industrial waste could be dumped without risk in the sea at depths of 5,000 metres, because owing to the prevailing conditions of pressure, extreme cold and complete darkness it would cause no damage to the environment.

In February 1992 the acting World Bank President Lawrence Summers in a memorandum (later, after international protest, downgraded to a "personal opinion") pronounced himself in favour of the export of toxic waste to the Third World, because it would cause less damage there than in the industrial countries. One month later Russian experts, whose regime had for decades been simply tipping their nuclear waste into the sea, suggested that toxic waste should be destroyed by atomic bombs . . .

Of course that is not the solution. Even in Brussels they know that. But the attitude of the European Union towards supervision of waste transports inside or outside the EU was itself until recently marked by divers contradictions and absurdities. An EU-Directive did lay down a ratification procedure, but in such a clearly ineffectual and inadequate form that the scandals have not been curbed by it. The European dilemma is obvious.

For Brussels waste is "merchandise" or, if destined for recycling, a "service" – and those are two of the four sacred cows, two of the great freedoms in the borderless Common Market which may not be meddled with. So they dithered between worrying about freedom of trade and worrying about the environment.

In principle nothing has been changed by the Waste Transporting Directive, by means of which the EU Ministers responsible for the environment in Luxembourg in 1992 tried to put a stop to Waste Tourism. It followed a discussion during which the Brussels EU-Commission rested its case on the famous and frequently quoted Common Market Article 100 of the Treaty of Rome, which provides "directives for the approximation of such provisions imposed by law, regulation and administrative action in Member States as directly affect the setting up or operation of the common market." That would have left individual Member States little latitude in the way of free movement of goods where there was a veto on the import of EU waste from other countries within the Union. Consequently a majority of EU Ministers came out against the Commission's proposal.

Cross-border waste transports within the EU should therefore not be subject to the decisions of the Common Market or be liable to prohibition. That holds for non-reusable waste for dumping, including domestic refuse. The export of recyclable waste can be made more difficult. At the same time, however, the Ministers agreed to a compromise which permits trade restrictions for the good of the environment, but only in cases where possible prohibition is "in accordance with the Treaty". The European Parliament has played a highly committed role in this waste-controversy, as warning voice and critic on all the sub-committees, and has always demanded substantially sterner measures than the EU–Commission or the Council of Ministers which has been inhibited by the conflicting interests of its members' governments.

"You have to pay for your pleasures," argued European Delegate Karl-Heinz Florenz, reporting on waste-control, and he advocated "keeping close to the source"; those who produce the waste should also deal with it, he maintained. Reusable packaging should be given clear preference over disposable, single-use packing, he said, asking for a "Psychological signal against the throwaway mentality of our time."

"Stay poor or become a dustbin," is the alternative many Third World countries dread. The situation could arise which European Parliamentarian Annemarie Kuhn foresees: "The EU decision to prohibit waste-export to Third World States is threatened by enticing but villainous offers, some of which originate with enterprises from those regions themselves."

Already by the end of 1989 the EU had committed itself to 69 African, Pacific and Caribbean developing countries to limit international waste-deals and to prohibit export of hazardous waste to those countries. The Basel Convention, too, is to become a fixed component of EU regulations.

However you look at it, waste will remain an endless problem for a long time yet. The enfranchised citizen does, however, have a chance here to prove his coming-of-age by strategies of rejection and avoidance, and thus to loosen the Eco-Twisters' grip on the brakes to progress.

Chapter 11

The spirit is willing, but the flesh is weak

If all went according to theory, the future of the environment in Europe would look pretty rosy. But the opposite is the case. In practice the good resolutions are not carried out. The best example of this is the frightening balance sheet of environmental events in the European Union, but also in other parts of Europe. Words no longer convince: we want to see action.

The unbearable heaviness of becoming
Pacta sunt servanda – agreements must be kept

Josef Ertl, Federal Minister of Food, Agriculture and Forestry, had cause for rejoicing. On 11 June 1976 he wrote in the Bulletin of the Federal Government: 'On the 21 and 25 June firstly the "Convention on international trade in endangered species of wild animals and plants (Washington Convention on Biodiversity)" and secondly the "Convention on Wetlands, especially as habitat for aquatic and wading birds of international importance (International Wetlands Convention, or Ramsar-Convention)" will come into force. With that the Federal Republic will have taken two significant steps towards international wildlife preservation.'

In June 1991 Klaus Töpfer, Federal Minister for the Environment, Nature Preservation and Nuclear Safety, was able to state in a special brochure from his Ministry on the 15th anniversary of the Washington Biodiversity Convention: 'The Federal Republic of Germany has contributed substantially to the ongoing development of the Convention. In doing so it has taken a leading role within the EU. Up to 1989 roughly 30% of the applications for protection of species came from the Federal Republic.'

An agreeable conclusion.

Actually, when you look at it, enough seems to have been done for years to protect nature and environment, rare and endangered animals and plants. At least on paper. But paper, as we know, will accept anything, and not everybody keeps to what is down in black and white and to which he is committed. The Ancient Romans, living in a world as yet fairly uncomplicated in comparison with ours, set up a guideline to secure their Empire (and it is still valid): *Pacta sunt servanda* – agreements must be kept.

How does that stand up in Europe?

Nature protection has a long tradition, and prepared the way for general environment conservation, which really only became a public concern in the '70s. In both fields over the last three decades a large number of recommendations have been made, conventions, agreements, settlements and protocols signed, directives issued, which mostly meant a strong moral imperative for the signatories, but only in isolated cases were legally binding.

Nearly all countries have signed these agreements; international organisations and institutions have also joined or even been initiators. No country can afford, in the face of ever-increasing public awareness, to stand aside and risk the reproach of being environment-hostile. Everyone is all for nature and environmental conservation; all want to join in. But how does it work out in practice? What is actually achieved? There are all sorts of question marks.

After the Council of Europe in Strasbourg in 1962 set up a standing committee for the protection of nature and natural resources, three years later, in 1965, the so called European Diploma was introduced. This was to be a prestigious and rare award conferred on European natural landscapes, reserves and national parks. Every member country can apply for this diploma for a certain development. If it conforms to the very strict specifications, the award is conferred for five years at a time, with the possibility of renewal. It is revoked if the demands are no longer fulfilled. In Germany there are eight of these areas. Lüneburg Heath was threatened with withdrawal of the diploma when plans were revealed to bore for oil. The Pyrenees lost it when a region awarded the Diploma was opened up to tourism. In this way sanctions can really work.

But without the support of the citizens no effective conservation can be carried out. That is why 1970 was declared the 'Year of European Wildlife Preservation', bringing a certain breakthrough into public awareness of the environment.

In 1971, 23 States met in the Iranian city of Ramsar on the Caspian Sea to prepare an 'Agreement for the protection of wetlands of international importance, especially as habitats for aquatic and shore birds' – the so called Ramsar Convention. In the Federal Republic it came into force in 1976, and since then has preserved over 30 important bird-resting places between the North Sea and Lake Constance – not nearly enough, in the wildlife protectors' opinion.

In 1973 the Washington Biodiversity Convention was signed, an 'Agreement regarding international trade with endangered species of free-living animals and plants'. The Federal Republic in 1976 was the first EU Member State to put it into force... In the meantime 110 States have joined, as has the European Union itself. In March 1992 at the 8th follow-up Conference to the Washington Biodiversity Convention in Kyoto, Japan, Germany received the award for the greatest commitment to species preservation. Germany had, inter alia, successfully advocated a trading prohibition on sperm- and fin-whales, servals, long-tailed cats and ocelots.

In 1976 the Strasbourg Council of Europe created a further

protective mechanism for preserving the wealth of 'genetic heritage', the biogenetic nature reserves, with a network of by now 200 such zones. The aim is to preserve the greatest possible number of different, representative natural habitats.

In the same year UNESCO began to list *Biosphere-Reserves* worldwide: protected areas of representative natural landscapes recognised as especially worth preserving. The list currently comprises over 310 biosphere reserves in 80 countries.

In 1979 came the famous Berne Convention of the Council of Europe, joined by most European countries and the EU (since 1982), and also the African States of Senegal and Burkina Faso. This Convention is, as Strasbourg sees it, the most effective means of carrying out the conservation and environment policy of the Council of Europe. By the Convention the signatory states commit themselves to protect endangered plants and animals as well as their natural habitats.

During the UN Environment Conference in Rio de Janeiro in June 1992 a further Convention was set out for signing, and was signed by 153 states and the European Union – that is, by nearly all the countries present. The aim of the Convention is again the global protection of animal and plant species and their endangered habitats, in order to secure the genetic potential contained therein. This Agreement is considered the broad international basis for the conservation and development of the global natural heritage, as worldwide protection of all animal and plant species, and as a supplement to the already existing international regulations and agreements.

With such a network one could almost talk of an inflation of international efforts on behalf of nature and environment conservation. Agreement is indeed worldwide, but in practice many things do look different than on paper.

What line does the European Union take towards the question, apart from having joined a series of non-binding agreements?

Already by the end of 1972 the heads of State and Government in Paris had decided to carry out a common policy on the environment. Over a hundred directives – laws, to be ratified by all Member Countries as part of their national legislation – have been issued since. They concern the fight against pollution of soil, air and water, protection against excessive noise, and control of chemical substances and waste.

It did emerge that environmental conservation had little space in the Treaty of Rome compared with economic aims, and that the unanimity principle in the Council of Ministers was more of a hindrance than a help when it came to carrying out environment policy. The turning point came with the *Unified European Document* of 1987. Since then the majority principle holds for environmental legislation. In the Treaty of Maastricht the special importance of environment protection for the Community was once again stressed. That gives some hope for the future.

That Member Countries have not taken EU environment laws very seriously in the past is shown by the statistics of the European Court in Luxembourg. More than 80 convictions have been recorded for crimes against the environment. Belgium, Italy and Germany head the list. Germany, of all countries, was indicted by the Court for inadequate quality of drinking water, while Greece, notoriously European sinner No. 1, gets off lightly. Here too the principle holds: Where there is no plaintiff, there is no defendant. In a few countries of the Community environment consciousness is just more strongly developed than in others, where conservation is still regarded as a luxury.

As regards wildlife protection within the EU, in 1979 the Bird Protection Directive mounted a signal. Its purpose was that protected birds – precisely listed – may not be hunted, caught, nor sold. Nevertheless along the Straits of Messina systematic murder of birds continues. And in Belgium bird catching is less than a tolerated delinquency; it is even officially licensed, despite the protests of the EU-Commission. Spain and Greece also stand accused. In North Germany, with the aid of a Court of Europe judgment, the environment-friendly dyking project in East Frisian Ley Bay was passed. Varying standards still prevail in Europe, and much remains to be done for conservation.

The Fauna, Flora and Habitat Directive passed by EU Environment Minister in December 1991 is to set new standards in a comprehensive Regulations-Handbook called *Natura 2000* – for the protection of animals and plants in the (then) twelve Member States. *Deja vu?* Or perhaps, *On verra*! In any case, we shall see.

The laws and agreements are in place, now they must be honoured: *Pacta sunt servanda.* The European Union has created instruments and organs for this purpose: the European Court of Justice and also the European Audit Office, which is not at all squeamish in tackling the misuse of millions and billions from the structural funds – to the disadvantage of the environment. And perhaps the concerted action (since 1993) of the European Union and the Council of Europe in matters of 'collective responsibility for damage to the environment' could at last achieve the truly desired breakthrough and put a curb on the offenders against nature and environment.

The Spirits I called up
Theory and practice in Eurocracy

Telling pronouncements: 'European environment policy is in a bad way', or 'There are no tools yet for stabilising the emissions of carbon dioxide up to the year 2000 on the actual level of 1990. There was no readiness to ensure that in future 0.7% of the gross national product should be set aside to help development in Third World countries. There was no prospect that the Americans would still agree to the Biodiversity Convention. For the Climate Convention, to save humanity from the catastrophic consequences of the Greenhouse Effect, no date has been set.'

Quotations from a disillusioned conservationist? Indeed. The first refers to Brussels' environment policy, the second, longer one, to the Environment Conference of 1992 in Rio. Both are from the former chief European conservationist, Carlo Ripa di Meana, ex EU Environment Commissioner, who by way of protest did not participate in the Rio Summit, and shortly afterwards left his post in Brussels. Ripa di Meana knows what he is talking about. He knows better than anyone the few strengths and many weaknesses of European environment policy, he knows the scandals great and small, the wrong developments, the successes of the lobbying tactics of the business representatives who are concerned with gain, not with the environment.

But these quotes are not the only evidence for the belief that the European environment as yet counts for nothing with the responsible officials. From other official documents one can easily tell how desperate things are. It is all in the report of the EU-Commission on the *State of the Environment in the European Union*. It is there in the papers dealing with the consequences of the Common Market. It is there in scientific assessments; environmental associations announce it every day. The quintessence is: Eco-Twisters are at work. Europe lives, the environment dies.

Climate catastrophe, ozone hole, soil contamination, soil erosion, chemical pollution, nuclear threat, species extinction, landscape spoilage, scrap mountain, water pollution, resources attrition, waste avalanche, dying forests. The threats and dangers are multifarious.

The Commission attempts, with programmes and pronouncements, regulations and directives, to assure the concerned citizen that one has read the signs of the times, that one will change direction. Even special meetings of Environment Ministers are called, for instance when too many oil tankers run aground in quick succession and discharge their sticky loads into European territorial waters. True, European environmental laws have been constantly refined in recent years, yet the result is sobering. The briskly galloping economy has left the limping nag of environmental protection behind.

What has been achieved by qualitative technical advances has been eaten up again by quantitative, State-initiated growth. The catalytic converter on cars is one example.

Yet it has been clear for a long time that a policy which misunderstands environment care as the mere absence of attempts at technical solutions is bound to fail. It cannot be simply a matter of technical standards, our whole economic system should be critically analysed – an economic system that attaches no importance to beauties of nature, but glorifies consumer symbols instead. What, nowadays, is the use of a lake without surfers? A mountain without a ski-lift, a landscape without a food stall, a region without a theme park? The youngest members of our society have long been able to name more makes of car than species of plant or animal.

Europe's citizens have acquired a lifestyle which is environment-hostile. We live in a market economy which claims to be ecological and social, but is not. It is antisocial to exclude a large number of our contemporaries from what we call affluence and progress. It is antisocial to rob succeeding generations of natural resources. And it is unecological not to manage a sustainable economy. The amount of energy used by industrialised countries, the amount of waste we produce, the quantities of kilometres we cover in ever more powerful motor vehicles: all that cannot last for ever. There must be fundamental changes of behaviour – which will not only hurt, but will cast doubt on previous economic and production structures.

Our lifestyle has to change, because the Planet cannot stand it. First we kill off our fellow creatures, and then ourselves. Look at it from this point of view: if you believe an agency report, in China at the end of 1992 there were just 37,000 private car owners. If the Chinese attained the car concentration of industrialised countries, the global CO_2 output from motor vehicles alone would be doubled, and the mineral oil resources used up even quicker. Everyone knows this cannot go on. The Western model is not transferable to the rest of the world.

All this has been known for a long time. And although we know it all, we carry on as though we had no problems. It is probably human nature to repress problems. To repeat the known facts once again in this book may not be original – these insights are not new – but it is essential. For we are further than ever from seeing a basic change of policy in European society. Of course protecting the environment is mentioned in every speech and programme. And we support nature, part of the time, as we do theatres, swimming pools and museums. We make nature and environment into purchasable and saleable goods. Because we can afford it. Sometimes more, sometimes less; least at a time of recession.

However, EU policy is determined as before by the spirit of a constant-growth economy, and that is ultimately what is eating up the environment, and finally ourselves. Economic crises and incipient slumps are not used actually to tackle the much-discussed remodelling of industrial society. On the contrary, all the old traditional methods of kick-starting the economy are invoked to send the sinking ship on yet another grand voyage.

Instead of approaching the remodelling of motorised society from a consistent perspective, instead of designing strategies for reducing traffic as a contribution to relieving the climate, instead of realising a truly 'regional' Europe in which regional identity becomes a main object of consideration, instead of building up public means of transport, the EU chiefs of government could think of nothing better than to design gigantic road-building projects within a billions-consuming 'EU growth initiative': 12,000 km. of new motorways to be metalled for the European network, more national asphalt roads and concrete runways. The European Investment Bank is to advance 15 billion ECU loans for this. Meanwhile the poorer EU countries are also trying hard to attract double-figure billions from a new EU resource, the so called Cohesion Fund.

Amid all this, conservation is just a drag. It is used solely as a green alibi, a cosmetic cover-up for global environment destruction. No other aspect of EU policy where communally decided law is so generally disregarded as in the case of the environment.

This already starts with the translation of EU laws into national regulations. It is only the rulings prepared by the EU-Commission and ultimately ratified by the Council of Ministers which become legally binding in the EU Member States. EU directives, on the other hand, only set a sort of framework to be filled within a certain time by national regulations.

The EU directives issued so far have been 95% converted into national laws. In certain sectors, e.g. the 17 directives concerned with the Customs Union, 100% has been achieved; the 50 directives in the sector of 'indirect taxation' the Commission can boast of a 99% conversion rate. 'The adoption of legal rulings concerned with agriculture involves 330 directives,' the EU-Commission states in its Ninth Annual Report on the control of Community Law. 'The conversion rate has reached 93%, but one should not forget the problems of veterinary affairs, above all the problems connected with artificial insemination and breeding procedures.' Are these the true problems of the EU?

In the environment sector there has so far been only 85% realisation of directives. That already tells you something about relative values. It is even more important to ask about observance of the adopted laws. Much in that aspect looks pretty dire, as proved by the Bird Protection Directive of 1979. It is the most important conservation directive of the EU, a sort of European Conservation Law. With none of the other 820 valid directives did the Commission have to take action against Member States as often as over this one – and it is not all that quick to take action ... Denmark, Luxembourg and Portugal are the only States against whom no proceedings have been taken for offences against this agreement. All the other Member States have so far proved incapable of protecting their remaining wildlife to the extent laid down by their own decision, the Bird Protection Directive. Where there is any doubt, it is wildlife interests that go by the board. Only where agriculture, transport, industry, dustmen, waterboard representatives, town planners, mineral wealth exploiters or Armed Services make no claims does nature, in theory, get a chance. If air pollution does not destroy it first.

It is not only the Member States whose drive for continued economic growth raises the pressure on nature, environment, landscape – and thus on the last remaining wildlife sanctuaries. The EU itself is also actively engaged in the war of environmental attrition. And it even admits it. In the above mentioned report on the observance of Community legislation one reads that: '. . . the Commission is increasingly concerned that special reserves within the Community are insufficiently well marked and more habitats are being destroyed, where some of this destruction can be traced back to programmes financially supported by the Community.'

The Commission does not give concrete data, but everyone knows what is meant: the structural funds of the EU, pouring out billions for the 'development' of apparently disadvantaged regions (always meaning their financial situation). With these funds massive environmental destruction is carried out. A large part of the negative examples described in this book are financed by structural fund money. Yet it has long been the rule that the demands of conservation should be an integral component of all branches of Community policy. An EU Directive lays it upon all Member States and the EU-Commission itself that initiatives financed by the EU must accord with environment conservation. Therefore no action part-financed by the EU should contribute further damage to the environment. On the contrary, it is provided in the EU contract that the Commission in all its proposals must start out from a high level of protection. Yet drainage of wetlands, hydro-electric dam projects and intensification of agriculture continue to be the order of the day. 'Very few effective measures have been taken to translate this obligation into practice,' the European Audit Office duly states in its deeply depressing report on EU environment policy.

At a rough estimate only ca. 6% of the invested structural funds money goes into environmental protection. By far the greatest part continues to finance environment-endangering and environment-destroying projects, although the Commission would have plenty of possibilities of countering them. In the areas where structural funds are invested, so-called operational programmes must be set up. These should be accompanied and approved by a controlling committee on which the EU should be represented. But the report of the European Audit Office shows plainly that the Commission does not meet its obligation.

Investigations of 13 operational programmes have shown that Board of Management XI, the Commission's department responsible for conservation, has neither taken part in such committee meetings nor received copies of the minutes of 20 meetings that have taken place. The Member States are allowed to get away with what can only harm the environment. The Audit Office further states that 'at the national level (. . .) investigation by the House since the reform of structural funds have shown no noticeable progress as regards procedures' which 'are to enable a stronger consideration of environment problems when working out programmes'. In most countries and regions the authorities responsible for environment matters had not been formally consulted when programmes were worked out.

When carrying out investigations in the regions of various Member States, the Audit Office itself had to give the necessary information about the existing Community regulations regarding the environment, and their import, to the departments engaged in preparing the programmes. One cause of that is the shameful understaffing of the relevant EU department. The permanent overload of work cannot be compensated for by sheer commitment. Moreover, the Management Board 'Environment' and the corresponding EU Environment Commissioner traditionally have only weak voices in the chorus of other interests. That situation has prevailed for years in Germany, too, where the Environment Minister has only played a subordinate role in the Federal Cabinet.

At present conservation is decaying at the EU just as it does in Member States. Economy beats ecology every time. Tax money is used to ruin nature. As well as the structural funds, the EU's agricultural policy is a classic example of that. You find the same mechanisms as in other branches of the economy; productivity and profit are the considerations, not social or ecological needs.

When the EU agricultural policy was formulated in the Treaty of Rome, food was still short and there was a lack of workers in industry. Both problems were to be solved by developing agricultural productivity. When fewer farm workers produce more, some can leave the land while the rest produce food more cheaply. With an ever more tangled system of so-called skimming off – to protect the somewhat more expensive produce of Europe against cheaper imports from abroad – and export subsidies, to enable our higher-priced products to be sold on the world market at all, and with price and markets guaranteed, an economy was fuelled which today confronts a heap of rubble.

There has been frequent talk of agricultural policy reform, even of ecological reform. Yet the illusion rolls on relatively undeterred. Despite surpluses, despite butter mountains and milk lakes, the genetic technicians are busy evolving high-performance cows. Despite sugar surpluses they are trying for genetically modified turbo-beet, despite starch surpluses, on new species of potato. All that in the cause of productivity – but will they know what to do with the products? Producing in order to throw away, or to pollute the environment?

What is the upshot? Agriculture which once shaped the multiplicity of our landscape has given way to agrarian industry. Increased productivity has become the measure of all things, not only in agriculture but in every department. The price for that is high, and not only financially.

So far the politicians have been pretty relaxed, watching the environment go to the dogs in the wake of economic growth. Against the rise in sea level caused by climatic changes the Eurocrats visualise higher dykes and new forms of insurance. Isolated national or EU initiatives towards improved global conservation are not on the cards; one might be handicapped in competition . . .

The political game has been honed to perfection. When a country thinks of making special efforts for conservation strategies, it is referred to the EU. Solutions have to be sought communally, that is right and proper as well as altogether more effective. At discussions within the EU the shoving to and fro of responsibility continues. One State pleads the subsidiarity principle, another stonewalls, or rather dilutes the matter in hand, fearing economic disadvantage. If the pressure increases, one delegates the problem to a supernational level.

A CO_2 and energy tax was a great idea, thought the government chiefs of all EU Member Countries, but not for Europe by itself. Only if the USA and Japan would co-operate could it be an effective measure. That assertion was made at a time when no one thought that an ecologically oriented man could become President of the USA. Now after Clinton and Gore have announced – without a vote, and in national isolation – a corresponding tax on energy in the USA, one of the two stumbling blocks has been removed. Suddenly the Eco-Twisters thought of asking for an OECD-wide solution. So once again more States have to be convinced, and that takes time. For the present one can sit back and go on as before.

It has all been described and said long ago. The Club of Rome pointed out the limitations of growth; the report to US President Carter in 1980, Global 2000, already described the climatic problems. In Germany in 1993 Action Programme Ecology, published as a series of papers by the Minister of the Interior, at that time responsible for conservation, celebrated its tenth anniversary of 'not being taken seriously'. One extract from it characterises our policy to date. The scientists and lateral thinkers who furnished the paper doubtless knew in advance of publication what fate awaited this progressive document. They wrote: 'It is incomprehensible to us why politicians keep demanding new evidence from ecologists for quite unambiguously obvious mistaken developments; why long overdue decisions have to be shored up again and again by expert opinions. The suspicion is inescapable that quite a few influential politicians misuse the work of scientists to justify a strategy of inaction.'

It is clear that we drive too many cars, farm too intensively, use too much energy. Nevertheless the EU with over a billion ECUs is promoting the development of a new-style high-definition Television, which is already outmoded before the series is produced, because it is not digitally controlled. The scandal is not just the billion subsidy for the industry – one knows that scenario from other media. The real scandal is that a technology which will use ten times more energy than the present receives such support in the face of shortage of raw materials and climate problems. 16(!) new(!) megapower stations(!) will have to be built if this television technology sells as its promoters hope. What about the principles of precaution and causation? A better TV image is more important to the politicians than climate protection. That is the reality, that is the present sorry scale of values.

Human labour power is too expensive, energy is too cheap, everyone knows that. Yet our system of taxation 'penalises' human labour and ignores the obvious shortage of energy. An ecologically motivated and executed form of taxation, making for more expensive energy, for instance more expensive motoring, would be a good thing. The Club of Rome even suggests developing a new science of economics based on energy expenditure rather than money, energy being the driving force of the economy, money only its substitute. And above all the consumption of energy in its varying forms is responsible for the problems of the environment.

'All people will have to make sacrifices, and only future generations will benefit from these. (...) The pressure of circumstances is so great that we must either change or vanish from the face of the earth.' That, too, is a message from the Club of Rome. Really decisive changes are needed, and the track has to be laid for them now. Yet the political will is lacking actually to turn the tiller round. Most politicians are ecologically illiterate, and their way of thinking echoes that of political economists in the '60s. The caravan moves on.

'My successor must stand for a contrasting programme,' said Carlo Ripa di Meana, cited above. 'Environment policy must be directed against the current rules of GATT, against the subsidiarity principle, against the agricultural policy. He should be the black sheep of the Commission.' Someone to speak out against a motorway programme planning for a further 12,000 km. Ripa di Meana ought to know: our society has long harboured such black sheep, and they serve as a token green alibi, without any of the necessary changes being effected. The outlook is pretty gloomy. Like lemmings we are rushing towards the abyss.

On the social scene the market economy has already been set narrower limits. This may sound banal, but it is an achievement of the social movement that small children no longer have to work underground. Trade unions today are fighting for other things, such as increased wages and more leisure. they have a decided advantage over the ecological movement: their successes benefit people directly, in the form of money or free time. That is why they have more political clout. The painful sacrifices the ecological movement has to try and force through will, as we have shown, only benefit future generations. So the pressure is less, the path is a stony one. It will be some time before the market economy can be forced into an ecological framework, where not only whinchats and yellow flag irises are protected, but human beings too – permanently – against themselves.

'The divide between measures required to protect living space and the natural world, and the measures actually translated into concrete action, threatens to become ever wider.

Putting the directives into force could, at the present pace, and despite persistent endeavours, take several more generations,' says the European Audit Office.

Will it succeed at all – and will there be time?

You can't see the ones in the dark
The sharp (blunt) sword of the Union

Looking out of the window of his office on the fifth floor of the European Court of Auditors, Dr. Bernhard Friedmann can see, below, in front and next door on the Luxembourg Kirchberg much of what spells power, influence and money in the European Union: the General Secretariat of the European Parliament, the European Court of Justice, and the European Investment Bank. Bernhard Friedmann himself is a powerful man. The former CDU Bundestag delegate and Chairman of the Audit Office is also the German President of the European Court of Auditors with the rank of EU-Commissioner. He is therefore one of the top 12 supervisors watching over the financial conduct of the Community.

A crucial part of his work lies in the realm of the environment, and that is no accident. In the Single European Act which came into force on 1 July 1987 environment decisions were formally incorporated into the Treaty of Rome. There it is laid down that the Union has the aim, among others, to preserve the environment, to protect it and improve its quality. Thus the Union is committed to prevent harm to the environment, combat it where possible at the source, and make the culprit liable for damage caused.

In the Treaty of Maastricht, agreed by the Heads of State and Government of the (then) twelve EU Member States in December 1991, it was laid down that the Community's aim of environment conservation should in future be given greater importance. For instance, it is proposed that the Cohesion Fund created for the four poorer Member States of Greece,

Spain, Portugal and Ireland should be used mainly for maintenance of the environment. In Maastricht it was also decided to give the European Court of Auditors – founded in 1975 and therefore the youngest EU institution, the official status of a fifth EU-Organ alongside the European Parliament, the EU-Commission, the Council of Ministers and the European Court of Justice, and thereby to increase its political influence.

The activities of the Court of Auditors are expressed in annual reports, regularly supplemented by special reports on important single subjects. Under the reference number C 245 on 23 September 1992 it published a special report on the environment in the Official Journal of the European Union. It had been drawn up at the request of the European Parliament and contains the results of investigations at the EU-Commission as well as in the six Member States: Germany, Greece, Spain, Italy, Netherlands and Britain.

The Court of Auditors through its researches comes to some fairly devastating conclusions, which allow a glimpse behind the scenes of the Brussels EU-Commission at work, where at times a terrifying mix-up of responsibilities reigns, and one hand does not know what the other is doing. Inadequacies and double-tracking, dilettantism and the blatant attempts to circumvent or wriggle under the regulations of the EU-Commission – it could be part of the scenario of a European-environment-set crime thriller.

Thus the report criticises, among other things, that the funds spent on the Community's environment policy are spread over the entire spectrum of EU activities, but exact figures are lacking. In 1991 at least one billion ECU would have been available for this. Again, the so-called action programmes for environment protection, in which the guidelines for the Community's policies are supposed to be laid down, could hardly do justice to the demands of conservation all over the EU. The tasks arising in connection with conservation are distributed among too many different departments of the Commission, which only occasionally meet for consultation.

This leads to an uneconomic use of resources. So, for example, initiatives for the intensive cultivation of coastal areas are funded, while at the same time conservationist organisations are financed in taking steps to protect wetlands by acquiring lagoons to *prevent* their intensive cultivation.

In Greece the construction of a dam, including access road and overhead power lines, was financed by EU structural funds. Subsequently further money was needed to ensure an adequate water circulation. In addition a part of the planned power network had to be dropped for fear of endangering bird life.

There was also criticism that actions covered by structural funds do not always take environmental interests into account. An appropriate and continuous follow-up of the EU's own environment schemes is not guaranteed. The surveillance of contracts also leaves much to be desired: the files are incomplete, and the documents to be presented by the parties often cannot be found. Nor is the reported expenditure fully backed by receipts.

At first glance, according to the report of the Court of Auditors, a significant part of the structural funds is destined for environmental improvements. The qualitative effects may, however, be of limited value. Construction of an underground train service in Athens – supported by 178 million ECU – is thought wholly in the interests of the environment, though no conclusive overall plan for avoidance of traffic problems exists. There has been no accurate registration of motor vehicles, a sizeable number of vehicles does not conform to standards of exhaust gas emission, the proposed biennial inspections are not systematically carried out.

The following examples also reveal that much remains to be done to ensure that measures financed by structural funds do not contribute to environmental damage:

1. During dredging works in the harbour of Thessaloniki the mud hauled up was to be dumped in the sea, despite harmful effects on flora and fauna.
2. In a steel works in the same town the dust collected after

installation of special filters was at first stored in one room of the complex and ultimately distributed in layers on surrounding plots of land.

3. In Saxony-Anhalt before a certain investment was made the question of waste water treatment had to be settled. In the event, the funds were granted before a corresponding commitment had been made.

4. In an application for a subsidy for a mining enterprise in Spain it was explained that the investment had no negative effects. But actually it entailed the clearing of a vast area of forest and the pollution of large amounts of water.

5. An enterprise in Britain that was not fitted with a water treatment unit tried to avoid spreading pollution by storing the polluted water in disused coal mines. However, this meant considerably endangering the groundwater.

The European Court of Auditors also critically assessed the work of the authorities charged with monitoring environment pollution as in need of improvement in many ways. The authorities were insufficiently equipped, only in isolated cases were the environment tests carried out, and there was no systematic check on offences against environment legislation. The converting of the Council of Ministers' Directive on assessing environment compatibility of certain public and private projects into national law was pronounced unsatisfactory, because several Member States would only partially do it.

A mere stone's throw from the European Court of Auditors on the Kirchberg in Luxembourg lies the European Court of Justice. It supervises observance of the Community's legislation. Roughly 100 cases concerning the environment have been dealt with to date. But the numerous judgments against Member States did not lead to a more efficient or complete application of the rules concerned.

In a comprehensive review the EU-Commission welcomes the special report of the Court of Auditors about the environment, 'appearing at the right moment'. It admits that a closer co-ordination between the various departments and more attention given to environment-oriented considerations at all levels of decision are required. Targeting of aims, assessment and action by the Commission can, however, only be successful if happening in the frame of closer partnership collaboration with individual Member States.

The European Court of Auditors and the European Parliament are only at the beginning of their work. Whether this will turn out an unsuccessful Sisyphus-labour or be ultimately crowned with success largely depends on whether routine muddle and incompetence can be done away with, paths cleared through the jungle of impenetrable regulations, and the necessary measure of power given to the organs of control and enforcement to prevent the misuse of gigantic sums to the detriment of the environment.

Twenty Years and little (none?) the wiser?
EU – ending or change?

Conservationists are pinning their hopes of finding the beginnings of a new policy for conservation on the Fifth Environment Programme of the European Union. This is valid for five years from 1993. Reading the document is rather amazing: certain passages could not be formulated more critically by the most fundamentalist of environment activists. Inter alia you can read this:

'The progressive deterioration in the state of the environment and the severe damage to the basis of life throughout the world are viewed with growing concern all over the world (...) The Community is aware of the fact that its own 340 million inhabitants together with the inhabitants of other industrial states are using a disproportionate share of global resources (...)' And later on: 'With the measures taken in the last two decades it has not been possible so far to maintain the quality of the environment.' And: 'Present-day speed and the additional burdens to which the environment and natural resources are subjected by the completion of the Common Market and the political and commercial developments in Central and Eastern Europe and elsewhere (...) make far more effective measures essential.'

To read these sentences does arouse hopes. Hopes of a renunciation of such scandals and misdevelopments as are described in this book; hopes, too, that the number of Eco-Twisters will finally diminish.

Every five years there are new Environment Action Programmes for the EU – there have been four to date. There are few official documents which express the dilemma of European environment policy so strongly as this 5th Environment Action Programme of the EU-Commission. Unmistakeably it describes the dire state of the environment and the policy for it. The authors are plainly aware that it simply cannot go on like this. You can tell they also know that there really has to be a total change of direction, the old concepts of the '60s have to be thrown overboard and new ideas developed. But they lack the courage to say this, to admit fundamental errors, to suggest radical reversals. Or are they not allowed to?

Need one ask whether the authors believe that the EU environment policy has failed? Or whether the 5th Environment Action Programme is a new and effective beginning of a common policy to protect life? Analysing the programme more closely, one finds that such a fundamentally fresh start is not considered necessary. According to Brussels logic the sell-out of nature and environment can still be presented as a triumph of environment policy. Thus one reads that in the past 20 years 'much has been achieved'. In view of the above-cited cases, the adverse quotes and the dramatic deterioration in the state of the environment, one may – without hurting the Eurocrats – safely deduce that what was achieved was at best so good that otherwise the deterioration would have been far worse.

'Much ... achieved.' That is the EU patting itself on the

back, on paper, something we could have done without. But perhaps they are just whistling in the dark?

'Much achieved, but not enough,' is one message that emerges from the Programme. Here is another, decisive message: The Common Market is definitely shown up as the overloader of the environment. According to the 5th Environment Action Programme, the most important task for the EU in the '80s was to develop and complete the Common Market. But, say the EU authors in this paper, in the '90s efforts must be directed towards 'making possible a sustainable and environment-friendly development.'

Of course the question immediately arises, 'Is this not a trifle schizophrenic?' Is it sensible, first to establish a policy which (inevitably) pollutes the environment, and then to mount a policy to help the environment? Of course it is nonsense, and the authors of the paper clearly realise it. They rightly recognise that 'much ingenuity and creativity' will be required to protect the environment adequately. 'In some cases that will demand far-reaching changes in consumer habits and life-style.' But the 5th Environment Action Programme fails to describe just where, concretely, this should be done, or how to overcome the resistance of those who have a vested interest in this very life-style and these policies, who lobby in Brussels and very largely mould the policy (and there are quite a few of them).

In some places there is a timid suggestion that 'Growth should be organised in an environment-friendly way.' But the necessary, fundamental criticism of the economic growth policy of individual European Member States, and thus of the EU, does not follow. One searches in vain in the Action Programme for any discussion of the alleged 'eco-social' market economy or the structural deficiencies of environment policy.

The fact that 'disquieting tendencies' like increased consumption of energy and water, proliferation of traffic and burgeoning of garbage, growth of tourism and intensive farming are truly described, but not recognised as the immediate consequence of the policies ensuing from the Treaty of Rome, is probably the greatest shortcoming of the paper, and of the EU officials responsible ... It should not delude one that many sentences in the paper could have come straight from the pens of conservationists. Which environment society activist would not agree that 'short-term advantage for single individuals, enterprises or institutions' should be balanced 'against long-term benefit to the whole of society'? Yet faith is lacking that the present EU, managed as it is by the governmental heads of Member States, either can or wants to achieve that. For have not the government chiefs, wholly in the interests of the economy while at the same time 'taking cognisance of the 5th Environment Action Programme' resolved, via the Environment Ministers at the Edinburgh Summit, to bring the Commission's decisions 'closer to industry' and make them more 'comprehensible'? And did not the same gentlemen resolve at the same time to start a new growth initiative, culminating in the pouring of billions specifically into road building?

The policy that has been carried out for years is miles away from the ecologically necessary change, which the programme does not detail sharply enough. And the Environment Action Programme, even during its conception within the Commission, was regarded so much as a tiresome side issue or duty exercise that one really cannot expect too much of it.

This action plan is, in any case, too system-conciliatory – on the lines of 'Peace, Love, and Chips with Everything'. It is praised as a great new achievement for the environment that market economy instruments are to be moved to the centre of (environment) political discussions. The times when politicians tried to shape the environment by means of laws and fines are said to be over, because that was shown not to be effective. Cooperation with 'partners', with consumers and commerce, is the current trend: financial incentives are supposed to improve the situation and attain ecological ends. In agriculture and forestry, for example, the 'granting of bonuses and other compensation payments, if environment regulations are kept' is to be introduced. Funds are made available for 'rewarding ecological achievements' in farming. One wants to encourage, i.e. subsidise, an environment-friendly agriculture, so that it can hold its own against the also subsidised but environment-hostile agriculture. How mad can you get? Can we look forward to a time when stopping at a red light will get you a financial reward?

The unfortunate thing about the EU programme is that it is only part-financed by the EU. 'Ecological programmes' in agriculture, which one has to call half-hearted simply because on the other hand factory farming is not stopped, must be partially financed by EU Member States. Yet countries like Greece, Portugal or Ireland have no funds in their national budgets to do this. For them the EU's ideas are just so much printed paper from Brussels, not a genuine policy.

Even less can such a policy be transposed to countries in the Third World or in Eastern Europe. States that cannot even afford to set up a reasonably acceptable social, health or educational system, will not and cannot subsidise environment-loving structures.

Tax incentives can, however, be perfectly suitable aids for reaching pre-arranged targets more quickly. But the horizon aimed for is often not recognisable in the 5th Environment Action Programme; it is not clear exactly what is wanted. Diffuse descriptions like 'Improvement of the competitive standing by environment-friendly means of transport', or 'Promotion of soft tourism' do not help much – and not only because you cannot sue on the strength of them. What is needed is clearly defined aims and concrete guidelines.

Altogether the use of fiscal instruments tends to be overrated, both in its effect and, even more, its chance of realisation. After the experience of recent years one must fear that the 'line' on taxes and fines only works as long as the basic working out of the policy is not queried. One knows this from the example of traffic. The price of petrol should be £2.20 per litre, to accommodate all ensuing and quantifiable costs and simultaneously to effect noticeable (and essential) reduction of traffic. But nobody dares risk such a rise, indeed, nobody wants it, because it would jeopardise the economic system. The 'most progressive' of German politicians talk of a rise of 10 Pfennig per litre (5p), which over the next few years would be quite unable to inhibit the increase of traffic generated by increased road building.

An additional difficulty is that politicians have hitherto taken the line that such taxation has to be at least partially compensated for by other means. In Germany, for instance, the higher tax on petrol has resulted in a much too generous tax remission as kilometre bonus. As a result professional and business motoring has actually become cheaper, by 1 to 3 Pfennig per kilometre!

Drinks cans can harm the environment, as everyone knows who does not think 'ecology' a misprint for 'economy'. Drinks cans should be banned by law or decree. It is absurd that fiscal measures can buy one off dealing with such unnecessary environment encumbrances. Nature and environment are not tradeable merchandise, but the very basis of our lives. Just as there are (often far-reaching) limitations on the economy in the sociopolitical realm, so there should be clear ecological framework of limitations. By means of prohibitions, not merely financial incentives or other market economy strategies. Child labour in mines underground was not abolished by market economy solutions, but by political restrictions. It is wrong for the 5th Environment Action Programme to represent the direct, clear, unmistakeable and politically enforceable instrument of prohibition so negatively. That exposes a policy which is not able to carry through restrictions against economic interests. Even the European Parliament noted in its expressed opinion that the Action Programme laid down 'no unambiguous limitations and aims' for industry. For instance, no sector is mentioned where the policy has to work by prohibition. To reduce waste, for example, there should be prohibitions, not merely regulations which, where effective, would be 'prohibitions by the purse'. Such 'prohibitions by the purse' are the least acceptable, because the least public spirited. Those who have enough money can afford to damage the environment in certain ways, those who lack the money remain on the outside (and ecologically blameless).

Of course in many cases the market economy instruments named in the 5th Environment Action Programme are sensible. To that extent the acceptance of this principle into the palette of political action is justified and welcome. The use of energy, for example, cannot be prohibited. A rise in price is, however, urgently necessary, to save energy and encourage greater efficiency of use. Yet practical experience shows that even here there are huge gaps between the original idea and the practical reality. To increase the price of nitrate fertilisers as a means of relieving the environment and reducing agricultural surpluses has not been considered to date. In countries where this idea was mooted by conservationists and farmers' associations (e.g. Germany), it was bluntly rejected. And the CO_2 and energy tax or duty which has at first sight been set far too low to effect the necessary far-reaching ecological change of direction, was rejected by the EU because of suspected losses to the European economy. So far we have not seen much of that special responsibility – praised in the Environment Programme – which Europe bears for Planet Earth.

To sum up: The mania for growth of the EU economy is not examined critically by the Environment Programme. There is no analysis of the mistakes made by previous environment policy. Various model solutions are praised which conservationists have long opposed, e.g. nuclear power to solve the climate problem. One looks in vain for demands such as using the resources of the Cohesion Fund to improve public means of transport and not for road building.

Certainly the 5th Environment Action Programme represents an improvement in comparison with its precursors. The environment situation is no longer dismissed as harmless, and in the technical sphere there are promising suggestions. But as long as the ecologists do not state plainly that (economic) structures like the car need querying, so long as we are not prepared at least to visualise radical changes in industrial society – perhaps to speculate about a post-motor-car society – the action plans of the EU are no more than signposts to slow down further environment damage. Technical strategies alone will not solve structurally conditioned environment problems. The danger is that such programmes could even serve as a green-mantle cover-up for aggravated global destruction. That must not satisfy us, nor the generations to come.

What the Individual Can Do

Much is desperately wrong with the environment and the quality of life in Europe. In many cases public funds are expended on the destruction of nature and the pollution of the environment. Here are a few tips for what every individual can do to protect nature and the environment, although this list is neither exhaustive nor final. Imagination is our strongest weapon in environment conservation.

- Write to the responsible politicians in your country and draw their attention to the deplorable state of affairs.
- Raise public awareness of the subject: at political meetings, by writing to the Press, in discussions with friends and acquaintances.
- Demand a democratic Europe. Chances of influencing or monitoring the activities of Euro-MPs, for instance, are much too rare.
- Voice your demand that all projects and measures supported by the public funds of the European Union – especially programmes imposed by the European Commission – must be subjected to environment compatibility tests.
- Ask your Euro-MP but also your local MP to support a tax on energy across the whole of Europe. Only this can reduce environment-damaging activities by market economy

mechanisms.
- This should include a tax on heavy goods vehicles, which would make long-distance transport of goods by road more expensive and thus mark the beginning of a reorientation of our economic system.
- Demand also the raising of tax on (mineral) oil, to make travelling by car more expensive and reduce road traffic.
- Change to using environment-friendly public transport such as passenger rail services.
- Ask your local politicians to press for extension and improvement of public transport.
- Monitor your own mobility. Which holidays, which journeys, can you do without? Which holiday or journey can be done by bicycle or by rail? Holidays at home can be very enjoyable. Long-distance travel harms the climate and squanders fossil energy stocks.
- Make your shopping 'transport-aware'; instead of exotic fruits buy domestic and seasonal produce.
- As a tourist, observe the regulations in designated nature reserves. Alert the responsible authorities if you find anything wrong. Also inform the tourist office in the resort, and also the travel agent at home with whom you booked the holiday. Urge the tourist organisations to use their influence to remedy any abuses you noticed.
- If on your holiday you come across any environment-destroying projects which are supported by European Union funds, do not hesitate to inform EURONATURE, the European Court of Auditors and the European Parliament.
- Demand from your parliamentary representatives a greater commitment to environment-friendly land use in agriculture, forestry and fisheries.
- Contribute by your own behaviour as a consumer to a change of direction to more environment-compatible

methods, by buying ecologically grown produce, also the products of nature-adapted woodland management and nature-friendly, resources-sparing fisheries. Produce of your own region, from a producer known to you, are the best guarantee of fulfilling the conditions of ecological management.

- Urge your local community to enter environment partnerships, especially with communities in Central and Eastern Europe. On the one hand these can help to solve the environmental problems of Central and East European communities by the transfer of knowledge; on the other hand they lead to twinning programmes with mutual visits by ordinary citizens, to greater understanding and a real feeling of partnership in Europe.

Addresses

Be aware of your rights and duties as a citizen of a Common Europe and participate actively in the process of shaping public opinion. Also address yourself to the following institutions:

Commission of the European Union
Rue de la Loi 200
B–1049 Brussels
(This address also applies for all Commissioners and General Departments.)

Audit Office of the European Union
12, R. Alcide de Gasperie
L–1615 Luxembourg

Bundesministerium für Ernährung, Landwirtschaft und Forsten
(Federal Ministry for Food, Agriculture and Forestry)
Rochusstr. 1
53123 Bonn

Neuland
Verein für Förderung tier- und umweltgerechter Nutztierhaltung
(Society for animal- and environmentally-friendly animal husbandry)
Baumschulallee 15
53115 Bonn

Deutscher Tierschutzbund
(German Society for Protection of Animals)
Baumschulallee 15
53115 Bonn

Bioland
Barbarossastr. 14
73066 Uhingen
Germany

Demeter
Baumschulenweg 11
64295 Darmstadt
Germany

Naturland
Kleinhaderner Weg 1
82166 Gräfelfing
Germany

Stiftung Europäisches
Naturerbe
(European Natural Heritage
Fund)
(EURONATURE)
Güttinger Str. 19
78135 Radolfzell
Germany

Bonn Office:
Stiftung Europäisches
Naturerbe
(European Natural Heritage
Fund)
(EURONATURE)
Koblenzer Str. 9
53359 Rheinbach
Germany

Austrian Section:

Stiftung Europäisches
Naturerbe
(EURONATURE)
Brockmannsgasse 53/1
A–8010 Graz
Austria

Spanish Section:

Stiftung Europäisches
Naturerbe
(EURONATURE)
Fondo Patrimonio Natural
Europeo
Marcenado, 24.6 1zqa
E-28002 Madrid
Spain

Addresses of Heads of Government

Albania
Bresidenca e Shqiperise
Boulevardi Deshmored
Kombid
Al-Tirana

Austria
Bundespräsident
Präsidentschaftskanzlei
Hofburg
Adlersteige
A–1010 Vienna

Belarus
Chairman of the Council of
Ministers of the Republic of
Belarus
Minsk/Belarus

Belgium
Premier Ministre
Rue de la Loi 16
B–1000 Brussels

Bosnia/Herzegovina
President
Sarajevo

Bulgaria
Presidendtsvo
Dondukov 2
BL-1000 Sofia

Croatia
President
Zagreb/Croatia

Cyprus
President
President's Palace
Z-Nicosia

Czech Republic
Kancelar Prezidenta
CH-11908 Praha-Hrad

Denmark
Premier Ministre
Christiansborg
Prins Jorgens Gard 11
DK-1218 Copenhagen K

Estonia
Prime Minister
Weizenberg 39
EE-0100 Tallinn

Finland
Prime Minister
Mariankatu 2
SF-00170 Helsinki

France
Président
Hôtel de Lassay
F-75007 Paris

Georgia
Prime Minister of the
Republic of Georgia
Tiflis/Georgia

Germany
Bundeskanzler
Bundeskanzleramt
D-53113 Bonn

Great Britain
Prime Minister
10 Downing Street
London SW1

Greece
Prime Minister
Vassilissis Sophias 15
GR-100674

Hungary
Prime Minister
Kossuth Lajos ter. 1–3
H–1055 Budapest

Iceland
Prime Minister
Stjormaradshusinu
IS–150 Reykjavik

Ireland
Prime Minister
Leinster House
Dublin 2

Italy
Presidente del Consiglio dei
Ministri
Palazzo Chigi
I–00186 Rome

Latvia
President of the Republic of
Latvia
LV–Riga, Latvia

Lithuania
Prime Minister
Gedimino 53
LT–2026 Vilnius

Luxembourg
Premier Ministre
4 rue de la Congrégation
L–2910 Luxembourg

Malta
Office of the Prime Minister
Auberege de Castille
Castille Palace
Valetta, Malta

Netherlands
Prime Minister
Binnenhof 20
Postbus 2000
NL–2500 EA Den Haag

Norway
Statsministerens Kontor
Post Boks 8001 Dep.
N-0030 Oslo

Republic of Poland
Chairman of the Council of Ministers of the Republic of Poland
Warsaw

Portugal
Primeiro Ministro
Presidencia do Conselho de Ministros
Rua du Imprensa 1
P-1300 Lisbon

Romania
Prime Minister
Palatul Cotroceni
RO-Bucharest

Russia
President
Kremlin
Moscow

Serbia
President
Belgrade

Slovak Republic
Premierminister
Nam.Slobody
CS-81370 Bratislava/Slovakia

Slovenia
President
Gregorciceva 20
SL-6100 Ljubljana

Spain
Presidente del Gobierno
Ministerio de la Presidencia
Complejo de la Mondoa
Edificio INIA
Madrid

Sweden
Staatsminister
sb Rosenbad 4
S-10333 Stockholm

Switzerland
Bundespräsident
Bundeshaus-West
CH–3003 Berne

Turkey
Prime Minister
TR-Ankara/Turkey

Ukraine
Minister for the Environment
Khreschtschatik 5
UKR–25200
Kiev

Bibliography

"Budget of the European Union for the year 1993", in the *Official Journal* of the EEC, L 31, of the 08.02.93

"*So klein and schon so weit rumgekommen*" (So small and yet so far-travelled), in: *fairkehr*, 7/92, p. 14 seq.

Aetologischer Verein für Umweltschutz (Aetiological Society for Environment Protection); *Die Ableitung des Flusses Acheloos* (The Diversion of the River Acheloos), Agrinion 1992.

Akademie für Natur- und Umweltschutz (Academy for Nature and Environment Conservation), Baden-Württemberg: *Nestos Delta. Feuchtgebietsschutz and Naturmanagement in Nordost-Griechenland* (Nestos Delta. Wetlands Conservation and Nature Management in Northeast Greece), Stuttgart 1990.

Official Journal of the European Communities, various issues of various years.

Arbeitsgemeinschaft beruflicher und ehrenamtlicher Naturschutz (ABN) (Study Group of professional and honorary Conservationists): *Naturschutz für Europa, Jahrbuch für Naturschutz und Landschaftspflege* (Conservation for Europe, Yearbook of Conservation and Landscape Maintenance), 45/1992.

Bölscher, Bernd: "*Emsvertiefung: Meyer-Werft Argumente verstanden*", in: *Wattenmeer International*, 1/92, p. 17 seq. WWF-Wattenmeer, Bremen 1991.

Buchwald, Konrad: *Nordsee – Ein Lebensraum ohne Zukunft?* (North Sea – a Habitat without a Future?), Göttingen 1990.

BUNDpositionen 19: *Die Nordsee* (The North Sea), Bonn, 1989.

Bundesministerium für Umwelt (Federal Ministry for the Environment): *Naturschutz und Reaktorsicherheit, Umweltschutz in Deutschland* (Conservation and Reactor Safety, Environment Protection if Germany), Bonn 1992.

Club of Rome: *Die globale Revolution* (The global Revolution), Spiegel Spexial 2/1991.

Council on Environmental Quality: Global 2000. Report to the President, Washington 1980.

Deimer, Petra: *"Kein Gnade für die Wale"* (No Mercy for the Whales), in *kosmos*, 10/92

Die Grünen im Bundestag (The Greens in the Federal Parliament): *Transitraum Alpen* (The Alps as a Transit Route), Lindau 1987.

European Communities Commission: *Die zukünftige Entwicklung der gemeinsamen Transportpolitik* (The future development of Common Transport Policy), Brussels 1992.

EC-Commission: "Proposal for a Council Directive on the development of the Community railways", KOM (89), finally in Official Journal of the European Communities, No. C34/8, 14.02.90.

EC-Commission: *Grünbuch Transport und Verkehr* (Green Book on Transport and Traffic), Brussels 1992.

EC-Commission: Commission Regulation (EEC) No. 487/90 of 27 February 1990, "amending, in regard to the sizing of apples, Regulation (EEC) No. 920/89 laying down quality standards for carrots, citrus fruit and dessert apples and pears", in: *Official Journal of the European Communities*, No. L 52, p. 7, Brussels, 28.02.90.

EC-Commission: "Council Directive of 02.04.79 on the conservation of wild birds (79/409/EEC)", in: *Official Journal of the European Communities*, No. L 103 p. 1 seq., Brussels 25.04.79.

EC-Commission: "Council Directive 92/43/EEC of 21.05.92 on the conservation of natural habitats and of wild fauna and flora", in: *Official Journal of the European Communities*, No. L 206, p. 7 seq., Brussels 22.07.92.

EC-Commission: "Council Directive of 27.06.85 on the assessment of the effects of certain public and private projects on the environment (85/337/EEC)", in: *Official Journal of the European Communities* No. L 175, p. 40 seq. Brussels 05.07.85.

EC-Commission: "Council Directive of 21.05.1991 concerning urban waste water treatment (91/271/EEC)", in: *Official Journal of the European Communities* No. L 135, Brussels 30.05.91.

EC-Commission: Report of the Commission to the Council regarding "The conservation of Whales in the frame of the International Whaling Commission", Brussels, 15.07.92.

EC-Commission: "The state of the environment in the European Union", in: KOM (92) 23 endg., 03.04.92.

EC-Commission: "*Neunter Jahresbericht über die Kontrolle der Anwendung des Gemeinschaftsrechts 1991*", in: KOM (92), 136 endg. 27.05.92. (Ninth Annual Report on the control of the application of Community Law.)

Ehrlich, P.R. & Ehrlich, A. H.: "The Population Explosion", New York 1990.

European Court of Justice: "Special Report No. 3/92 on the Environment", in: *Official Journal of the European Communities*, C245 of 23.09.92.

European Environment Bureau (EEB): *Ihr Recht nach der Umweltschutzgesetzgebung der Europäischen Union*, Brussels 1989. (Your rights under the environment protection legislation of the European Union).

Eurostat: *Europa in Zahlen* (Europe in Figures) Luxembourg 1992.

Fenner, Rudolf: *Boreale Wälder,* (Northern Forests), ROBIN WOOD, Hamburg 1993.

Fremuth, Wolfgang (Ed.): *Das manipulierte Leben. Die Gentechnik entlässt ihre Kinder.* (Manipulated Life. Gene Technology releases its children), Cologne 1988.

Friedrich, Michael: "*Wie ein Fluss den Bach heruntergeht*" (How a river goes down the drain), in: Greenpeace Magazine, 1/93, p.48 seq.

Frühauf, W. & Giesinger, Z.: *Europa ohne Grenzen. Alarm für die Umwelt* (Europe without boundaries. Alarm for the Environment), Spiegel Special 1992.

Gore, Al: Earth in the Balance, London, 1992.

Grimmett: *Important Bird Areas in Europe,* pubd. ICBP, London 1989.

Gruhl, Herbert: *Ein Planet wird geplündert* (A planet is plundered), Frankfurt 1978.

Hampe, A.: *Extramadura. Naturreichtum durch Tradition.* (Natural diversity by tradition), Radolfzell 1993.

Hau, Gerald: *Projekt: Mönchsrobben im Mittelmeer* (Project: Monk seals in the Mediterranean), Radolfzell 1991.

Hau, Gerald & Hutter, C. -P.: *Nördliche Sporaden – Leben zwischen Inseln und Meer* (The Northern Sporades – Life between islands and sea), Überlingen 1995.

Hey, Christian & Jahns-Böhm, Gutta: *Ökologie und freier Binnenmarkt* (Ecology and Free Common Market), Freiburg 1989.

Hey, Christian et al.: *Dead End Road. A Greenpeace Scenario* 1992.

Hutter, Claus-Peter & Thielcke, Gerhard: *Nature ohne Grenzen* (Nature without boundaries), Stuttgart 1990.

Iten, Oswald: "*Der letzte Kampf des Acheloos*" (The last battle of the Acheloos), in: *Neue Züricher Zeitung*, 30./31.10.1993.

Jerrentrup, H. & Resch, J.: *Nestos. Leben zwischen Fluss und Meer* (Nestos: Life between river and sea), Radolfzell 1990.

Keller, Horst: Europäische Zeitung 03/93.

Keller, Horst: ZDF-Europamagazin EURO 26.03.93.

Knake, Manfred & Lamp, Jochen: "*Meyer plant neue Werft vor Steilküste Rügens*" (Meyer plans new dockyard by the cliffs of Rügen), in: *Wattenmeer International*, 4.91, p. 19 seq., Bremen 1991.

Die Grenzen des Wachstums. Bericht Meadows, Dennis, et al.: *The Limits of Growth. Report of the Club of Rome on the Human Condition*, Reinbek 1973.

Megerle, A. & Resch, J.: *Die Crau. Steinsteppe voller Leben* (The Crau. A stony steppe full of life), Radolfzell 1987, 1991.

Michel, Jeff: *Saubere Kraftwerke in der CSFR* (Clean power-stations in the CSFR), unpublished manuscript.

Neuschulz, Frank et al.: BUND, *Naturreservat Elbtalaue, Hitzacker/Elbe* (Nature reserve Elbtalaue, Hitzacker/Elbe) 1991.

Norwegische Gesellschaft für Naturschutz (Norwegian Society for Nature Conservation): Written communication, 26.01.93.

Olsson, Roger: "Forest and Forestry in Scandinavia. A Staus Report", in: *Taiga News*, 2/92, p. 4.

Requardt-Schohaus, Eva: "*Emsvertiefung ohne Ende?*" (No end to the deepening of the Ems?), in: *Ostfriesland-Magazin*, 1/92, p. 28 seq., 1992.

Stiftung Europäisches Naturerbe (European Natural Hertiage

Fund): Press release 07.06.91.

Szijj, Josef: *Ökologische Wertanalyse des Acheloos-Delta* (Westgriechenland) (Ecological value analysis of the Acheloos Delta, Western Greece), University of Essen 1983.

Stüben, P. & Thurn, V.: *WüstenErde. Der Kampf gegen Durst, Dürre und Desertifikation* (DesertEarth. The fight against thirst, drought and the creeping desert), Giessen 1992.

Thurn, V. & Clase, B. (Eds.) *Klassenfeind Natur – Die Umweltkatastrophe in Osteuropa* (Class enemy Nature – the environmental catstrophe in Eastern Europe), Giessen 1992.

UNEP, *Convention on Biological Diversity*, Nairobi 1992.

Vassilakis, Kostas & Bousbouras, Dimitris: *The Diversion of the Acheloos River*, Hellenic Ornithological Society, Athens 1991.

VCD/DNR: *Öffentlicher Verkehr in der Fläche* (Public transport in the area), Bonn 1988.

Vlachoutsikou, Ada & Lazaridis, Yiannis: *Monk Seals in Greece*, Radolfzell 1990.

Weinzierl, Hubert: *Das grüne Gewissen* (The green conscience) Stuttgart 1993.

Wesemüller, Holger: "*Erneut Wirbel um Emsvertiefung*" (Renewed agitation about the Ems deepening), in: *Wattenmeer International*, 2/92, p. 26, WWF-Wattenmeer, Bremen 1992.

Wohlers, Rüdiger: in: *Der Spurkranz* (Trail ring), Vienna 1/93.

Wolf, Winfried: *Eisenbahn and Autowahn* (Railways and car craze), Hamburg/Zürich 1986.

WWF-Wattenmeerstelle: "*Keine Großwerft vor Steilküste*" (No to giant dockyard in front of the cliffs) in: *Wattenmeer International*, 2/92, p. 26, Bremen 1992.

Index

Acheloos 87, 96
Agricultural subsidies 8, 124, 150, 158
Agriculture 7, 23, 78, 97, 122, 143, 149, 156, 164, 194, 217
Albania 75
Alonnisos 13
Apples, Sizing Regulation 78
Bananas 134
Bear 77, 88
Bird Conservation Directive 70, 99, 185, 211
Black Triangle 117
Brussels (sewage works) 173
CFCs 49
Chernobyl 111
Cohesion Fund 10
CO_2 42, 62, 110, 161
Dams 32, 87
Debt remission 112
Eastern Europe 75, 102, 110, 116
Eco-Tax 110
Environment Action Programme 228

Eucalyptus 90
Extremadura 21
Finland 61
Fishing industry 16, 127
Forest depletion 117, 175
Forest fires 26, 35, 82
Forest management 20, 61, 90
Frogs 180
Fruit 78, 134
Germany 60, 69
Greece 13, 35, 74, 82, 83, 95, 122
Growth initiatives 215
Health hazards 103, 116
Hunting 74, 184
Iceland 130
Italy 74, 82, 89
Latvia 76
Lignite excavation 160
Majorca 53
Marble 34
Marine pollution 13
Monk seals 13
Netherlands 11
North Sea 187

Norway 67, 130
Poland 104, 110, 165
Portugal 11, 89
Shetlands 44
Silesia 104
Spain 21, 28, 32, 44, 54, 82
Structural funds 10, 28, 36, 72, 87, 90, 98, 218, 223
Subsidies (see Agricultural subsidies)
Sugar 10, 12
Thasos 34, 84
Tourism 28, 37
Traffic 38, 43, 194
Waste 198
Whales 127, 209

List of Authors

...... *The Eco-Twisters* should not really exist as a book. If everywhere in Europe there were as much care for landscape, wildlife and environment as is necessary for the survival, for handing on the precious natural heritage intact to coming generations, such a book would simply be superfluous. Unfortunately our allegedly environment-conscious society in reality looks quite different. The hypocrisy with which on the one hand the official voice loudly appeals for conservation, and on the other hand deliberately permits destruction of nature merely to set the cash registers ringing, is utterly outrageous.

It is a crying shame how our officials deal with the remaining natural and cultural landscapes of Europe. Out of personal involvement and anger the authors decided to document the dual morality to be met with everywhere in Europe. In this Dossier of crimes against the European environment the most incredible, spectacular, and surely the most symptomatic examples of Eco-Twisterdom (to coin a term) have been assembled.

Behind every case history mentioned in this book lies thorough research and a wealth of inside information about the relevant background. For years the authors, each specialising in his own field, have been actively engaged with international conservation and in touch with numerous individuals and environment groups for nature in the most varied regions of Europe. Together with the like-minded of other countries they have stablished a sort of Eco-Alliance, with a cross-border commitment to the interests of nature and the basis of human life.

The Eco-Twisters is therefore a team work. All the participants are behind each contribution, though it has been researched and written by one author. The individual contributions are the work of:

Claus-Peter Hutter: Eco-Twisters are everywhere; Here's dust in your eye; Money down the drain; The destructive power of stupidity; Put money in thy purse; Aid which does not help; Going for uniformity; Don't look beyond your own plate; Planning with blinkers on; The art of waiting.

Horst Keller: My home is my castle; Spellbound into the abyss; Just like the ostrich; For they know not what they do; The instant feast; None so blind . . .; Two minds in one body; Out of sight, out of mind; But you can't see the ones in the dark; The unbearable heaviness of becoming.

Lutz Ribbe: Living at other people's expense; The lust for killing; Exporting your mistakes; Don't get it right, don't stop the wrong; You have to have something in the bank, Frank; Better look this gift horse in the mouth; I could eat you up; More, more, more - means less; Big, cheap and cheerful; Animals as merchandise; The spirits I called up; Twenty years – and little (none?) the wiser?

Rüdiger Wohlers: The Men of Gotham at work; Accelerating into Chaos; The privatised environment; Many trees do not make a forest; I want my fun; Rules where there is nothing to regulate; Sweeping your own doorstep; Never mind what I said yesterday; Refusing to learn from one's mistakes; The beam in your own eye; Sweeping it under the carpet.

The overall co-ordinating editors were Claus-Peter Hutter and Roman Hocke.

Acknowledgements

The authors extend their warmest thanks to all who have contributed to the making of this book

Firstly we thank all those numerous nature-committed people in many parts of Europe who, themselves enraged, reported to us the appalling state of affairs, the planning failures and scandals at the expense of nature, and for the detailed data and background information with which they supplied us. In spite of all the setbacks and disappointments they experienced in the course of this work, we strongly urge these people not to give up, but to continue giving their full commitment to the conservation of nature. For there are grounds for hope. The many friendships all over Europe forged during the work on this book have given rise to many new initiatives and have shown that it is only through communication and understanding between people that one can fight the wrongs committed against nature.

We particularly wish to thank all those who supplied us with as yet unpublished information and alerted us to dire circumstances not yet publicly known. Unfortunately we cannot name them here, as we do not want to cause them difficulties.

For their close collaboration we especially thank Jürgen Resch (of the German Environmental Group (*Deutsche Umwelthilfe*) and Ingmar Streese (in Brussels). We are grateful to Monika Schaaf, Ilse Koller, Sylvia Ollesch, Wolfgang Fremuth, Frank Neuschulz, Heiko Müller, Gerald Hau, Marion Hammerl-Cavanna, Jesús Garzón, Claudia Brözel, Inge Merz,

ACKNOWLEDGEMENTS

Barbara Honner, Bärbel Strasser and Albrecht Buhl, for multifarious collaboration and help. For help going far beyond the call of publishers' editorial assistance we warmly thank Roman Hocke, Gunter Ehni and Hansjörg Weitbrecht, of *Weitbrecht Verlag*. We would like to thank Merlin Press for publishing this English edition.

We are grateful to the German Federal Environment Foundation *Deutsche Bundesstiftung Umwelt* and its General Secretary Fritz Brickwedde for funding this translation and we thank Inge Goodwin for translation.

We would also like to thank Larry Williams, director of the international programme of the Sierra Club (Washington D.C., USA) very much for his co-operation.

And if you, the reader of this book, after becoming aware of all the unpleasantness and all the obstacles constantly put in the path of conservation all over Europe from all sides and levels, would like to contribute personally to the preservation of nature in Europe, you might wish to send a donation to one of the conservationist organisations active in Europe. We recommend the Foundation for European Natural Heritage (EURONATURE), whose work for the environment is dependent on public support. Their Account Number is 333, Baden-Württembergische Bank, Stuttgart (Bank Code Number 604 300 60).

Directory for the Environment
4th Edition

Organisations, campaigns and initiatives in the British Isles

Monica Frisch

It provides an overview of organisations concerned with environmental issues, from general groups like Friends of the Earth to specialist bodies such as the Barn Owl Trust or Industrial Water Society. It includes not only charities, pressure groups, partnership, networks and other voluntary sector bodies, but also government departments and agencies, professional institutes and learned societies, and regional and county organisations from Alderney to Orkney.

It outlines aims, activities and publications, enabling users to get an idea of the nature and style of organisations. A detailed index makes it easy to identify groups concerned with specific issues, and is designed to take some of the work out of networking.

It includes organisations concerned with:

Information on each organisation:
- green issues including energy
- built environment, planning and urban issues
- wildlife, its habitat, natural history and conservation
- animal welfare and animal rights
- peace and third world development
- specialist aspects from archaeology to zoology

ISBN 185425 083 3 Pbk £15.99